FAIRY TALES

by Sharon Moore

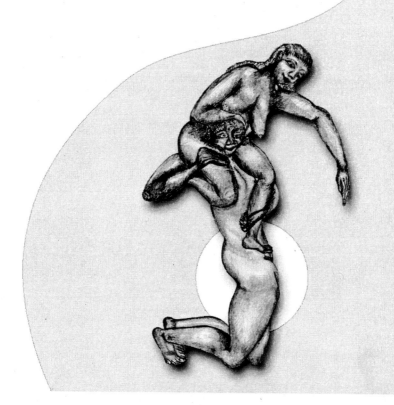

 **Trafford** PUBLISHING® www.trafford.com

North America & international
toll-free: 1 888 232 4444 (USA & Canada)
phone: 250 383 6864 ♦ fax: 250 383 6804 ♦ email: info@trafford.com

The United Kingdom & Europe
phone: +44 (0)1865 722 113 ♦ local rate: 0845 230 9601
facsimile: +44 (0)1865 722 868 ♦ email: info.uk@trafford.com

10 9 8 7 6 5 4 3 2 1

About the Author

Raised in Stourbridge, Sharon attended King Edward VI Sixth Form College. She gained her Honours Degree in Law at Liverpool University and her Solicitors' Finals at Lancaster Gate Law College, London. After two years training, she qualified as a solicitor and joined a busy medium-sized practice in Birmingham in 1991 following two years of extensive travel abroad. During her last ten years in practice she was a partner heading the Matrimonial Department, a regular advocate in the County Court and throughout her career family law predominated.

Over that time she assisted the local Citizens Advice Bureaus and staunchly supported the provision of Legal Aid (now Public Funding). She held specialist qualifications with both The Law Society and The Solicitors Family Law Association and was responsible for training several of her colleagues.

'The Unconventional Sharon Moore' was how the editor of a magazine profile described her. Perhaps this was not a hard reputation to earn within the legal world's confines. The accompanying photo showed a besuited woman standing against her motorbike (as the senior partner felt it inappropriate for her to be sitting astride it!)

She has lectured, spoken on local and national radio and written for relevant publications about family law. This is her first book and one which she has increasingly felt compelled to write.

DEDICATION AND THANKS

I would like to dedicate this book to all those whose lives I have touched deeply and to all those who have deeply touched mine.

And I would like to thank:

Stef the Lone Ranger who has given me constant friendship and support for nearly two decades and whose observations on this book from its infancy have been invaluable.

Cecil 'Levi' Williams who was my brick through one of the most difficult times of my life and who has unwaveringly believed in this book way before it even became a twinkle in a windows word document and even when I questioned my own belief in it.

David Estridge for his sheer enthusiasm and positive feedback during his proof reading.

Adrian Adams of Creation Cafe who has unscrambled some of my technical anomalies and rescued me when I thought I would never manage to get the work into publishable form.

And finally, my former business partners without whose actions this book would have remained a thorn in my mind.

FOREWORD : YIN AND YANG

Most of us recognise this symbol (shown on the front cover) as it increasingly appears on clothing, jewellery, cards and such like but few of us really understand the origins or significance of this remarkably simple yet complex representation. The first record of its illustration in Britain has been found on a fifth century Roman shield but it was the brainchild of much older and more distant ancestors. It is otherwise known as the Tai-Chi symbol and heralds from China. The pictorial representation of Tai-Chi is found in the I. Ching, a book of changes of Divination which is regarded as the greatest foundation of Chinese philosophy.

In simple terms, it is a reflection of Mother Nature Herself, of The Universe, of 'Everything' and all the phenomena that develop from these wholes. It is about opposites. The two shapes which lie so perfectly symmetrically opposite each other in their circle of 'Everything' have what looks like a fisheye of the colour of that opposite. Each contains the seed of the other. The outer circle represents that 'Everything' which is filled by these two symbols, neither of which is completely black nor white, as in life, as in nature. It represents two primal opposing but complimentary forces which are found in all things in the Universe.

These complimentary opposites form the Yin/ Yang dichotomy; each is its opposite when viewed from the other side. The two are in movement rather than being in absolute states, each flowing into the other illustrating continual momentum whilst each contains a part of the other. The darker shape of the female Yin descends just as black cold falls whilst the lighter shape of the male Yang ascends just as white heat rises. It is like a 70's lava lamp though circular

i

rather than rocket shaped and containing as much wax as water, moving in perfect symmetry, an air bubble in the wax and a globule of wax in the water.

The blackness of the Yin triggers the Summer Solstice. It is the moon; it is woman; it represents three of the five elements - earth, water and wood - which are soft and yielding. The whiteness of the Yang triggers the Winter Solstice. It is the sun; it is man; it represents the heat and hardness of Fire and Metal. The fisheyes mark the Winter and Summer Solstices and the symbol as a whole represents the length of shadow over a year (measured in six concentric circles, each with twenty-four segments). The sun rises in the East and sets in the West; the shortest shadow is in the South whilst the longest is in the North.

The movement inherent in the symbol also expresses time. When applied to a twenty four hour day: noon is full Yang; sunset is the Yang turning into Yin; midnight is full Yin; and sunrise sees the Yin turning into Yang again. Similarly, when applied to a year: Summer is full Yang (the globiest bit of the white); Autumn sees Yang turning to Yin (the tail end of that glob); Winter is full Yin (the globiest bit of the black) and Spring sees Yin turning to Yang again (the tail end of the black glob!)

Thus the Yin and Yang come to represent moon vs sun, night vs day, dark vs light, cool vs warm, rest vs active, feminine vs masculine, north vs south, winter vs summer, right vs left, introversion vs extrovertism, even vs odd, water vs fire and indeed the physical earth vs the spiritual 'heaven'. However, quite contrary to the dualism of Good vs Evil, both the Yin and the Yang are equally important and worthy of respect. Crucially they are interdependent; the Yin cannot exist without the Yang and vice versa because everything is relative. Beauty, Love, Heat … can only be truly appreciated by knowledge of Ugly, Hate, Cold …

It represents Mother Nature's balance; as one increases the other decreases to fill the circle. Thus it represents continued balance and continual change. As no condition can dominate eternally, all conditions are subject to change, to transform into their opposites. And so we have the eternal cycle of reversal with varying ebbs and surges. Being dependant opposites means that 'health' contains the principle of its opposite 'sickness' and so its presence is felt by its absence.

Whilst the symbol we recognise was first evident in Britain in the fifth Century, the philosophy of Tai-Chi came long before then and did, and still does, permeate many cultures throughout the world. During the Chinese Shang Dynasty (1523- 1028 B.C.), it is known that people would write a question on a tortoise shell which would be heated and then doused in water. If the consequential crack in the shell formed a broken line (----) this represented the Yin and meant the answer was 'no' whilst an unbroken line (___) represented the Yang and meant 'yes'.

In Asian cultures the Yin and Yang was often used with reference to disease. If the patient displayed a Yin symptom, such as coldness, it would be treated with a Yang treatment such as hot foods. Conversely, a Yang symptom, such as nervousness, would be treated with a Yin treatment of cold food and fruits. A parallel might be seen in our saying 'feed a cold and starve a fever'.

The currently popular 'art' of Feng Shui or Chinese Geomancy has its roots in the principles of Yin and Yang as illustrated on the compass face below. The diagonals represent the Spirit Gates and assist in determining auspicious or inauspicious situations and the orientation of places.

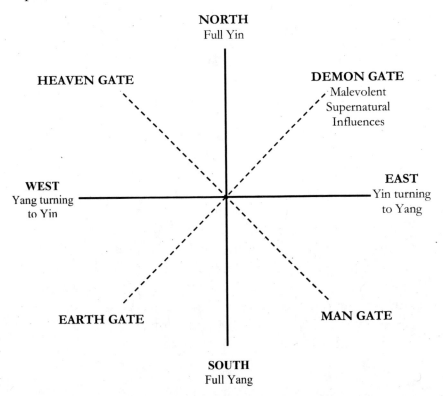

The diagonals represent spirit gates and the Demon Gate is a pathway for malevolent supernatural influences. Feng Shui is used to determine auspicious and inauspicious situations and the orientation of places by reference to these gateways.

Perhaps it is not surprising that in different cultures different attributes are placed on the 'male' Yang by the minds of a

patriarchal society, creating gender stereotypes. To the
Greeks the Yang represented straight, light, good and 'resting'
(a state considered superior to 'moving') whilst the female
Yin represented their opposites. To the Chinese it
represented odd, light and active (a state considered superior
to female Yin's 'passive'). In India the male Shiva is detached,
remote and unmoving whilst Shiva's female side is active,
creative and powerful. In India detachment was considered
superior to participation. Thus these patriarchal societies
attributed the male with the 'worthier' attributes, as they saw
them.

Given that when Yin reaches its extreme it becomes Yang
and vice versa, ironically this may make little difference and
these cultural anomalies possibly reflect sexual archetypes
rather than gender stereotypes. Paglia suggests that the
darkness of the female Yin is reflected in her concealed and
internal sex organs which she cannot see whilst the lightness
of the male Yang with his exposed organs allows him to
easily examine them! And so the opposites go on.

The Yin creates the physical senses of the body. When an
earthly dead spirit is returned to the air of Yang it receives its
nourishment just as the body was nourished by its senses. But
as with all things, love and sex, spiritual and physical,
everything is a mixture of its opposites. A female may be
mostly Yang and a male may be mostly Yin and things which
are clearly represented by the Yin or the Yang may be the
opposite. Cool concept.

Part of the way we recognize the extreme emotion of Love is
by the absence and knowledge of Hate but in every example
of love there is some hate – even if it emanates from the
recognition of emotional vulnerability and dependence that

Love befriends. It's a thin line between love and hate just as love contains the seed of hate. Nowhere is this more evident than in a divorce lawyer's office and after years of that questionable privilege (from the 'working' side of the desk) I cannot entirely enjoy the apparent ecstasy on a bride and groom's face without thinking of the divorce statistics. Why does love so often turn to hate and why are so many of us unable or unwilling to allow it to flow back? How many of us, at the zenith of an ugly row with our beloved, really feel in that instant, that we hate them? How many of us have enjoyed that fantastic feeling as hate wanes and love waxes lyrical!

CONTENTS

1. WHO AM I? WHAT IS THIS BOOK ABOUT?   1

2. OUR CHANGING SOCIETY.   14

3. WHO ARE YOU?   26

4. FORMING OUR OWN SEXUAL MORALITY.   43

5. SEXUAL ORIENTATION.   53

6. PORN AND SEXUAL FANTASIES.   65

7. SELF-PRESERVATION IN THE FACE OF SEXUAL FREEDOM.   76

8. FINDING A PARTNER.   83

9. HONESTY AT THE OUTSET OR ELSE?   89

10. TRUTH.   105

11. HONESTY THROUGHOUT.   113

12. MEDIATION.   123

13. SUPPORT EARLY ON.   134

14. SEX, SEXUAL FREEDOM AND ADULTERY.   141

15. INFIDELITY AND LIES.   161

16. WHY DO WE DO IT?   172

17. IS IGNORANCE BLISS?   179

18. MONEY.   188

19. THE DANGERS OF FILLING IN THE GAPS.   209

20. MEN AND WOMEN.   216

21. CHILDREN.   231

22. THE END OF MARRIAGE AS WE KNOW IT?   264

23. SO WHAT'S THE SHAPE OF THE FUTURE?   275

CHAPTER ONE

WHO AM I? WHAT IS THIS BOOK ABOUT?

I walked into my partner's appraisal meeting. As ever, there weren't enough hours in the day so, although I knew the standard form's question content, I had not provided a written response in advance. The Practice Manager and one of the most senior partners conducted the interview - as usual. My appraisals had become something of a necessary which were viewed with dubious anticipation by both myself and those charged with conducting them. Much to the relief of all involved, the appraisal remained light and relatively amiable. I had had a good costs year, had some 'good' results on several of my cases and managed to 'behave' myself in the eyes of my partner piers, so far as my nature allowed.

My Practice Manager asked what I would say were my three personal goals for the next twelve months. This is a standard question within the partner appraisal system designed, aside from the six hour monthly partners meetings we had, to ensure we kept ourselves in touch with what might be motivating us or otherwise taking our energies outside of our legal family. Without having to think I replied amusedly,

"finish the house, have a baby, write my book. In no particular order!"

She laughed,

FAIRY TALES by Sharon Moore

"Same as the previous four years then!"

I laughed. But when I got home that evening, I thought about it and I wasn't laughing. Realistically, they had probably been my goals for the last fourteen years when my then partner and I bought the house.

My Practice Manager once admitted she was unsure as to whether she even liked me when she first joined us to beat us into good shape, bombarding us with her Accountancy-trained pearls in graphics, figures, good ideas and dogged determination. Ironic that you only ever get to discuss such impressions once the tables are firmly turned (in that moment at least). She certainly did not approve of me. When lifestyles differ so dramatically, it is harder to understand the other and easier to view them disapprovingly. Part of that is self-defence, a reinforcement of our own justifications for the lifestyle we 'choose' to lead. As a wife with two young children it is impossible to truly empathise with the life which one inevitably leads as an unmarried, childless, financially comfortable and emotionally fired adult with lots of 'get up and go' upbringing cursing through your red blood. My mother has similar problems understanding me!

A Black Country girl never judges a sausage by its skin. People throughout my life have misunderstood me. I am sure I have done the same to others. A relationship requires an interaction, beyond the physical, which requires time. The more time that is spent, the more we are able to communicate both directly and indirectly. If we also learn to listen, rather than just hear, the unavoidable conclusion is greater understanding. If we understand those that we have relationships with — be they neighbours, colleagues, family, friends, lovers - a great deal of pain and suffering can be avoided and a great deal of trust built. Time is difficult to buy and we never have enough of it so we also have to prioritise our time so that there is enough of 'quality' to nurture our closest relationships and create true intimacy.

Working full-time long hours and heading a busy matrimonial department meant the house got done when there was time, motivation and a tradesmen who actually arrived, available. The baby? Well that's a whole chapter in itself but, like many successful professional women of my era, time was something I juggled on a 'he who shouts loudest' basis and the 'right' time and the 'right' man always seemed to be somewhere in the future. And the book? Realistically I knew that was something which would have to wait until my probably distant retirement.

As an only child with parents ambitious for my success and happiness, I was always pushed out into the world on my own, encouraged to join the Brownies, dancing classes, gymnastic club, art classes… I grew up feeling almost uncomfortable when I was without a challenge. I had decided I wanted to be a lawyer in my fourth year of Grammar School because I used to love the T.V. programme 'Crown Court' and, being a bit dramatic, could see myself in a wig and gown as a criminal barrister.

I wasn't a genius at school and although I did well, I always had to work hard for my achievements. A good friend of mine with whom I lived in my third year at uni, now a Consultant, never ceased to amaze me during the long hot summer of my finals revision, at the way that she appeared to work so little and achieve so much. It's surely not the case that you can be psychic about body parts, Latin words and all the technical impossibilities of a medical degree. Such memory always leaves me feeling dumbfounded, somewhat inadequate and unquestionably envious.

I had faced the challenge for me of a life away from home at eighteen, getting a Law Degree whilst loving the Liverpudlians and their Liverpool, moving to The Smoke with no grant, no money and a pile of boxed papers which had to be understood, learnt and then intelligently regurgitated nine months later. I had seized the opportunity of taking my first 'year out' in Europe and America and then gone back to live with my parents. I spent two years as a trainee solicitor. My university tutors had persuaded me that, being a 'people person', I would enjoy the greater people contact which that side of the profession offered, and they were right. I found myself increasingly asked to deal with anyone who came in looking vaguely emotionally upset by my two male employers to whom I owe a priceless contribution to my position both actually and mentally but who didn't feel comfortable with women in tears! Taking a second year off to travel Australia, India and South East Asia I then found a job where I did not feel like a square peg in a round hole as I had anticipated from my Principal's (the guy to whom I was officially apprenticed) misgivings. My Principal, who became my friend, my second father, my mentor, had always warned me (usually over a pint of Bathams) that the rest of the legal world wasn't like our loving and relatively liberal ship. It would be years before I really understood what he meant.

Well, on my arrival back from that last long trip, I got a job despite the fact that I was barely over seven and a half stone and black after nine months of Australasia's relentless heat. I had my hair scraped in a bun on the top of my head and gave the immediate impression to my interviewers, an amusement only subsequently divulged, of being a lesbian (the implications of which I will play with later). Having built a successful and well reputed department, having been accepted by my partners despite a much improved but enduring tendency of being unable to arrive at 9 o'clock, having broadened my knowledge in my field sufficiently to have confidence in my ability, having realised my dream of setting up a separate twelve strong family law office, I had no challenge. Almost thirteen years had gone by.

Of course, my challenge in the Life Bible according to 'the man on top of the Clapham omnibus' (the legal definition of a 'reasonable man') should have been fulfilled by appraisal life-aim number two and the responsibility of children. But after spending my entire menstrual life ensuring that I could never possibly have conceived, to just settle for what seemed like a doomed situation felt like giving up.

The purpose of all which is to explain to you, my greatly appreciated reader, how I came to write this book. How I initially managed to persuade my partners to agree to my taking a three month sabbatical in Jamaica three years ago which began a perhaps feted series of events which has ensured I was able to deliver it to you.

Whilst common sense is not common, mankind is. Common - in our basic instincts, drives, needs and desires. Having spent fifteen years as a family law solicitor I increasingly wanted to write this book, to ask questions about our relationships with ourselves and others, how these are changing and may change further in this twenty-first century and analyse our common humanity. A humanity driven by Mother Nature's inescapable, sometimes unpredictable, rules, by a need to preserve ourselves and have a new generation to preserve. A humanity driven by Father Time's unpredictable inescapable rules, by a need to use such time between birth and death as He may grant to us, as profitably as possible.

This is also a book very much intended to concentrate on life in the U.K. I hope it might be interesting for those who don't share this 'sceptered Isle' but it is clear that Europe itself varies quite dramatically, both religiously and culturally, such that many of my observations would simply be inaccurate when applied to them. For example, in 2004 when 42% of births in the U.K occurred outside marriage, 95% of newborns in Greece entered their world with married parents. Sweden had the highest 'illegitimacy' (what an expression!) rate at 55%. Anyone visiting Greece will immediately be aware of the very strong influence of religion and the family hierarchy - perhaps as one might have seen in the U.K. fifty years ago. If you are Greek you must wonder whether the writing is on the wall for your social structure. Somehow I doubt that it will take fifty years until 50% of Greek children are born to unmarried parents. As technology shrinks the world, everyone is bombarded by influences from outside our traditional cultures. In this increasingly multi-cultural society within the U.K., where we have a wide spectrum of beliefs and traditions, anything said about our society must, by definition, involve generalities. As a white professional 'middle class' woman I doubtless bring my own preconceptions to the table.

Why choose the family field? No-one stays in it for long unless they are motivated by something other than money. It is true that the more you do something the better you become at it and so the better you enjoy it but day in, day out, all the people who come to see you would far prefer they didn't have to. Dentists have one of the highest rates of suicide and divorce of the professions. I was once told by my retiring dentist, who had tended my teeth for the first thirty years of my life, that he would never be a dentist if he had his time again. It wasn't so much digging around in people's mouths all his life but rather the hour upon day upon week upon month upon year mantra of people declaring their wish to be anywhere else other than in his company. The mantra is prompted by dental discomfort – 'Nothing personal of course' - except it does become so for the recipient.

The same with a matrimonial client. That part of their being which is not already worn out with anger, pain, desolation, self doubt and all the other horrible side effects of losing a once loved one, tells them they need to get legal advice. They haven't seen their children; they have had their worlds devastated by declarations of lack of love; their boyfriend won't move out and is paying nothing towards bills…. the potential combinations creating the chaos is endless. Perhaps you have to be some kind of sadomasochist to choose to deal with these issues over happier topics of buying a house, selling a company or even making a will! The huge difference is the absence of control which people feel in the 'family' situation. Not only lack of control over our estranged, and perhaps our children, but lack of control over ourselves and our emotion. By definition, it is impossible to 'fall in love' if we are completely in control of our emotions and it is equally as impossible to control our emotions when we 'fall out of love' or someone 'falls out of love' with us. After fifteen years of professional voyeurism you are inevitably driven by questions of how this could be avoided.

FAIRY TALES by Sharon Moore

As a 'family' lawyer I have shared the intimate details of other's lives. In my more sanguine moments I hear myself stating that I spent fifteen years elbow deep in other people's emotional mire (or 'shit' as I was more prone to say). As an individual, I have formed close relationships for their duration with a myriad of personalities. And as an animal, I have enjoyed my earthly passions.

As is probably the case throughout most of Europe, the vast majority of people raised in a 'U.K. culture', somewhere inside, cling to the safe quasi-Victorian Fairy Tale of a coupling for life and children to nurture. This applies to heterosexuals and homosexuals alike, to whites, blacks and browns.

Look at the Christian vows and the wild promises purportedly made and burned into our subconscious after years of attending church weddings. Presbyterians vow to:

> 'love, honour, cherish, respect ... forsaking all others and holding only to him/her (?)... to have and to hold, in sickness and in health ... for richer or poorer ... and promise my love to you'.

Can anyone really do that?

The Episcopalians, Lutherans and Methodists vow to

> 'live after God's ordinance in the Holy Estate of Matrimony'.

And from the often used Anglican Book of Common Prayer

'with this ring I thee wed, with my Body I thee worship
(probably accurate at the time) and with all my worldly
goods I thee endow"

... until you run off with my best mate in which case I will
fight you through the courts over every last penny!

This language is not only archaic in thee obvious sense, it
fuels the belief that this 'perfect' state of being is both
possible and common place. Not that human nature has
changed over the centuries but all the impact which
technology has had on our everyday lives means we are being
forced to 'get real', to stop pulling the wool over our own
eyes, to be honest with both ourselves and those with whom
we seek to engage in a 'meaningful' union.

One website helpfully suggests the following readings for
couples planning their wedding "to help express the joy and
love in your Christian wedding vows". Ecclesiastes 4: 9-12

'two are better than one because they have a good return
for their toil. For if they fall, one will lift up his fellow but
woe to him who is alone when he falls and has not another
to lift him up. Again, if two lie together ... (now that
sounds more real) ... they are warm ; But how can I be
warm alone? (no comment) and though a man may prevail
against one who is alone, two will withstand him.

So, we should get married because we'll have someone to
help us out at the fight in our pub on a Friday night, to pick
us up when we stagger into a lamp post on the way home and
to act as our private hot water bottle when we eventually get
there. Great. I jest but really!

FAIRY TALES by Sharon Moore

The second suggestion, Song of Solomon 8, requires little additional comment.

> 'place me like a seal over your heart, like a seal on your arm; for love is as strong as death, its jealousy unyielding as the grave. It burns like a blazing fire, like a mighty flame. Many waters cannot quench love, rivers cannot wash it away. If one were to give all the wealth of his house for love, it would be utterly scorned'

This seems to be more about ownership than real love. I use Christianity as an example since I know most about it. (That said, I wonder how many of my readers know the real difference between just the Christian religions referred to above; I don't but my generation's mothers would most likely have known). In every religion's text there is an equivalent portrayal, a misleading idealism, when it comes to our most intimate relationships, with which we are brain washed from birth.

Is it a Fairy Tale? Increasingly we, as a society moving with the speed of light into the infancy of the Twenty-first century, have to stop and ask ourselves one simple question. In the ideal world of our fantasy, do we innately want and believe in a partnership for life? Other questions then follow. If so, how do we have to change our views in order to have a chance of achieving it in the reality of affluent multicultural safe Britain as seen through the eyes of an Iraqi? If we do not believe that such is possible, how do we adapt our views and expectations to best enjoy such a reality.

All I know is that a huge proportion of my clients in whose troubles I have been elbow deep for years, feel let down. They did not question the Fairy Tale but slavishly followed it.

WHO AM I? WHAT IS THIS BOOK ABOUT?

Childhood summer days spent wrapped around a pretend boyfriend (a tree, a down pipe…) do not metamorphosise into romantic, unwavering, thoughtful adult males. No more than women become that impossible combination of relenting, available horny beasts who run a career and a household whilst remaining calm, witty and practical to the end.

The desire to now write about what has consumed much of my adult life is prompted by an ineradicable after taste of that experience. I want us all to ask questions and not stumble on blindly as a society taking a fatalistic approach. In my work and in my wide and colourful personal life, I have touched intimately on others relationships - relationships which haven't made their first Paper Anniversary to ones beyond Gold. Relationships placed under a microscope in my office, representing those couplings which have almost frazzled beyond repair, and which are only the tip of a cold and painful iceberg in society at large.

I hope you do not agree with all that follows, that would make all of us very dull. I hope you will explore with me the realities, whether we like them or entirely accept them, and the possible options which they present. I don't think that there is 'an answer' but every individual must find their 'answer'; I don't necessarily wish to offer solutions but suggestions and possibilities; I want to make us think about our society, made up of individuals, strongly influenced by our 'relationship status' and join me in wonder as to where we may be heading, which solutions we may find and, indeed, what Fairy Tale we may offer to our own grandchildren. If, as a result, a handful of relationships grow stronger, deeper, more intimate, then perhaps that will be my atonement for the part I have played in breaking so many apart.

I have discussed many of the ideas and issues contained in this book with my friends and family over the years and that has invariably caused some very heated debate. When it comes to relationships, fidelity, children, honesty ... we frequently find we are quite passionate about our views. If I can provoke such passion from my reader, rather than a 'whatever' response and make you ponder on your own views then I will have achieved my aim.

I spent several years actively involved in running a jazz club/Kashmiri restaurant with one of my dear Muslim friends. Once the punters had finally left, the tables had been reset and the floors and surfaces cleaned we would sit around, 'chill out' and debate all kinds of things. One evening the conversation turned to evolution. This was something that for me was a known, an unquestioned certainty after years of visits to natural history museums, viewing documentaries and Darwinian schooling. In my ignorance I had not previously realised that Muslims do not agree with this theory since it flies in the face of their deeply held religious views. Ironically, it also flies in the face of the Christian teaching that on the sixth day 'God' created man before taking a much needed rest on the seventh. The fact that highly intelligent and thinking people could really not believe that we had evolved from pond life came as a real shock to me. At the time it raised in me a passion of certainty which I was anxious to share but subsequently it made me ponder upon this never-before-contemplated possibility. It has not changed my view but it did open my mind to re-examine what I believed and why. Hopefully this book will do the same for you within the context of your relationships.

CHAPTER TWO

OUR CHANGING SOCIETY

Is Prevention better than Cure? Are we feted to ever shorter couplings, decreasing commitment and lack of real intimacy?

In 1950 the number of marriages in the U.K. was more than eight-fold the number of divorces; there were around 330,000 first marriages, 78,000 second marriages and 33,000 divorces according to Government statistics. By the year 2000, for as many people as there were getting married (306,000) more than half as many were getting a divorce (155,000). Despite a growing population there was a 25% decrease in the number of first marriages over those fifty years. Marriage rates peaked in the early 1970's (around 471,000) and have been in decline ever since. The highest level of divorce appears to have occurred around 1993 when it peaked at almost 180,000, a more than fivefold increase on the 1950's figures. As marriage has continued to decline, the number of divorces has leveled off and will naturally decline with the years except in the unlikely event that we 'mend our ways' and alter our course back up the aisle.

There are no statistics about happy married or cohabiting couples as such but we only have to look around at the other lives which touch our own. Long marriages and partnerships are becoming a thing of the past and many of those which 'hang on in there' are struggling. Do we accept this as a fact of 'modern life'? If we do, how do we adjust our emotional expectations and social structures to take account of it? If we don't, what do we do to buck this ever pressing trend?

Of course, there has been a huge increase in those of us who 'cohabit' since the mid 1980's partly explained by the fact that, if we marry, we marry later and so some of us who presently cohabit will go on to marry later, though not necessarily the same partner! By 1986 11% of none married men under the age of 60 were cohabiting, according to Government statistics, and 13 % of similarly placed women. By 2004 those statistics had increased to 24% and 25% respectively.

We are animals. Before we are daughters, fathers, friends, we are animals. My dog was one of the most well behaved creatures you might have the pleasure of meeting. Collected from Birmingham Dogs Home without a jot of history aged about 3 he had obviously been strongly disciplined in training. We had to teach him how to bark! The only time when his great discipline went out of the window was when he saw a cat, running. I was immediately reduced to becoming the local 'fishwife' screaming after him as he raced blindly across roads, down alleys and over fences. Only a great deal of training can dull this most basic of instincts - the chase, the hunt, the kill. In Jake's case the cat only had to stop and face him and he behaved almost as though he had just been woken from some dream, looked embarrassedly around, usually stretched or yawned and then carried on about his business nonchalantly. He was more frightened of her than she was of him but his deep-rooted instinct still drove him to chase her and forget all he had learnt, including his road sense!

Mother Nature dictates that our most basic instinct is to survive: directly, by feeding and defending ourselves; indirectly, by procreating our genes. Survival no longer involves our hunting and killing for our daily bread but rather crossing the road safely and eating healthily. Procreation for most is equally as basic an instinct - passing on the genes which thousands of our forefathers have struggled to preserve, which natural selection has saved from extinction and which natural and manmade disasters have avoided. To mate, to have sex - Mother Nature needs to preserve that desire.

If we have time to reflect upon the 'meaning of life' and procreation, which is the strongest instinct after personal survival, Mother Nature will meet us at the door. If we have time to reflect upon the best ways to serve Procreation we must consider the choice of our mates and what would be best for the offspring of our couplings. There is a point beyond which children's interests are best served by the parties in a disfunctional relationship breaking up, splitting, getting the hell out of there and building a new relationship with a new mate with whom they can find a new happier state of living. But that 'point' is debatable and depends upon the alternatives. If the alternative is happy parents in different lives with time and attention for their loved offspring, then there can be no choice.

But ideally most of us innately believe that our children are best provided for in a stable home, in a loving environment where their different needs can be met by their next of kin, their parents. That ideal, like the Fairy Tale Princess, who grows up, meets her Prince, falls in love and forms a sexually faithful, permanent partnership with him, has children and lives happily ever after is unhappily, rarely, a realistic likelihood. We struggle on as best we can, meeting whatever needs we perceive our other masters might have, blurring further from Intuition's eyes those needs which are prompted by Survival, and those prompted by Greed and a search for Power, of whatever form, with which to better survive.

Does it matter? Our children are everyone's future. The manner in which they are raised and the norms of the society in which that occurs, will ultimately produce their values and so, the values of the society which raises the next generation, the values of the society in which we shall be the elders and reliant on them. We have selfish as well as altruistic reasons to ensure that we achieve the best for the next generation. There is always a shift which should be progression and which produces the inevitable 'age gap' of all generations. Even those who do not want or cannot have children of their own for whatever reason will need them, almost invariably, to provide for them during their old age via the provision of taxes.

So why, increasingly, do so many of our relationships turn sour and rot on the vine? Some, clearly, should never have been formed, mismatches feted to failure from the first fondling embrace. But many have a sweetness which could be preserved if their seeds were carefully nurtured in the arms of Intimacy. It is that which produces blossoms of sweetness - Closeness, Understanding, Trust, Reliance, Security and all their fellows will bloom from such a beginning and mature to produce the finest wines, the best relationships. It's nice to be nice. It's good to be around other people with good strong relationships. From a selfish point of view they usually make for far better company but they are also infectious. When we see something which seems to be better than our own, we naturally want to emulate it and share in the good fortune which it produces.

A very special lady in the U.S. once gave me a book to read by Eric Berne entitled 'Games People Play'. It explains itself as 'a book on the psychology of human Relationships' in which Byrne discusses the various masks which we don as we perceive suitable for different occasions, relationships and interactions with others. The games which these different masks produce might be distractingly pleasurable but ultimately the game has to go if we are to achieve the kind of lasting relationships which are good for us and our society.

He writes:

"Fortunately, the rewards of game free intimacy, which is or should be the most perfect form of human living, are so great that even precariously balanced personalities can safely and joyfully relinquish their games if an appropriate partner can be found for the better relationship".

He concludes:

"After games what? the somber picture presented… in which human life is mainly a process of filling in time until the arrival of death or Santa Claus, with very little choice, if any, of what kind of business one is going to contract during the long wait, is a commonplace but not the final answer. For certain fortunate people there is something which transcends all classifications of behaviour and that is awareness; something which rises above the programming of the past, and that is spontaneity; and something which is more rewarding than games, and that is intimacy. But all three of these may be frightening or even perilous for the unprepared. Perhaps they are better off as they are seeking their solutions in popular techniques of social action such as 'togetherness'. This may mean that there is no hope for the human race, but there is hope for individual members of it,"

So, sharing intimacy can create the most fortunate of people but they are not innately fortunate. They may not necessarily verbalise all of their respective relationship strategies. But they perceive, on whatever level, that the hard work required to produce such an intimate relationship is well worth the investment both in their own lives and for the greater good of society. We all treat our relationships as very personal things, our own affair, and yet the way we conduct them, both directly and indirectly, affects everyone.

So is there no hope for the human race? Are we bound on a path of relationships of different lengths which inevitably end in destruction? Does every relationship have an inevitable inescapable shelf life? This may be of no immediate concern to Survival who pays no heed to the method of your service to Her, the end unquestioningly justifies the means in Her book. If all of our relationships which are not blood-linked become transient, how long before blood-linked ones become strained, weakened, tenuous, part of a game, something which we have our special Sunday mass for. To what extent has this already happened?

I found myself watching a documentary on BBC 2 one day, watching the News while channel surfing to make sure I wasn't missing the talk of tomorrow's tea break. It expounded a persuasive theory. In the first half of the last century - world wars not excepted though expectancy reduced dramatically - a job was for life. This was particularly so if, as the male of the species, you managed to haul yourself up to the heady heights of middle-management. But middle-classdom, in all its glory, could only be truly achieved if he had a female of the species at home - heading committees, organising charities, being the voice of her man in the community. This system clearly benefited the sanctitude of marriage. It was almost part of a man's social duty to provide a capable counterpart; the pier pressure of the majority which created the norm and his own social standing and security. Bollocks to the rest of it, the system worked best for you if you played it that way.

The system also benefited society, or the way we lived in it then. It kept the community together, charity did start at home and a lot of women were able to look out for others in their immediate society in a hands-on way which is ever waning. Though women have always 'worked', the Second war brought many women into the workplace who, hither thereto, would have pursued the prime ambition to 'trap' a man of the species capable of the ladder haul. Often due to the advances made during The Wars, Invention ever being the birth-child of Necessity, technology was to take up all the spirit which would be the precursor of the at-the-speed-of-sound velocity to which we are now exposed daily.

Technology's demon - men and women lose jobs. Even those white collared paper chasers (yes, we still had paper then!) were not safe. If they were one of the lucky ones they would shortly be able to buy their own car, perhaps a Mini, which opened further new horizons whilst others quietly disappeared forever.

So, add into the cauldron of post war freedom and relative prosperity, at least of the essentials in life, greater populace movement, far more physical interactions of people, affordable mass-produced cars, the package deal, the telephone and televisions, the pill whilst security of a life-time's job was preserved for the relative few. People were able to interact with many more people. The circle of potential courtiers was widened - and of courtiers passing in the night.

Other than when my Nan used to make the inevitable enquiry as to whether l was 'courting', the only context in which I can think we actually use the verb 'to court' is 'courting with death', 'courting trouble', 'courting favours' ... perhaps we choose to do all three ever more wantonly in our couplings. It is a phrase which I suspect will die with my Nan's generation but when they have left this mortal coil, it will tellingly leave a descriptive gap in the English language, one which is no longer relevant or of any application to modern life.

A girlfriend of mine, having recently got through her second, emotionally charged divorce, had spent some months seeking out men via a dating agency on the net. She had had several pleasant dates, had met people from different parts of the country and dined in restaurants (and seen a couple of hotel bedrooms) she would never otherwise have seen. Then she met a guy, eight years her senior, whom she really liked.

He wasn't an obvious choice in terms of rugged good looks but she found herself increasingly drawn to him as their dates

21

progressed and, being very aware of her own vulnerability, was scared by her own inability to draw her emotional horns in. I was frankly amazed at the extent of her 'falling', particularly given the fact that their physical interaction was limited to hugs and kisses.

She was in the process of transferring her house to her ex and moving into rented accommodation; she did agree with new man that it would be better to have all that sorted and then go away for a weekend somewhere chilled. She did! She impressed it on me when I expressed my surprise, knowing her as I do, at her willingness to accept this continued delay. There had even been a couple of times when, charged with excess alcohol and another full stomach, she had begged that they get a room (much to her embarrassment in the clear sober light of morning!) Four months down the line she snapped and, again similarly charged, effectively said that if they didn't go to bed the relationship was over. Not the best backdrop to a first session but that wasn't in her consciousness at the time!

I was chatting with my mom who enquired after her well being. I explained that she was pretty low and alluded to the cause. "How refreshing!" my mother said. That was certainly not the word my friend would have used. What a difference a generation makes!

I rapidly learnt in Liverpool that there was a subtle but substantial difference between 'copping off' and 'trapping off'. Whichever way round it was, one meant you had had sex, the other meant that you had, or did, anything other than sex. We all understand courting to mean a kind of gentle, gentlemanly, stiff upper-lip dating process which, in reality, probably also meant a great deal other than sex in some cases but, in its pure form, involved nothing so 'gross' and was a precursor to marriage. Will the next generation ever have the chance to be so naive? So unexposed? Where is the need for such a word in our modern day society? Courting is very largely consigned to the history books.

So, people moved around in their jobs, in their neighbourhoods and, increasingly, in the world. They started moving around in their relationships too. Suddenly women had far more control over their own destinies. Hot baths, gin or a steep staircase were no longer the only options for the unwanted consequences of a night of passion out of wedlock. They were in control of when they took that little pink pill which, practice was showing them, could be relied upon. At the same time, outside cultures reached us when travelling, in relaxed publishing laws and even satellite links. Red Hot Dutch graced the airways of anyone with an early satellite dish - and that was hardcore porn - before the Government got the signal blocked (momentarily and prior to the Twenty-First Century's deluge from all sources!)

The impact on our relationships and the way we conducted them was immense. The structural framework, the very infrastructure of our society, changed irreversibly. The movement, the freedom, the variety attracted us like sweets in a shop window once did. Unless we were raised in Mao's China, moral pressure of a society on a society is generally localized. People who live in close communities where everyone knows everyone, and their business, exert and have more influence exerted on them by others than those living in an anonymous metropolis.

This freedom … of travel, of sex without the consequence of birth, of information, of being … dramatically changed our own lives and the lives of our relationships. However, we were left holding the old blueprint for a happily fulfilled life, expecting The Fairy Tale to survive the total scene change. As if we could drop Cinderella onto a Star Wars set and expect her to fit in. It is imperative that our expectations of our relationships change with this never-before-encountered freedom. Greater freedom brings greater translucency.

In true Yin Yang fashion, with Individual Freedom has come Her opposite, Big Brother.

When we travel, the immigration services know it, our fingerprints and irises are photographed when entering the States; when we are allowed to travel it allows those of different beliefs to tour their terrorism, which means we need Big brother whilst despising Him.

When we have sexual freedom, the government knows if we're on the pill (because it 'gives' it to us); it knows, if we have a child, whether we are married, cohabiting or single; when we are allowed our sexual freedom we risk both our sexual health and our long-term couplings. We despise being sexually inhibited and yet perceive that we need rules which prevent sexual anarchy.

When we can access such a broad spectrum of information via the Net, we are incredulous at the number of hours previously spent in libraries largely locating the source rather than information gathering; when we are allowed to access so much information Big Brother collects the spectrum of information which makes up the minutia of our individual lives.

When we are, we have to face who we really are; when we are allowed to be, we have to allow Big Brother to be. The difficulty is that Big Brother is increasingly anonymous and distant from ourselves. When the main influence in our lives was our parents or our pier group, their advice was tailor made to us as individuals and, as such, was a lot easier to heed or at least consider. With our dispersed families and city living we resent being increasingly told in the minutest of detail what to do or not to do by a faceless force but the changes in the very infrastructure of our society make such dictates unavoidable.

CHAPTER THREE

WHO ARE YOU?

It is not as easy as it sounds to be Honest with yourself.

'To thine own self be true' - if we can find ourselves in the sea of an emotional and social tug-of-war which pulls at us throughout our lives and then recognise our own image and our own nature.

If you ask a Caribbean how long they have thought or felt something their answer will often start

'As long as I've known myself...'

It may be a wise man who knows his own father but it is an even wiser man who knows himself, truly.

Ultimately, how well we know ourselves dictates our ability to convey this to a proposed soul mate. Reason and Passion, Head and Heart, do battle for supremacy.

Kahil Gibran, poet philosopher and artist writing The Prophet in 1923 suggests:

"Your reason and your passion are the rudder and the sails of your seafaring soul. If either your sails or your rudder be broken, you can but toss and drift, or else be held at a standstill in mid-seas. For reason, ruling alone, is at once confining; and passion, unattended, is a flame that burns to its own destruction. Therefore let your soul exalt your Reason, that your Passion may live through its own daily resurrection, and like the phoenix rise above its own ashes."

Undoubtedly wise truth, simple obviousness, but difficult to achieve as mere mortals.

Mother Nature, in her wisdom of relativity, produces mortals who lack either Reason, through mental illness, or Passion, like the cold psychopath deprived of the riches which empathy breeds. Those of us whom, through the fortune of birth, have both, spend our lives trying to curb our Reason and our Passion whilst simultaneously driven to indulge both. Our Passion will produce the babies which Mother Nature needs for our perpetration and our Reason will guide our choice of mate. When Reason and Passion find equilibrium, women decide upon the breeding mate and men decide the gender of our children through provision of an X or a Y!

Self analysis is not something which we are taught even indirectly. Some of us are naturally more inclined than others to question ourselves and our motives. We have always known ourselves and we are aware of our idiosyncrasies ... we may not wish to dwell on them too much!

To know ourselves we have to be honest with ourselves and lift some of the shutters which we might choose to keep bolted down in the corners of our minds. We have to take our own self-knowledge and try to stand outside of ourselves in an attempt to bring some objectivity into what, by definition, can only be subjective. To approach true objectivity we need a third party whose objectivity will, of itself, be subjective.

How well do we know ourselves? Every year my partners and I would take ourselves off to a 'nice' hotel in the 'country' with a pre-booked conference room to talk about marketing, strategies to 'grow' the business, areas within our particular legal fields which we needed to develop, attempting to agree where we wished the business to head... it was always a hard, seemingly unending and tasking day, not least because the aspirations of a commercial lawyer or a senior partner who needs to ensure the business is 'healthy' enough to fund a long-established 'capital account' tend to vary quite considerably from those of relatively 'young' lawyers immersed in criminal or family work. It was the zenith of our Practice Manager's year since it was she who was responsible for preparing the subject matter and the accompanying paperwork. She always fretted that there would not be enough to keep us occupied and accordingly showered us with an impossible mountain of tasks and exercises which we were never able to complete!

To ease the pain which must be endured prior to an over-indulgent evening meal, plentiful booze and inevitably crashing the wedding disco in the function room of the hotel to have a wobbly bop, we would have a post lunch reprieve, some light relief whilst our lunch and wine wore off. Over the years we were variously 'amused' by presentations on body language, how to 'network' alone in a room of strangers, remembering people's names...Other than the golf lesson which preceded dinner (the only time I held a club in my hand annually), it was the high-light of the day. We even learnt how to Karate chop a piece of wood though I can't quite recall the intended purpose of that. Mind over matter? A bit scary in the context of a lawyer's training!

One of the most memorable 'light relief' sessions related to our testing our own personalities. As far as I am aware, none of us had ever encountered anything quite like this before. I had chosen to study Criminology at uni in which, for example, I studied the likelihood of identical twins, separated at birth, both becoming 'juvenile delinquents' … nature vs nurture etc. Fascinating but one step removed from our own lives. What follows is an abbreviated version of what we were given (the full text can be found in the annex at the end of this book). There is something decidedly unnerving about being given a test which apparently categorises you into one of four personality types. We all like to think that we are unique individuals with an unmatchable series of traits and characteristics, moulded by our one-off genes and life experience. Whilst this is doubtless true on a detailed level, it is very enlightening to find that we can each be fairly accurately boxed into one of four personality types! The more extreme your character, the more accurate the related description.

Take a piece of paper and note down the letters next to your answers to the following questions. Give yourself a couple of seconds only to answer each. There will obviously be instances when your general answer will not be accurate to specific situations but they should, in most circumstances with most people, be fairly representative of your behaviour/personality. Make sure you have all 22 answers.

FAIRY TALES by Sharon Moore

COLUMN A		COLUMN B	
1. S	Tends to deal with facts more than opinions	1. O	Tends to rely on opinions more than facts
2. S	Punctual	2. O	Leisurely about time
3. O	Easy to get to know	3. S	Reserved
4. S	Enjoys following an established schedule	4. O	More spontaneous, lives for the moment
5. O	Animated facial expressions during speaking and listening	5. S	Few facial expressions when speaking and listening
6. S	Focuses conversation on issues and tasks at hand, stays on subject	6. O	Conversation consists of many stories and Anecdotes; gets off subject
7. O	Shows and shares feelings freely	7. S	Keeps feelings hidden
8. O	Considerable hand/body movement during conversation	8. S	Limited hand/body movement when conversing
9. O	Openly shows enthusiasm	9. S	Less likely to show enthusiasm openly
10. S	Makes decisions rationally	10. O	Makes decisions based on feelings/emotions
11. O	Mostly speaks in generalities and opinions	11. S	Mostly speaks in specifics facts and logic
12. I	Risk avoider	12. D	Risk taker

WHO ARE YOU?

13. I	Infrequent contributor in group conversation		13. D	Frequent contributor in group conversation
14. D	Fast paced		14. I	Steady paced
15. D	Uses voice intonations to emphasise points		15. I	Little use of voice to emphasise points
16. I	Speaks softer than average		16. D	Speaks louder than average
17. D	Speaks faster than average		17. I	Speaks slower than average
18. D	Makes gestures to emphasise points		18. I	Few gestures to emphasise points
19. I	When don't agree, most likely to go along		19. D	Most likely to put up an argument when don't agree
20. D	More likely to introduce self to others in social gatherings		20. I	More likely to wait for others to introduce selves
21. D	Communicates readily		21. I	Hesitant to communicate
22. D	Makes emphatic statements (black and white)		22. I	Makes tentative statements (shades of grey)

When you have your totals of O's and S's, take the bigger number off the smaller number, the same for your D's and I's. e.g. 7 S's minus 4 O'S equals 3 S's and 8 D's minus 3 I's equals 5 D's. Then plot your score on the following graph:

BEHAVIOURAL STYLE PROFILE GRID

SELF-CONTAINED

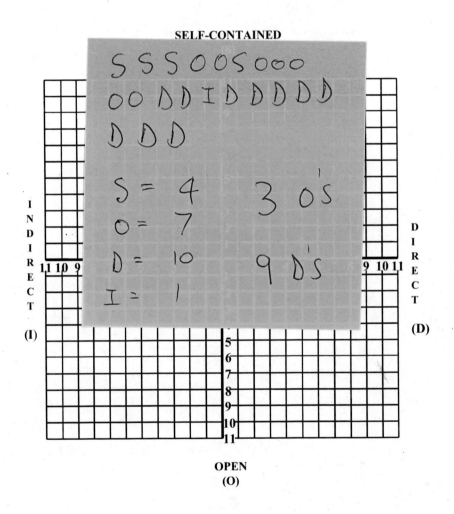

SSSOOSooo
OO DD I D DDDD
D DD

S = 4   3 o's
O = 7
D = 10   9 D's
I = 1

INDIRECT (I)

DIRECT (D)

11 10 9   9 10 11

5
6
7
8
9
10
11

**OPEN
(O)**

To take the example above, the person would be quite self-contained and quite direct. The further away from the centre of the graph we fall in any particular direction, the stronger that aspect would seem to be in our personality. Once we have established which quadrant we fall into and to what extent, we can gain an insight into what makes us tick.

OPEN: If we are open we outwardly show and share our personal thoughts and feelings. We tend to be relaxed and warm though also dramatic using animated facial expressions to tell stories and anecdotes. We like to be around people but are rarely on time. We are both opinion and relationship orientated. We use our bodies to emphasise our speech and provide immediate non-verbal feedback. We can place little emphasis on facts and details and metaphorically tend to live within the 'spirit' of the law rather than the letter of it.

SELF CONTAINED: If, conversely, we are self-contained, we are more formal, proper, fact-oriented, guarded, controlled, disciplined about time and task oriented. We tend to hide our personal feelings and we are thinking and non-contact oriented. We may be somewhat expressionless, have controlled and limited hand and body movement and be slow in using non-verbal feedback, if we give it at all. We are disciplined and punctual and our conversation focuses on issues and tasks. We push for facts and details and we are slow to share personal feelings. We live by the letter of the law.

DIRECT: Directness is the way we seek control. If we are direct we take risks, make swift decisions. We are impatient and confronting, talkative and extroverted, readily expressing our opinions. We are verbose and our questions tend to be rhetorical. We use a high volume fast voice to make emphatic statements. We use gestures and challenging voice intonation to emphasise points and question others opinions. We are likely to have a firm handshake and maintain steady eye contact.

INDIRECT: As such we will avoid risks; think about our decisions; be supportive, easy going and introverted. Whilst we are good listeners, we reserve our opinions. We do not talk so much and our questions are for clarification, support and information. Our statements are tentative, our gestures limited. Our voice is quieter and slower with few variations in our vocal intonation. We are slow moving and communicate hesitantly. Our handshake is soft and our eye contact intermittent.

Quite frighteningly these huge generalisations transpire to be surprisingly accurate, especially for those of us whose score takes us to the outer edge of our quadrant where our characteristics are more marked.

Not only is this test an interesting mirror on our innards, it reminds us that we act and react instinctively according to our nature and are not so much in control of our behaviour as we would have ourselves believe. We must also remind ourselves that it is the same for those around us both in our workplaces and in our beds. To try to walk around in someone else's shoes we first have to tiptoe around their minds and understand their likely behaviour. This will be affected by numerous other influences from gender to which side of your particular brain is dominant.

The following illustration will not reflect everyone's work situation but has proven uncannily accurate if viewed in general terms to mirror the way we may approach our workspace and, with a little imagination, our relationships in general and our love lives in particular!

When we are stressed our somewhat immature 'back-up style' will kick in in an attempt to dissipate that tension. Though this is true in a work situation it is also true within the context of our relationships and is particularly evident during disagreements and arguments. The Thinker will withdraw under stress and their dominant needs are to receive reassurance that they are right and to achieve an understanding of the principles and details involved. The Director will dictate under stress and their dominant needs are to control themselves and their situation and to gain fast tangible evidence of their progress. The Relater will submit under stress and their dominant needs are to gain reassurance, slow the pace and secure tangible guarantees for the future. Finally, the Expressive will become confrontational under stress and their dominant needs are to act and interact quickly whilst gaining credit for their point of view. If we can not only be aware of our own 'back-up style' but that of our partner then we can quickly reduce tension by trying to meet, or at least acknowledge, our partner's dominant needs in the first instant. If your partner shares the same behavioural style under stress it may be harder to restore harmony and compromise will be key.

It is perhaps easier to predict our likely behaviour within the relatively controlled environs of work as our options are, for the majority, limited. It is often the case that we really don't know how we will react, feel or behave in a given situation until that situation actually presents itself to us. As armchair watchers of a grisly war flamed by Greed, Fear and Prejudice do we really know that we would not behave as some of the shamed soldiers have behaved. Violent cruelty and rape have been synonymous with warfare for as long as we have records. It seems incredible but then it is literally an 'incredible' (un-knowable) situation for those of us who have never been placed in it.

Many of our strengths and weaknesses may never be fully tested and so we never know the true extent of our black and white sides if we have a grey life or choose the latter because it feels safer, easier, less challenging.

I recall the story which hit us from the U.S. in the mid 80's about 'the girl in the box' the detail of which was presented in a book 'The Perfect Victim'. She was a young, bright and lively student hitching along a busy road when she was picked up by a young couple with a baby. Pleased to have found what appeared to be a 'safe' ride she got into the back seat and chatted pleasantly with her transporters. After some time they indicated that they wanted to pull up into a small side road since it lead to an excellent photo opportunity spot. When they stopped the car the man made to open the door for their companion but snapped a home-made box on her head, secured around her neck.

The couple drove her back to their home where she was stripped, blindfolded and hung from a beam in the cellar. They fucked on the floor in front of her. She was put into another prefabricated box in which she was forced to lie because it wasn't big enough for her to do anything else. Over a period they were able to completely brainwash her into believing she had no identity other than that of a slave. He copied a 'slave contract' from some alternative magazine and got her to sign it.

Captured aged twenty, the couple would let her out increasingly over the next seven years to perform household, as well as bedroom, chores culminating in her actually going out of the house to work each day. Though this was relative freedom, she had not been allowed out of the house, and seldom out of her basement box, for the first year. In those early days

"… the list of sadistic fantasies he acted out on her lengthened. Once, while he had her hanging by the wrists, he held a heat lamp next to her skin, watching her writhe in pain as it burned. Another time, he touched her with live electric wires. He hung her upside down and bound her in strange ways. He made her orally copulate him. He strangled her. She was little more than his guinea pig, and he subjected her to just about anything he could imagine and devise, short of braking his (then) promise of fidelity" - Christine McGuire and Carla Norton.

She had been allowed no contact with her family over the years. When the story broke people were not prepared to believe that a normal young woman had been brainwashed to the extent that she would not run away from slavery even when she had had the opportunity. But she hadn't. There for the Grace of… ? Fortunately we shall never know. Perhaps an extreme example to prove a point but we are all 'brainwashed' - usually to a lesser extent - and moulded by our experiences especially those in our formative years. We need to unravel why we feel a certain way in order to understand ourselves and indeed open our minds to other possibilities and think outside of our box, however it may be customized by our particular brainwashing.

Mother Nature does plant an essential drive in all of us for self-preservation, nowhere more than in the fragile balance of the mind. Whilst She has given us the ability to look into ourselves and explore, She also has an interest in maintaining our mental balance. If the scale tips too far one way this may lead to depression and self-loathing which in turn may lead to acts of self harm, from that inflicted with razor blades on our own bodies, to suicide. When we feel as though the scale is tipping too far we increasingly turn to various props like alcohol or drugs. The number of people currently taking Prozac, a prescribed antidepressant, is at an all time high, there is so much heroine on the market we can buy 'a wrap' on the street for a fiver and the demand for weed increasingly outstrips supply. They help us to lose ourselves, or perhaps find ourselves from a different approach, like seeing our house from the back door rather than the front. If we have never been drunk it is impossible to know how we would behave inebriated and so the extent of our self knowledge is again bordered by our experience.

In 1923 in his 'Structural Theory' Sigmund Freud proposed a division of our personalities into three main contingents and though much of his theory has been discredited by some over the years, his model still provides a useful reference point.

The first was our Id, our core, the animal that is born whether in a gutter in Calcutta or a sanitised hospital bed in this green and pleasant land. The genes of our ancestors are passed down by those who manage to procreate and clone themselves into the core of the next generation. Our basic instincts he accredits to our Id such that the fundamental drive to survive by feeding, sheltering and defending ourselves comes from this innate and almost primeval facet of Human Nature. It drives us to protect, preserve and promote ourselves and our offspring. It is the natural product of our genes. A newborn has nothing but this to drive it. It is wholly part of our unconscious self and is our pleasure seeker. A baby cries if it wants food, is uncomfortable, is in pain or simply wants attention. It is, according to Freud, the Id which cries; the Id doesn't care about anyone else's needs and is removed from reality.

He goes on to expound that, in the next three years, a child develops its Ego, the second part of what becomes our personality. This is our learnt behaviour prompted by the reality around us. The Ego will try to satisfy the needs of our Id whilst taking account of the reality of any given situation.

Finally he suggests that, by age five, we start to develop our Superego, which exists in our preconscious. This is the moral part of our personality and reflects the moral and ethical restraints imposed on us by our carers. It is our conscience and dictates what we see as right and wrong. It is the polish on the stone, like the fairness of our Equitable laws which have grown up to soften the harsh corners of our black and white Common laws. Table manners ingrained to prevent the display as Nature would otherwise present Herself at the dinner table. My mother taught me to drink my soup by dipping the spoon and the bowl away from me (was that in the event of spillage?) and never breaking the bread into it or using it to mop up the residue. She admonished me as a teenager and advised that one day 'some young man' would take me to a restaurant and be forever repelled by my otherwise natural soup-eating methods. She did not discuss how difficult it is to get the right man at the dinner table and, if he were there, my soup-eating habits would have likely nothing to do with whether the experience was repeated!

According to Freud, our Ego, which floats between our unconscious, preconscious and conscious, has to be the strongest facet of our personality, seeking a healthy balance between the needs of our Id and the necessary learnt social constraints of our Superego. If our Ego fails to keep that balance then either our Id will be too strong, and our impulses of self gratification will take over, or our Superego will take over and we will become morally rigid, judgmental and unbending. He believed that our Id is the source of our drives, the reservoir of our libido being predominantly sexual but underlying all our mental processes.

The man who might, whilst wandering around a supermarket and seeing an attractive woman bending into a freezer, if his Id were able to rule supreme, take her from behind there and then, is prevented from doing so (in the vast majority of cases!) His Superego dictates that this is socially and morally wrong (quite aside from the fact that it is likely to land him in jail). His Ego, aware of both driving forces, might save the day by prompting him to ask her out on a date, by finding a compromiseed.

When I was in India some seventeen years ago, the Government in Delhi was running a campaign to educate people to wash their hands before eating and after defecating. This is drummed into us from such an early age that we forget it is a learnt behaviour and even such a basic hygienic action does not come naturally, is not part of our innate knowledge, is not part of our Id.

The key lesson is that however disciplined, educated or balanced we believe ourselves to be, there are facets of our personalities which effect how we think and behave of which we are largely unaware and over which we have little control. Though our egos will do their damndest to keep them in check they have a massive influence upon who we are. The comforting and yet scary reality is that it is the same for everyone such that those we have any kind of interaction with are also labouring under this veil of self-ignorance.

When my former business partners and I completed the Behavioural Questionnaire it was revealing to find that I scored 11 for openness and 11 for directness. None of my answers had been either self-contained or indirect! The guy presenting the lecture had never encountered such an extreme Expressive and I suspect this will reveal much to you about the person behind this book. I have to add that, within the context of my legal work itself, I never took the attitude that 'rules are there to be broken' though I did take such an attitude with some of the 'social norms' which prevail within the legal profession. Perhaps amusingly amongst a group of seven partners, involved in a service industry, none of us were Relaters but maybe that was why we had all achieved the heady heights of partnership!

Who we are and the particular attributes of our individual personalities will not only shape the form of and our success in the workplace, it will also have a bearing on the relationships we choose and the extent of their success. Once we become consciously aware of what presses our own buttons we can pursue a course to true self-discovery.

CHAPTER FOUR

FORMING OUR OWN SEXUAL MORALITY

We can take the girl out of the city but we can never take the city out of the girl. We can remove ourselves from a certain experience but we can never take the experience out of ourselves. It is what we do with the knowledge that experience affords us which can help us change and grow, if we allow it to.

Our morality is part of our Superego. Our Id, our very animality, what we are at birth, does not know that it should not covet another man's wife. There would be no need for religions to promote edicts such as the Ten Commandments if we innately knew these things already. Even so far as murder. Our basic potential sexuality may have been fixed by Mother Nature in our genes but how we explore that sexuality, with whom and in what circumstances, is partly created by sheer opportunity but, more importantly, by our nurturing, by the experiences creating influences which we are exposed to throughout our lives, our taught morality forever being realigned by our learnt morality.

I grew up in a fairly small town. There were two boys' schools and one girl's school in the actual town itself. Even by seventeen, few of us had cars and you don't go out on the piss on a motorbike. We socialised in and around the town throughout our teens. For those who grew up there, the

43

difference between the various Black Country accents was marked and changed within a matter of a few miles. Your identity was very much related to your town, your accent, your tribe. Though you didn't know everyone, you would certainly know several people if you went to a pub, party or just took a walk down the High street.

There was one girl in my class of thirty-two whose parents were divorced. That was little more than twenty five years ago but at the time it was something which we would only whisper about behind raised palms at break time. 'Sexual intercourse', when (as we were taught in our biology class) "the penis is placed in the vagina", sounded a rather uninteresting concept for something which had, up to then, been a mysterious untalked about act, to our twelve year old ears listening so intently you could have heard a pin drop. When you've never seen or realised how dramatically the male form changes when his blood gets pumping, the "placing" bit sounded particularly tricky. Unlike many of today's twelve year olds, at that age we had never seen a picture, let alone a film, of what sex actually looked like in the having. We would have been totally awestruck at the thought of having a personal computer let alone being able to view explicit photos and video clips for free with a simple tap on our search engine.

A child's personality may be formed by the age of seven but our sexual morality is usually instilled much later. Our parents may have set an example by staying 'happily married' but it is usually only when we enter our teens that we even begin to understand what sexuality is. And even then it is shrouded in an intangible greyness of knowledge. My classmates and I were brain burningly aware of what genital warts looked like

from gross films shown at school but we weren't really any
the wiser as to how it would actually feel to have a boy's
penis thrust, pushed or even 'placed' in our vaginas.

I grew up going to Sunday school and 'Christian' schools
promoting 'Christian' morality, guiding our Superegos. Nice
girls really did not have sex until they were married. Whilst,
had we been asked, which we were not, whether we believed
that a ceremony was a prerequisite, we may have refuted it,
we certainly felt we should be older and 'in love'. Nobody
had ever talked to us about oral sex. With the Curiosity which
only Ignorance can fire, this became a kind of allowable
halfway house. Our hormones were having a Rave in one of
those typically hidden locations and we wanted to release
them without breaking the ultimate sex taboo. Our Ids
wanted to have sex, our Superegos told us we could not and
our Egos were desperate to find a solution!

We had boyfriends whom we snogged endlessly and held
hands with always. We exchanged notes with the Boys
schools, all with multiple contributors, such that they became
a group experience - less scary than one to one
communication. These were our tokens of love. For a boy of
fifteen to walk round town, where people you knew would
see you, holding your hand, wearing your school scarf, was an
announcement to the world. It made us proud to be finally
wearing the badge of entrance into sexuality, though we were
only hanging out in the vestibule of that massive house.

Our form of thirty-two girls had spent five years of our lives
together, from uncertain eleven year olds, through all the
trials and tribulations of the early teens, to confident sixteen
year olds. It was almost a group decision for many of us to
cross the divide, pursue the ultimate taboo. From a shy

fumble under the T-shirt in a cold garage at a party fuelled with the fire of love and a bottle of Merrydown Cider, we progressed to being naked, giving oral sex, having sex. As Time sped on at that heady speed of discovery, we savoured each moment. The Rave was in full swing and we were enthusiastic partygoers with hormones for E's.

Some ten years later when I started my first 'proper' job as an assistant solicitor, I learnt a bizarre reality. Several of the girls in the small office were twenty years my senior. We worked together closely and became close. There is a need to get on in a close stressed working environment and an interdependency which goes further than merely getting the job done. The two male partners were out and we found ourselves talking about sex and sexual experiences.

The oral concept raised its head. The older girls started to resemble the look of our playground whisperings - giggling, embarrassment, averted eyes. It became clear that for them this was an act of such intimacy that it was only ever practiced within a longstanding love-filled relationship, preferably condoned by a ceremony. It was something they had come to, presumably prompted by the frustrations of their husbands, well on into their marriages. For this generation, who had swallowed the 'nice girls' mantra, oral sex was beyond the vaginal placement, more extreme (and the swallowing created even greater reaction!)

Our core sexuality may be in our Id but whether we give good (or indeed any) 'head' is very much part of the way our Ego manages that against our Superego, our taught and learnt morality. When my friends and I crossed the divide, our raving boyfriends knew no more than we. They didn't know it was impolite, contrary to bed etiquette, to cum in situ without prior agreement. And we didn't know that we had any choice. No-one talked to us about oral sex never mind about a swallowing option. And we knew it was full of protein! No-one leaves a rave just before midnight. No-one in those early days of sexual experience wanted to stop the love of their life just before climax and make his boys go flying into midair. Our Egos in those mid teen years believed they had found a solution.

Though the even stickier subject of masturbation was not one which we discussed that day, the way in which our society views that pastime has shifted quite dramatically in a short period of history. Boys are no longer told that it will send them blind, problem pages are actively encouraging young women to explore their own bodies and medical ignorance which went so far as blaming it for infertility (and for various other physical ailments) has been firmly corrected. Though it is something which is as instinctive as scratching our nose when it itches, this activity was vilified for centuries creating guilt and phobias which lasted lifetimes. One boyfriend of mine once suggested that the reason I couldn't always reach the heady heights of orgasm during penetration was because I "wanked too much". I had to explain that whilst it might encumber his own performance 'in the sac', if anything it enhanced mine. It seems a shame that Mother Nature had to limit men in this way, from the perspective of both sexes! (or perhaps you thank her for small mercies).

The 'About marriage' website states that the consensus of those doing a statistical analysis suggest that 90% of the total male population and 65% of females "masturbate from time to time". It asserts that it can be therapeutic, relieving sexual tension , helping couples with different sex drives cope and,

47

in non-sexually-active men, can help 'prevent congestion of the prostate'! From a 'moral' point of view it is argued that it can serve to 'hide repressed anger and lessen spousal intimacy'. Catholics, Mormons and Ecclesiastics (to name but a few) consider it a sin as it is clearly not for the purposes of procreation (though it is free, healthy and should harm no-one). Just as men over egg, and women under egg, the pudding when it comes to recounting their number of sexual partners, I suspect that the same is true when it comes to wanking. There is still a greater social taboo about women talking openly about it than for men, except if you're on the cast of 'Sex in the City'.

Sexual practices and morality move with the generations. In 2004/5 13% of men aged 16 to 69 and 9% of women aged 16 to 49 indicated in a survey that they had had four or more sexual partners, according to government statistics. That surprised me (since far more than 9% of my female friends, myself included, would have fallen into that category). However it confirmed that one third of men and one quarter of women under the age of 25 indicated having had four or more sexual partners. As our lives have become less restrained by religious and ethical dictates it seems that our Superegos are less restraining of our Ids – which must make the job of our Egos a whole lot easier. Interestingly, of all the married or cohabiting adults surveyed, 5% of men but only 1% of women indicated that they had no sexual partner, were not sexually active.

The morality taught within certain cultures and religions shows itself in related statistics. Asian and Chinese ethnic origin families with dependant children are most likely to be married and the least likely to be lone parents. In 2001, 85%

of Indian families with dependant children were headed by a married couple, in the UK. Conversely, cohabitation with dependant children is most common in Mixed, Black Caribbean and White families. In turn, that morality effects whether we have children and how many. The Office for National Statistics issued a news release in 2001 concerning 'Diversity within Ethnic Groups'. Bangladeshi families are the most likely to have children with almost 4/5ths of them in the UK having a minimum of one dependant child. The least likely are White families for whom only 2/5ths have at least one child.

Of all the 39,333 known HIV sufferers in 2004 in the UK, 52 % were white, 38 % Black African and 3% black Caribbean leaving only 7% to all other ethnic origin groups. Our Superegos, by definition, vary widely between different religions and cultures which dramatically effects the extent to which our Ids, which are largely the same and ignorant of such divides, are allowed to have their way by our Egos. Though I have nothing but my own life's experience to base this on, I can't help but wonder whether the fact that Black Caribbean's in the U.K. have such a relatively low incidence of HIV is not related to the fact that homosexuality within that particular culture is so strongly frowned upon. Though heterosexuals are now more likely to contract HIV, in the early days it spread predominantly amongst the male gay community. The Caribbean Superegos might have been much less likely to allow a homosexual Id, via its negotiating Ego, to have its way. But then all of the figures are relative to the percentage of the population which these various ethnic groups represent (statistics, damn statistics and downright lies?)

FAIRY TALES by Sharon Moore

The effect of the influence of our Superegos upon our behaviour, our morality upon our social structures, is also reflected if we look at the number of individual households in the UK. Between 1971 and 2005 there was a 30% increase in their number from 18.6 million to 24.2 million. This was over proportionate to the general population increase and again reflects the trend of there being more lone parents, smaller families and a general increase in one person households.

One person households have become much more prevalent and again government statistics suggest that around seven million people were living alone in Britain in 2005. In 1971 one person households represented 18% of the total number of households in Britain, that rose to 27% of the total in 1991 and since that time it is believed that the percentage has risen to around 30%. Whilst in the mid 80's to 90's a high proportion of those households were made up of older women who had outlived their male partners, in the last ten years that tendency has become increasingly irrelevant. The age of individuals in one person households is getting younger and the largest increase is in people aged 25 to 44 which has doubled in the last twenty years. The number of men living alone is greatest in the 45 to 64 age group (again the number having more than doubled in the last twenty years) reflecting the increase in marriage breakdown and the fact that women are much more likely to be the main carers of children when that occurs.

By definition, in our everyday lives, we are not aware of the complicated mental processes going on in our inner psyches. We have to deal with all the pressures and vicissitudes of the everyday . To maintain our mental balance we have to love ourselves and our traits as much as we hate them. This can colour our true view with rose tints on occasions, a necessary Subjectiveness for mental balance. We also have to trust ourselves and our sixth sense. The danger of this technological age is that we lose sight of our spirituality or learn to ignore it. Everything in life requires balance, Yin and Yang. As our lives become increasingly technology-driven we have to 'up the anti' on Nature's impact. The most amazing computer in the world is housed in our own bodies and we have to be reminded to listen to it.

In his introduction to 'Listening with the Third Ear', Theodor Reik writing upon the inner experience of a Psychoanalyst reports the following speech:

> "…In vital matters, however, such as the choice of a mate or a profession, the decision should come from the unconscious, from somewhere within ourselves. In the important decisions of our personal life, we should be governed, I think, by the deep inner needs of our nature".

This had been spoken to him by Sigmund Freud during an evening stroll.

That may have been so in 1948 when he was published. Has anything really happened more than fifty years on, to make his statement any less relevant? I think not. Was it wise advice then and is it now? A friend of mine suggests that, once you reach forty, any important decision you make in your life especially one relating to living together, marriage, children… becomes one in which the head must rule the heart. We are older, wiser and better informed. We know ourselves better and know what we do and don't want. We are more reluctant or less able to throw caution to the wind and 'fall in love'. But a rudder with no sails can go nowhere; Reason without

FAIRY TALES by Sharon Moore

Passion makes for a dry old age and, when it comes to the choice of a mate, our intellect only follows our instinct to preserve our genes.

So when we feel that initial spark when we meet someone, that underlying animal attraction which can hit us suddenly and take us by surprise, take our breath away, make us blush and feel like a butterfly got trapped somewhere, we should listen. These unspoken internal communications which disclose the 'deep inner needs' of our natures - pheromones, unconscious body language, 'sixth sense' stuff – are all too easy to ignore or discount. It is only an inkling which has to be explored and nurtured if it is to grow into a strong and healthy relationship but it's a good start. Passion and Reason are not mutually exclusive and a 'gut reaction' will intoxicate the head as well as the heart in our soul's mixing bowl. All of the ingredients are thrown in and the consequent cake may surprise us in its form or taste and indeed be incapable of our conception prior to the baking but if we've left out the salt, the flavour will always be lacking however much jam we slap on it.

CHAPTER FIVE

SEXUAL ORIENTATION

If we have not been placed in a particular place of opportunity it may be difficult to predict with certainty what we would do.

Sex in the context of a relationship is usually vital (at least for the first few decades!) It is what distinguishes it from family or friendship alone. So the beginning of our self-knowledge is impossible without an awareness of the true nature of our own sexuality. That of itself may not be so easy since our self-knowledge will inevitably be limited by our particular experiences. Matching our sexual orientation and drive with our partner is often essential to achieve a fulfilled and happy relationship. The compliant homosexual in a heterosexual relationship will only be happy if he shares such an intimate relationship with his partner that she understands his need to explore that sexuality elsewhere. Someone with a naturally low libido coupled with a healthier one will be unhappy and their partner will be frustrated to the point of supplementing elsewhere. This was not always the case when Religion and Family had a tighter grasp and it may not be as we would wish it to be but, in our easy access society, it is now. As sure as eggs is eggs.

In many cases the 'match' or the mismatch may not be immediately obvious. The man who learns that his partner was bound and abused as a child will not indulge his own penchant for tying her to the bedstead, unless they become so intimate that such trust is created that she ultimately learns to enjoy this rather than fear it. That's a tall order. The woman may have had such bad experiences of sex in the past that her once healthy libido has been reasoned into submission and needs renurturing within an intimate relationship. We all change with time and the relationship has to be truly intimate enough to deal with those changes, from a waning and incapable libido to the discovery of some bisexual tendencies later in life. We can find these truths difficult to recognise and accept ourselves let alone share with the person we hold as our dearest.

If men purportedly reach their sexual peak at around nineteen whilst women do so at around thirty-six this can inevitably lead to differences and changes which can be frustrating and challenging to both sexes within a relationship. The simple fact that many men can not 'get it up' or 'keep it up' as often or for as long at fifty as they could at twenty-five can create feelings of inadequacy and insecurity not only for those men but also for their female partners who can then feel less attractive, less sexually alluring. When combined with the fact that women, having matured and relaxed into their own sexuality, might just be at the stage of wanting more from their partner, this can create a potentially explosive cocktail. Human nature being what it is, the danger is that attack can appear to be the best form of defence and then the blaming game begins. The man suggests that he does not 'perform' as well because of the pressure which he feels she is placing him under, the mere fact that she has mentioned it has created the 'problem'. The woman suggests that he has simply become complacent or even selfish, not bothering to try to extend her pleasure before taking his own. Alternatively, no-one says anything, fuelling our own theories as to what is happening within our own minds without the understanding which only honest and open communication can bring.

But, before we are able to do that, we first need to know and understand our own minds, our own selves, our own sexuality and be open to the fact that even that may change. I have acted for as many male clients over the years who have been left by their wives for other women (one found his wife under the kitchen table at a party with the hostess!) as I have for female clients left by men who have 'come out'.

From the outset, Nature and Nurture play their parts in the end result adult. Two of my good friends are gay and have an ongoing lengthy living-together relationship. One originally married his childhood's best mate - it lasted six months (though the law dictates that you have to wait a year before you can start divorce proceedings). He had known from a very early age that he was gay, long before he was sexually active. He came from a small town with a small town mentality and it did not then hold any kudos to be 'theonlygayinthevillage'. He conformed to social pressure and married the person he cared most about in the world outside of his immediate family. He learnt relatively early on in his life that he has no choice as to his own sexual orientation and that there was only pain to be gained by being dishonest about that; pain for himself and those whom he loved and loved him. In some ways he is so much more a woman than I could ever be and the thought of being sexually active with a woman repulses him just about as much as the thought of being with him would be to the average Joe.

His partner on the other hand, had a 'long' marriage in today's terms. He says there was nothing wrong with his wife at all, she was just the wrong sex! It is one thing to commend Honesty but that can only be provided if the truth is known and accepted by the interrogated. He enjoyed sex with women and then with his wife but he increasingly preferred to fuck men. He had a high profile senior position within an industry, engineering, renowned for its homophobia. He had two children whom he loved above all else. It was inevitable that he would 'play away' but he chose with the majority to conceal the evidence, delay the day of reckoning. Easiest solution - get laid, no hassle, no expectations, if she doesn't know the 'terrible' truth it can't hurt her, or me, or my kids. It took a longer time, and a lot of pain suffered and caused, for him to learn that his only chance of a contented old age would be as, and with, an 'old queen'.

On a sexual orientation line from homosexual to bisexual to heterosexual he would be hovering on the homosexual side of the net whilst his partner would be firmly out in the back tram lines with the boys. Their sexual orientation is homosexual but, just as with heterosexuals, there is a wide range of behaviour, preference and inclination covered by that label. It is not always so easy to know and understand ourselves particularly when we lack experience but at least we have finally seen an end to the days when homosexuals felt pressured to marry heterosexuals simply to be accepted by society. How far we have come from there to the Civil Partnership Act and straight women having gay men's babies!

It is also impossible to ignore the fact that our nurturing just as much as our nature plays a huge part. In societies where male bisexuality is considered quite normal it will become far more common. In pre- Christian Rome it was a social norm for the male adult population to sodomise adolescent boys. In the intricate carvings on the amazing temples at India's Kajaraho the holy men sought to teach their people the many pleasures of sexual interaction illustrating sodomy, group sex and bestiality along side more conventional sexual indulgences. It may be hard for us to accept but history clearly teaches us that had we been nurtured in the same way, we would behave in the same way. Much as we would astound ourselves to realise that we would be screaming for a 'Holy War' had we been raised by Muslim extremists.

You may be saying this is all very well but you were not raised with these norms and you are definitely a heterosexual - straight, you're clear on that, you can be honest about your sexual orientation, the sex to which you are personally attracted, just as it seems there was a genetic certainty for my friends, the second of whom had two gay sons though raised predominantly by their 'straight' mother. He had hoped that they would be straight - purely because he knew from personal experience how hard it could be to be a gay in a straight world. His sons' experience will thankfully be very different from his own (unless they decide to be engineers!)

But what of Nurture? Far more women would openly admit to at least having contemplated engaging in sexual relations with another woman whilst many men would, outwardly at least, feel genuinely revolted at the thought of stroking another man's pulsating penis. As new born babies, the girl child is no more (or less) predisposed to her own kind than would the boy child be to his.

I went straight from an Inter-railing month around Europe to Law College. When my folks delivered the bulk of my stuff a week later my father had obviously discovered the old porno mags (the tame days of the likes of Fiesta) stashed with my drawing paper. Without taking a breath after the usual salutations of greeting he remarked, apparently to no-one in particular, that he could not understand why a woman would want to look at another woman's 'fanny'. Nothing else was said. Some years later over a Sunday dinner table I remember him saying that, OK, he could accept some people were born gay but he couldn't get his head around bisexuality, "You're not born bisexual". It was as if he was saying 'it's just indiscriminate sexual greed. Nymphomania without barriers'. So is it?

Just as my gay friends could be logged on a graph of the X Y chromosome pull, so can we all. Like alcoholism, there is a pre existing genetic propensity to deviation. The nearer the median line we fall, the more likely we might be, in certain circumstances, to deviate. Imprisoned I would certainly have lesbian tendencies. Nature and our socially accepted norms play a big part as do our specific experiences.

As a child, neither of my parents chose to hide their nakedness, not flaunting it, not hoovering around the house or watching T.V. nude or anything like that but getting dressed, walking to the bathroom, bathing. I was never made to feel that I shouldn't see their flesh nor that they had any hang-ups over their own bodies. It is of course mere speculation but I feel convinced that the fact that I have always felt comfortable and unabashed about my own body stems from a subliminal message which was conveyed in my pre teen years. A friend at university had attended a very posh private girl's school run by nuns. They were made to dress and undress in bed presumably through fear of any improper behaviour or temptation. I have rarely met anyone so hung up about their body and its nakedness.

At about age nine or ten my father suggested that I perhaps should not go into the bathroom whilst he was showering. It struck me as such an odd thing to say at the time and made me feel as though there was suddenly something wrong in what had hitherto been quite normal. Like I had done something wrong. As an adult of course I can understand why he felt he had to change our behaviour but as a child it was a difficult message to interpret.

Whilst this changed, the physical closeness I had with both of my parents, but particularly my father, did not. I had always sat on his lap as a child to watch T.V. He would take his comb out of his pocket so that I could groom him. He would take me to the baths every Sunday morning to swim. I would hold his hand walking down a busy High Street well into my teens. Other than perhaps our gay friends, those of us who had a close physical relationship with our cross gender parent rarely again experience such a non-sexual yet physically close relationship with another man/woman. Which is perhaps one reason why mother : son and father : daughter relationships are so special to many of us. The instinctive need which most sons have to protect and 'stick up for' their mothers crosses all cultural and religious boarders and is doubtless why the profanity 'mother fucker' is so heinous, the ultimate perversion of Nature.

I do believe that sharing such physical closeness with parents from those early years again dramatically effects our behaviour as adults, our ability to give physical affection to others and to seek it from them, whether it be merely physical contact or sexual pleasure. If we feel an uncomfortable need for others to 'stay out of our space' then we will find it harder to feel comfortable in any closer physical situation. And so again, the way we are nurtured has a massive impact on us as an adult.

The fact that 'girl on girl action' is much more widely accepted in today's society than the male equivalent seems to lie in the fact that we do still live in a Patriarchal society. Its rules and regulations are rooted in a male dominated church and are produced by men, or women working within the male dominated machine. On a sexual level, many men are turned on at the thought of watching, and even joining in with, two women excited by and exciting each other. They can relax and be honest about this 'fantasy', to their mates and even to their lovers, because it is one which is widely accepted within this male dominated society. The average heterosexual male would not share a gay fantasy with his heterosexual mates even if he entertained one. Porn sites on the net might offer video clips and separately, gay video clips but the latter involve men only. Unless there is a specialist section for lesbians on the particular site, all 'girl on girl action' appears in the heterosexual section and the girls used conform to the stereotypical attractive female still promoted by our media as seen through the eyes of a heterosexual male. Girls with no makeup on and hair scraped up in a bun do not feature (unless the 'producer' is trying to make them appear under 18!) Bisexual female tendencies are not only accepted but encouraged by many heterosexual men who would often be the first to disapprove of viewing 'boy on boy action'. Our children are nurtured by an adult society which holds this view and so it self-perpetuates.

If we lived in a Matriarch - and the only example which will come to mind is the mythological warrior Amazonians which hardly assists the point! - I strongly suspect that the 'norms' in sexual fantasy land might be very different. A reverse scenario may seem bizarre and unimaginable to most of us but then why does the current situation not strike us as such?

It seems from my web surfings that most modern anthropologists and sociologists assert that there exist no examples of human matriarchy in known history. One example often thrown forth in contradiction of such is the 200,0000 strong population of the Musuo people who live in South West China, on the left bank of the Yangtse River and predominantly around the Luguhu Lake, high in the Tibetan Himalayas. They have apparently evolved a system where marriage, as western society perceives it, does not exist and women's promiscuity is not socially frowned upon. Men visit their women in a special 'Achu' house where the couple can secure privacy in an otherwise communal way of living. Men reportedly visit their women under cover of darkness (hence named a 'walking marriage')but otherwise have not even the society of conversation during the daylight hours barring the special occasion of festivals five times a year. Children often are unaware of their true parentage (not so different from the West) and are raised by their maternal family, take their mother's surname and receive their inheritances through that line. Though the men have no responsibility for their children they share responsibility for their sisters' children who live in their family home. Their mother Goddess is the Gamu Mountain and they have no written language. Women run the household and make most business decisions though they remain politically disempowered, reducing any claim to a true Matriarchy. The actual situation could better be described as

61

serial monogamy since, in reality, women tend to form a bond with one man for a given period and illustrating a matrilineal system in which names and possessions are passed through the female line rather than women ruling the roost. Needless to say, nothing in any of the reports refers to women becoming sexually excited whilst watching 'boy on boy' action and it seems that this unusual social order originally grew from a feudal system in which the nobility married but peasants were encouraged towards matriarchy to keep any male challenge of the nobility at bay.

It seems that in theory and in practice a truly Matriarchal society for humans is a non-starter whilst ants, bees, bonobos, elephants, killer whales, spotted hyenas and bison are reputed to have achieved this within the wider animal community.

And what if we lived in a gender Egalitarian society? If the strides which women have made towards equality continue at the present rate, then that would logically appear to be where we are heading. It is not simply the fact that the majority in our society now accept that women are intellectually as able as their male counterparts but also the fact that the male's natural stronger physique is losing its former significance in this technological twenty-first century. The more we learn how to make machines do the unskilled, manual labour and 'blue collar' work, the less brawn, muscles and height are going to be relevant in the work-place, the less gender will impact on our ability to earn money. The true impact of such gender equality, in so far as it would affect society's attitude to sexual norms, is no more predictable than was that of the pill when it was launched. But it will be significant. Perhaps bisexuality will be the norm for our great grandchildren!

SEXUAL ORIENTATION

Perhaps we will have machines which make blow-up-dolls and vibrators look prehistoric! I do hope sex never becomes 'virtual' … well not exclusively anyway.

I am put in mind of a man I met on a rooftop in Penang, Malaysia. That was the place where most Europeans, going to Thailand on a visitor's visa, would go to renew it since it had to be obtained outside Thailand. It is a small, beautiful but rat-infested island off the top left hand corner of Malaysia. He was looking out on the star spangled sky whilst I devoured another paperback. He was the first person to explain to me in words I could understand, the true spirit of the 60's sexual revolution. He was at least thirty years my senior. He described how he had travelled through Wales as a young man; he had stopped to get work at a farm owned by an amiable husband and wife. He lived with them in what became a 'ménage a trois' situation. Or not, in that they shared the woman separately which is not the same thing at all.

He lived in a foursome. He lived in a commune. He came to the conclusion that, for him personally at least, monogamy was, finally, his 'bag'! He had married a young Thai girl and was set to spoil her through his remaining days. I recall admiring his self knowledge reached through trial and error, not swallowed on a plate from the congressional. He had asked questions. He had pushed at boundaries. He had found his own answers. Respect.

To have the ability to think independently, to think outside the box, to question what the majority say is the 'right' way to behave, react or live is what distinguishes us in the animal kingdom and yet how often do we truly utilise our ability. We like to fit in. From the respect of others we acquire part of our own self esteem but the self esteem to be acquired from taking action against the sway because we have delved into ourselves and instinctively believe in our own opinion, can reap far greater rewards. This does not have to involve life changing decisions. Just as in business, where small financial changes can have a massive effect on success, this is no less true in our relationships. Small changes and adjustments can vastly improve the quality of our lives and that of our partner. Greeting them when arriving home, holding their hand as we walk into the supermarket, not over reacting to relative trivia … can help massage the lifeblood of our partnership and restore the desire to work on a relationship in those inevitable, difficult times which our relationships need to endure, survive and grow from. Actions do speak louder than words.

The concept that, whilst we may have a predilection towards a certain form of sexual activity, we are largely influenced by the mores of the society which raises us, can be a hard one to get our heads round. However, once we take that information on board, it can have a balming influence and perhaps assuage the guilt or shame we may feel over some of our sexual fantasies or indeed experiences. It may also help us to have more understanding and tolerance of our fellow human beings.

CHAPTER SIX

PORN AND SEXUAL FANTASIES

Porn has become so stereotyped within its own media to promote lens access rather than genuine enjoyment and so widespread in its availability, that it is in danger of encouraging sexual Fairy Tales which only serve to extend ignorance.

Studying criminology at uni, I learned that in the early 60's the Dutch government abolished the majority of law relating to porn with predictably necessary exceptions - children, animals, the use of force ...

In the first three years the relevant cinemas did an immense trade and earnt lots of money from the irresistible pull that this had on the Dutch public. They gorged themselves on the hard core whilst the sociologists and politicians, wearing those particular faces, looked on in uncertain expectation. In those three years, sexually related crimes reduced by around a half and Holland has since retained one of the lowest rates of such crime in Europe. After the initial period, the engorged Netherlanders went about the rest of their lives secure in the knowledge that it was there if ever the urge arose. They'd reached saturation point and perhaps the novelty, if nothing else, had worn off.

FAIRY TALES by Sharon Moore

One of the earliest 'advertisements' was found in Pompeii - a left foot carved into the stone pavement with a heart engraved on it. Translation - prostitute up here, on the left. Those women who, through the centuries, have voluntarily worked in the sex industry have provided an invaluable service, sometimes directly but always indirectly, to all of us. Their profession involves the most honest and clear-cut of all sexual exchanges and, by providing an accessible pressure valve to a few, society benefits.

I like watching porn - whether by myself for a quick fix or in company to help with a prolonged one. It's been a habit since my biking days. It does usually turn me on, the voyeur in me free with my flitting fantasies. Sometimes I watch and imagine I am the man, try to experience what it is like to be him, what he might be thinking. Perhaps this is partly due to natural curiosity - most women will have wondered what it must really feel like to have a cock and to enter her pussy with it. The same applies to many men watching in wonder as a multiple orgasm unfolds. Strangely though, when I have asked men about this, they say that they have never watched porn and imagined they were the woman (only that they had multiple orgasms!)

The problem is that the vast majority of these films are designed by men for men (just like seatbelts). Women are viewed grinning groaning growling and gasping in the depths of sublime orgasm whilst the man pounds hard, all the way in, all the way out. No hanging about between strokes. His hands may be grasping her arse as he controls it to meet his attack or holding it back to better view the scene. Pan into the woman - sublime orgasm ongoing - who is taking the brunt of the force on her knees which are 'comfortably' ledged on the side of a bath, kitchen work surface, patio, desk, tractor… standard stage sets. Her clitoris is experiencing sublime contact with thin air and the arch in her back and elbows is beginning to dissolve under the strain.

Putting aside the possibilities of the elusive 'G' spot, few women would be subliminally anywhere near orgasm in such positions and so it can be difficult to watch and enjoy by putting yourself in the same position. Those I enjoy the most are those in which I am utterly convinced as to the woman's enjoyment (the man's hardly seems questionable) and then want to imagine myself in her position (that after all is the way men view porn). These are hard to find and if you'd like an interesting storyline with half decent acting, forget it.

When most people have sex, whether protected or not, it usually culminates in a man shooting his sperm into another's body. Even this is a rare sight in porn since it spoils the inevitable 'cum shot' which the camera man is anxious to capture. Women may enjoy watching a man take his flaccid manhood, stroke it into life and even bring himself off without inhibition or vocal reserve (it can save a lot of time and wrist ache in learning how this particular male likes his handled!) and it is a turn-on to watch someone else turning themselves on. Not a very subversive enjoyment but not the kind of thing which regularly features in heterosexual porn. The men who make the majority of these films can watch themselves masturbate and have no particular desire to see another, usually better blessed, male pleasure himself. Nor does their predominantly male audience it seems.

The unsuspecting male punter laps up the delights of 'Fanny's Multiple Orgasms' and the like, then tests out his hard won lessons on his wife, girlfriend, date or one-nighter. The results are never as earth shattering as Randy's and he never really knows why if he isn't told or shown. He can become preoccupied by penis pertaining phobias, specifically length, girth or his lasting power. Alternatively he blames her for being unresponsive or abnormal in her lack of shuddering ecstasy at his mere touch, attack being the best form of defense. That is if he even considers it beyond the fleeting moment before he is overcome by sleep!

Size does count, whether it's the size of the man or the woman, but knowing what to do with whatever Mother Nature blessed you with, counts more. However She did not give us via our gene chain, any innate understanding of the other's sexuality. Mean really cos you'd have thought that would be a doddle for Her! Given the inadequacies of the porn industry the obvious solution would be for us to talk to each other about these things. As we have been raised not to talk about sex (the definition, I once truly believed, of 'oral sex') we find it difficult, often if not always. Perhaps the great payback for the next generation being exposed to so much sexual knowledge at a relatively early age is that they will grow up comfortable with their own sexuality and in talking about sex to their life partners, able to freely express their needs and desires without our uncertainty or embarrassment.

None of us are born with a crystal ball on the finer arts of sexual interaction. Mother Nature needed Procreation and threw in an itch to ensure participation in the activity. Beyond that, we're all on our own. If we accept that sexual matching is extremely important in finding a long-term mate and maintaining the sexual health of that match, then we all have to communicate better. It can be the ice breaker which leads to greater intimacy in other aspects of the relationship. Some things can be learnt by watching others, reading relevant information and even gleaning some gems from the pages of Penthouse or the Sunday Sport but it is the unique personal details and fantasies that create intimacy and a feeling of sharing something special which we would not readily want to risk losing or giving up.

As a motor biking rock lover, who had opened an account at Abbey Nat at sixteen and secretly saved, religiously, for a bike from my Saturday job, my reward was a 'nail' of a Honda CB 100 N and singular female admittance into my local bike club. You had to have a bike to be a full member and attend Club meetings so we would all meet up in a pub in Lye then leave the girlfriends downstairs whilst we retired upstairs for our meetings. Many of the beleathered members were more senior than my tender sixteen years and it was tradition that, after we had agreed on the next club run, paid subs, discussed mechanical faults … and closed our meeting, they would play a porn film and have a drink before descending to the womenfolk. It was my first experience of porn in somewhat singular circumstances with a load of 'hairy' bikers. Perhaps it set the scene but it was a strange experience of being 'one of the lads' but equally feeling very much a young, though morally-encumbered, hormonal woman.

Everyone's reaction to porn is different dependant upon what we are exposed to in our formative years and our own particular sexual preferences but one thing I feel confident in asserting is that the more we are exposed to in life the more 'normalised' that behaviour can become. Kids today have it with violence – they are exposed to so much more than my generation was both in their video games and on the street. If we have a voyeur in us who does get a kick out of watching porn, visiting porn sites on the Net, watching strippers … the more we want to see. Watching two people together becomes a little tiresome after a while and Mother Nature serves up Curiosity to fuel the thirst for pastures new … in whatever direction that might take our particular predilection. Slippery slope.

Is someone 'unfaithful' when they secretly visit porn sites or enter chat rooms/dating sites and flirt? Is there a thin but important line between mentally 'cheating' on someone rather than doing so in reality? If so, why should that be? Isn't a relationship as much mental as physical? It may be related to our animal instinct to ensure we have a 'one' to further our genes and retain a carer/protector for the produce of the exchange. To achieve that in our free accessible society requires a facing up to the Truth that no other generation has ever had to deal with. It's in our faces.

Communicating our sexual desires, things which really get our blood flowing, can often be an almost impossible feat but doing so and listening to our partners can only develop a closer, more understanding and fulfilling coupling. Every sexual person shelters fantasies which often become very personal and very private, like a hidden box of favourite fantasy cards which we take out and shuffle in the seclusion of our own imagination. They may be fairly tame or fairly extreme but if they can be truly shared with an intimate partner they can enhance our relationships and our understanding of each other and ourselves. It is vital that we remember that true fantasies are just that. There is a big difference between those sexual situations/accomplices which/whom we would truly like to experience and those

70

which are truly props we use with which to titillate ourselves. If we fantasise about sleeping with Madonna it may or may not be the case that, given such a reality presenting itself to us, we would follow it through. There are fantasies which, by the very tabooness of the situations or people they involve, we would not entertain conducting in reality. The very tabooness of them is both exciting and guilt-racking. Why on earth would your mind fantasise about shagging the local sports team/your dog/a stranger in a lift/a parent/your best friend's partner ...?

These can be things that we struggle to deal with ourselves let alone sharing them with the person we fear losing the most but if we are able to achieve at least a modicum of honesty about what goes on in our heads and about what our particular bodies enjoy, the chances of one or other of the couple's members looking elsewhere for greater pleasure with someone who has had better training by experience, must be reduced.

There is an incumbent danger in indulging our sexual fantasies and exploring them; if we allow our minds that freedom it can be something of a slippery slope. If we try to analyse them, the glimpse into our darker selves can be frightening and unnerving. Historically we Brits were protected by our big brother government from anyone who might conspire to corrupt our public morals. That very idea appears to suggest that we cannot be trusted with ourselves and we need an externally imposed restriction on our potential morally delinquent personalities to protect ourselves from ourselves.

I have never been raped. The nearest I have ever come to such an experience, which is still a world away from the real

FAIRY TALES by Sharon Moore

Macoy, was one evening when, most unusually, my live-in boyfriend of the time would not take my most unusual 'no' as an answer. I was tired and not best pleased with him but he would not leave it alone. He stepped over the line of his usual gentlemanly behaviour and forced himself upon me. It developed into one of the best bed sessions we ever had in years.

Women who fantasise about rape are usually excited at the thought of a man being so excited by her irresistibility that he cannot help himself. Such a situation within a loving relationship, when the woman knows that if she really doesn't want to go there she can make herself understood and heeded, is a very different thing to true rape. We can fantasise about a certain aspect of rape whilst, within that media, we can block out the horrendous realities of such a situation. The reality is that rapists are rarely driven by an overpowering sexual desire for their victim but rather a hatred or fear for women generally.

As I write the Government has announced that one in twenty reported rapes end in conviction. It is suggested that the law is taking too relaxed an approach to such crime and that the general public are more inclined to think a woman had been partially responsible if she were drunk or even if she had flirted with the perpetrator. Young men are reported as thinking that 'no' doesn't always mean 'no'. Slippery slope. The grey areas of this crime are difficult to judge. I said no to my boyfriend but he carried on.

Ultimately it seems that those who make the laws, as well as being subject to them, can not abide by them. How many more politicians' sexual revelations must we be bored by?! Barbara Bush, the former US First Lady, is credited with saying "Clinton lied. A man might forget where he parks or where he lives but he never forgets oral sex no matter how bad it is!" From the Oval office to the prison cell, every man and woman alive comes from the same basic mould which is vulnerable to seduction of many kinds and which fears having its contents too closely examined.

Geoff Thompson worked some of the worst 'doors' in Coventry for years. He became a legend in his own lifetime as a bouncer and a film 'Clubbed' based on his book 'Watch My Back' should be hitting our screens in Spring 2008. He talks about being bullied at school and how he eventually found a way of dealing with the many fears which he had accumulated since childhood. He writes:

> "So I admitted all the things that scared the crap out of me, and wrote them into a list. I drew a pyramid on a scrap of paper with as many steps to the top as I had fears – there were a lot of steps, I have to say. Then I wrote each fear on a step, starting with my least fear and finishing at the top step with my greatest fear.
>
> Once they were all down on paper I systematically confronted them, one at a time, from the bottom step to the top, confronting each one until I mastered it. It was a difficult time, I have to tell you, but on the way up the pyramid, as my confidence grew, I found myself confronting things that would normally have had me running to the loo like a tester in a laxative factory. I even stood up to the people I loved, who had become dominant and bullying. My wife for one. She didn't like the new me at all, but I figured that she had no respect for the old me because I was such a pushover, so I had nothing to lose. She went on the pyramid like the rest of the scary

creatures. I went through my fears like a man on a mission, I had found a new lease of life, and the depressions I suffered from in my youth were smashed like brittle toffee and tossed to the side. My problems started when I got to the top of the pyramid.

My greatest fear was violent confrontation …. "

And so he goes on to regale us with a fascinating, and often brutal, insight into life as a sober peacemaker in a twilight world of drunken protagonists and criminal prides. It is an extremely powerful story that spring boards from his decision to be honest with himself, to recognize his fears and to actively do something about them.

What if we all wrote our own personal pyramids for our own relationships detailing the things we fear to disclose or talk about, we least feel comfortable to admit or face up to. I mean to include both non-sexual and sexual issues. If we see that we could never, even over time, deal with those top layers then, if we continue in the relationship, we have to be aware of its innate shortcomings from the outset. We may take the attitude that there are certain things that we could not share with our significant other, but is that because we would prefer to take the easy option rather than because that other couldn't deal with it or want to understand it? If we attacked our own pyramids with the determination that Geoff imparts in that short passage how much more intimate would all of our relationships be (provided our partner hadn't shot us after disclosure of layer 4 of our 40 stepped pyramid!) Of course, that is why we must choose our partners wisely and ensure we are not so blindly taken with their looks/ brains/ wit/ humour/ money … as to make us blind to other potentially incompatible traits.

PORN AND SEXUAL FANTASIES

The bottom line is that both porn and our fantasies are props, like drugs or alcohol, against the backdrop of life's realities. They can be useful, enjoyable and perk up our lives but, like drugs or alcohol, if we over indulge in either we risk 'losing the plot'. We can become so removed from the reality in which we actually live that we become frustrated, self-indulgent and critical. Though both porn and sexual fantasies are fabricated daily throughout the world, they both have an element of Bollywood and Hollywood and we have to remember to see them as such.

CHAPTER SEVEN

SELF PRESERVATION IN THE FACE OF SEXUAL FREEDOM

Applying our Reason we curb our sexual behaviour generally, consigning our daily physical attraction to others to the realms of our fantasy lands. Our Superegos manage our Ids under the tireless supervision of our Egos.

Having established our own sexual orientation and found a partner who is matched in that respect, that is a beginning. What of drive, libido? An apparent mismatch on that front leads to all sorts of pain. Sure, there are hormonal, weight, emotional, factors but assuming all is otherwise rosey in the garden, do men really need sex more than women? I've known too many women both through my work and my play, to know that isn't true.

We are talking about a pastime which requires no props, no money, no special extras (other perhaps than a condom). Just two people oriented on the same course. It makes us feel good, it allows us to be completely ourselves, it allows us to put ourselves over entirely to the pleasure of ourselves and of our partner and it is physically and mentally good for our health. Why would anyone not want to do it?

SELF PPRESERVATION IN THE FACE OF SEXUAL FREEDOM

When I still lived with my folks, my mother undertook an O.U. degree in psychology, particularly appertaining to children. I used to get up with her in the early morning to watch the accompanying T.V. programmes. We all have images of Pavlov's dogs with their saliva glands transplanted to a comfortably viewable position, oozing juices at the ring of a bell. From those programmes I carry images of mice in cages with a bowl of food in one corner and a hooped wire circuit which emitted the equivalent of a mouse orgasm, presumably with the assistance of an electric charge. The mice starved. All of them. l00% chose to orgasm themselves to starvation. They did not have our reasoning ability to delay pleasure for an essential prerequisite.

We generally curb our sexual impulses prompted primarily by our need to self-preserve and, with Aids now added to the list of nasty diseases on offer in that forum, this has become a matter of life and death. Add to that the likely social fallout of behaving sexually in whatever manner you may feel Id-driven to pursue, and we have an effective curb to complete sexual anarchy. Whilst the primary fear forty years ago might have been an unwanted pregnancy, today that can be very simply dealt with via the Morning After Pill, available over the counter at all good pharmacies, from the UK to Jamaica, but there is no sure fire remedy for many of the diseases which have spread along with our greater promiscuity.

As a grammar school girl I was shown the most awful slide show of the horrors which await any wanton woman. I still have images in a comer of my mind of pussies ulcerated by genital warts which must have been left unattended for years, body bits which looked more like particularly nobly gourds rather than genitalia. I have spent the subsequent decades failing to meet anyone who has suffered such an ordeal! But today, here in our shiny new twenty-first century, if we have unprotected sex we risk, amongst the more easily diagnosable and treatable infections, HIV, Syphilis and Herpes.

The most common sexual infection is Chlamydia, the number of cases having tripled in ten years since 1995 to around 110,000. It is highest amongst under 25's and London has the highest incidence. The most common bacterial disease is uncomplicated gonorrhea which again is highest in under 25's and in London.

For HIV there is no quick fix, neither in its diagnosis nor in its cure. HIV is about weakening our immune system but cannot be detected even via medical testing for at least three months after the 'incident' and may take up to around two years for its deadly grasp to be identifiable. A positive result leads to a lifetime of medication and oh-so-too-late precautions. Following such a diagnosis we cannot even have unprotected sex with a similarly afflicted mate since there are several aspects to the disease and whilst we may have a high level of one strand we may have a low level of another and accordingly a fellow-sufferer could still make us worse and we them. Though condoms are not prone to split in the way they once were, they are still prone to slip off. Our sexual partner is permanently at risk which cannot do great things mentally to assist sexual abandonment and indulgence.

At the end of 2004 the estimated number of people with HIV in the UK was 58,000, one third of who were unaware of their affliction. There were 7,275 new HIV cases diagnosed in 2004, almost double the number in 2000. Three quarters of the total new cases are thought to have been acquired in

Africa or through a travelling African though this seems
impossible to validify.

Syphilis shows itself by a small pimple-like bump which
ulcerates and is much more evident in a man. For a woman it
may be much harder, if not impossible, to detect. The pimple
is small, hidden within the 'beef curtains' or even inside the
woman where it is even more difficult to detect by self-
inspection. It is not usually particularly painful and
'disappears' within a few days, seeping into the body's
systems and potentially not rearing its head again for twenty
years to a shocked host who is then riddled with arthritis,
neurological decline...

Genital Herpes is recurrent and remains a black cloud to its
owner. There may be none, or only minimal, signs when
contracted but, once contracted, it can never be cured. It
usually shows itself in the form of blisters around the sex
organs and the hapless recipient can expect typically four or
five such outbreaks in the first year, the frequency declining
over the years. Anti viral medication can shorten the
outbreaks, or even prevent them whilst taking the drugs but it
is, as a puppy should be, for life.

For the uncertain, responsible or paranoid amongst us, tests
and subsequent medication are readily available for their older
and more familiar cousins as well as some newer additions to
the family. A less known but increasingly prevalent condition
is known as TV or trichomonas vaginalis caused by a tiny
parasite. It passes easily on sexual contact and often there are
absolutely no symptoms. Even for those who do have
symptoms these are easily misinterpreted being common to
many complaints such as stinging on pissing, discharge and

tenderness when having sex. It is easily treatable with antibiotics but it is very unlikely to go away on its own. One specialist nurse suggested to me that if the entire nation were to adopt the habit of regular testing when sexual partners have been changed, the results would be staggering in their extent.

We have to escape the traditional taboo of going to a clinic to be tested if we have unprotected sex. The whole disgrace of such a necessity used to be reflected in Birmingham by the very name of the testing centre itself, 'Ward 19' but if you were having a drink in the city with a plaster on your arm some wisecrack about a visit to 'the clap clinic' was inevitable. Insurers have finally amended their stock question as to whether you have had an AIDS test to whether you have had a positive test but the nurse at my doctor's still advised me, in this century, to go to a clinic for a test rather than through the surgery because "it's anonymous".

For a woman, the only thing between herself and an HIV infection is a thin piece of rubber wrapped in a plastic-coated packet which, at the height of passion, must be unwrapped and correctly fitted, taking care to pinch its end nipple to evacuate the surplus air which will push the rubber further up his impatient shaft and make it more secure. Despite the woman's intoxication, hormonal or otherwise, she has to rely upon the compliance and cooperation of a fellow being who, at the time, has very little on his mind other than a successful penetration. He need not harbour the same level of fear for himself because his risk is, in any event, so much smaller.

Human Nature is Human Nature and the 'I'm alright Jack' attitude is never more illuminatingly unmasked than when a man wants to 'get his end away', or a woman desperately

wants a man to. Add to all this the fact that, especially at the
height of stimulation, the condom is: difficult to unwrap, to
put on outside-out (there must be a simple colour coding
they could use for that), to keep on throughout the ups and
downs, in's and out's of the proceedings; that it feels, tastes
and smells horrible; that it changes the temperature; that it
takes away that completely unique feeling of 'that' skin on
'that' skin lubricated by the affections of each others passion;
that it often makes men's passion quell or even disappear…
Like Domestos it "kills all known germs dead" (a tautology
any mother would point out every time the bloody ad came
on - anything killed must be dead!) It does an essential job
but everything else about it stinks!

When the news of Aids first hit in the 80's the UK
government reacted and in 1987 each household received
their leaflet:

> 'AIDS: Don't die of ignorance … anyone can have it, gay
> or straight, male or female. Already 30,000 people are
> infected.'

No-one really knew what impact it would have. The
perceived wisdom seemed to be that it was the equivalent of
showing the nation the genital warts slides and terrifying us
into 'appropriate' behaviour. We were told that within five
years we would all have had a close friend who had died of
the killer. The 30,000 figure was world wide prediction; at
the end of 2005 it was estimated to be 63,500, in the UK
alone.

A documentary was aired at around the same time depicting
an Australian woman who had been on a business trip to

New York and had a weekend fling with a gentleman who, it transpired many years later when someone was paid to find out for the purposes of the documentary, was bisexual. She returned home to her husband and her "normal" sexual relations - a phrase which I have come to appreciate can mean the widest spectrum of behaviour from total abstinence to swinging but, for the purposes of this documentary, was presumably intended to convey three weekly missionary. It was only when she became pregnant eight years later when tests were routinely carried out, that it was discovered that she was HIV positive. Her husband was fine. Unless the woman is cut and the man is cut enabling an exchange of blood, a man has no risk. If an infected man cums in a healthy woman her only chance of escaping the inevitable is to fly to her nearest hospital where she will be given a big dose of AIDS drugs. This will either avoid the catastrophe or bring the disease on tripplefold.

And that is only the physical side of having various partners or not settling in at least one main one which neither fits into our world of couples nor satisfies any deep emotional need which most of us have. Perhaps Mother Nature felt that to weave sexual disease into the fabric of our world would promote male: female partnerships post coitally to better improve the survival chances of its potential product, our offspring. She is the ultimate Big Brother with Yin and Yang as Her male- and maid-servants.

CHAPTER EIGHT

FINDING A PARTNER

**The other side of 'when in Rome…' is 'wherever you
are, be yourself'. Both hold admirable sentiment and it is
rare for either doctrine to be pursued exclusively. We
dissemble with our faces which we keep in a jar by the
door. Our Ids make it impossible to resist ripping the
mask off on occasion. With whichever end of the scale
we feel more comfortable, we are still pulled towards the
centre of our meridian line by the strength of the other's
irresistibility. Etiquette vs Id. Nurture vs Nature. Nature
will out or we wither through its suppression. Truth is
its unavoidable bedfellow.**

We are animals before we are civilised beings. No amount of
religious suppression nor hierarchical social structure can
change that. We don't like it. We pretend that it is otherwise
but we know it is not. Through their eyes, I have lived
through too many people's lives. Of course, this doesn't
mean that there are those who largely succeed in taming their
natures. Many women of my mother's generation have only
ever slept with their husbands and they would claim such a
victory. But life is no longer that straightforward in our
twenty-first century Britain.

When a child of sixteen loses their virginity behind the bike
shed or wherever, it is gone. They are free of it. They have no

responsibility for it. They can pursue the pleasure of it from then on - or otherwise, should that prove to be their particular nature, tolerate or avoid it. But the twenty-one year old, retained intacto, feels the constant pressure of its responsibility. The older it gets, the more difficult and frightening it is to give up. A child's fear of the unknown is not fuelled by its life experience, it is uneducated fear. When a young girl or young woman 'falls' pregnant - without intent or otherwise - she has 'the child issue' out of the way. But as we increasingly leave motherhood to a later age, having ensured that any earlier pregnancy was impossible or having exterminated any that did arise, this produces the same constant pressure. Finding a mother or a father for your unborn children becomes a harder issue.

We are also 'blessed' with far more choice of partner in the shrinking world of our twenty-first century than at any time in history. A recent study in the US unsurprisingly reveals that the huge stress levels within 'civilised' society can be directly attributed to the huge choices we face on a daily basis. You only have to go to a steak house there and battle your way through a barrage of questions from the waitress to rapidly experience this inevitability. Though you do learn to say you want a ribeye steak, medium rare, with fries and salad with blue cheese dressing, the indomitable series of choices you have to make to reach that order the first few times makes you feel like mimicking Munch's 'The Scream'!

The choice we now have in terms of a potential mate is equally as extensive. Compare the situation just twenty years ago when the vast majority of us were computer illiterate and few of us had mobile telephones. Finding a partner is a stressful business!

FINDING A PARTNER

As we mature through our life's experience, our mental checklist of the qualities which we are looking for in the prospective parent or partner (or both!) both changes and gets longer. We know we want salad but the jury is out on the dressing. We know what we don't want in a partner but, more importantly, we know what we feel we can't do without at least, that is, in order to have a chance at anything like a long-living love-match. We sacrifice much in ensuring the nest is ready, building our careers, pursuing our work and saving, trying to get on the property ladder. But we are finding, sometimes too late, that we cannot then furnish it with our choice chics.

The danger of this partially subconscious inevitable check list is that it can blinker our reaction to others, exclude potential mates because they don't apparently fit our criteria and prevent us taking on less familiar experiences which might ultimately lead to better ones. An ironic factor in the falling in love game is that we are rarely overcome with this extreme of emotion with someone we would have chosen to feel that way about. How many of us could say 'If only I could have fallen in love with that particular person, it would have made life a hell of a lot easier'. But love doesn't always work like that.

So, the older we get the harder we are to please? Or the older we get the more we are prepared to compromise? Or the older we get the more we have experienced to realise that we are compromising? The bliss of our earlier ignorance escapes us. Anyone of twenty, even if they choose their fellow procreator-to-be, does not have the life experience for that to be a fully informed choice. They are blissfully ignorant of the myriad of possibilities which life unveils to us.

FAIRY TALES by Sharon Moore

If you've never had an apple and you are given a Golden Delicious, you will think that apple is the best in the world. If you've tried a Granny Smith's, a Cox's, a Pippin etc you may then become driven to find the apple which has all the best qualities, and none of the worst, of all those apples. Our search for a permanent partner with whom to have children, increasingly late in life, presents a similar conundrum. By our thirties it is likely that we will have had several relationships and perhaps a few love affairs. We know what it feels like to be 'in love' when Passion and Romance dance wildly together in an emotional internal spectacle.

We may know how it feels to have someone who disrespects us, who becomes evermore possessive and distrusting with us, who physically abuses us, who is driven by money and selfish goals, who uses us, who lies to us. But we may also know how it feels to have someone who respects us, is secure enough in themselves to allow us our freedom, who loves our bodies as much as our minds, who can be selfless and thoughtful, who cherishes us, who tells us the truth.

Unlike the Fairy Tale, we have known these things as a reality. We know that life is one big learning curve and, just like the child who will not put his hand in the flame a second time, so we wish to avoid those characteristics and traits which have caused us pain in the past. We want to hunt out those which brought us the greatest pleasure, happiness.

On top of all that is the fact that our checklist is then customised further both to suit our individual characteristics and interests and to suit our individual circumstances and aspirations. The thirty-five year old who now wants to start a family will be looking for a different type of mate than one who does not have children on their agenda. And so the checklist gets longer. Reason kicks in and urges us to realise that our bodies will have been burnt before our perfect checklist partner walks into our flesh and blood lives. Even with the amazing technological choice the internet brings where we can find a Russian, African, Asian … bride or groom, our checklists, and our choices, can become impossible.

Reason then makes us compromise. The desire to have a meaningful other will generally outweigh the disadvantages which come with the package, the warts. You can't change people, they can only change themselves? Our instinct, having made the compromise, is to then get them into shape, metaphorically, by reference to the checklist. People have to want to change themselves or naturally do change as they grow wiser. Someone who has a truly honest and intimate relationship with their partner will have respect and show it, love will make them selfless. The quality of the coupling, its depth, will determine the extent to which it changes the individuals in it. We are all innately selfish, it comes from our survival instinct but when love makes us selfless the payback feeling is overwhelming! Ask most parents.

How fearful then, the longer we maintain our relationships, and associated family and social support, to give it up. Whatever the age of our virginity loss it seems unlikely, in twenty-first century Britain, that the bike shed mate will become our lifelong soul mate. We no longer couple with the first person to take our cherry, the first Golden Delicious we meet. Once we have made our choice we might have one of a myriad of possible relationships of different strengths and weaknesses and different levels of understanding. And the Animal fights on with the Homo Sapiens both hoping against hope that they will reach an amicable truce without ripping each others heart out or indeed upsetting the equilibrium of their particular apple cart.

In may seem surprising that although the incidence of marriage is decreasing, the majority of male: female cohabitation still occurs within the context of the beloved institution. According to Government statistics around 7 in 10 households in the UK were headed by a married couple in 2005.

As we race around in our twenty first century lives juggling work stress with domestic stress, we hardly have time to think about the fact that we don't have a close, honest, unshakeable relationship with a soul mate. Or we hardly want to. We struggle on, to a greater or lesser extent, dependant on the quality of the foundation, and make the most of it. Nothing is perfect. That's life. We are strengthened in our conviction by what we see around ourselves, in our friends and relatives relationships. Strength in numbers creates a norm. That's all normal is.

What if a massive majority of those relationships could be close, unshakeable, honest? If there is a pill, does it taste too bitter and come at too high a price? Complete honesty with both ourselves and our partners about who we and they are. The nearest we will ever come to seeing ourselves as others see us is through our partner's eyes. No-one is perfect but how often are we subconsciously attracted by someone's frailties as much as their strengths, by the weaknesses which we feel robust about tackling. Perhaps it makes us more comfortable with our own.

CHAPTER NINE

HONESTY AT THE OUTSET OR ELSE?

Honesty's price may be greater friction, the avoidance of which is the purpose of our lies, but this will be as a small storm next to the tornado which erupts from a failure to acknowledge Her necessity.

Spending time in honest communication with someone builds the level of intimacy and trust which will form the bedrock of any relationship. Obvious stuff which we know to be true. We only have to look to our best friend. So why do we either never start that process with our lover or, worse, having learnt it, forget or ignore it?

'Start as you mean to go on'. My mother will complain that my father has never ironed a shirt in his life, something she presumably failed to object to with sufficient force in the early days and to which she found increasing objection as the world changed around her. For not only do we individuals change, grow, mature, in a lengthy relationship producing need for compromise but so does the society and its norms, practices, laws. The goal posts are continually changing in our modern society and, with few jobs for life, Necessity commands Versatility both in the workplace and in our relationships.

"We just grew apart"

FAIRY TALES by Sharon Moore

"He said he'd fallen out of love with me"

"I want a divorce based on our irreconcilable difficulties"

"I feel like I'm living with a stranger"

… and a billion versions on that theme are spoken hourly in family lawyer's offices across the country. However expressed, they all add up to the same thing. Lack of communication producing lack of intimacy leading to a party crashed by the Bad Boys. Distrust, Self doubt, Insecurity and all their mates. They're sure to turn up, boots blacked.

That common denominator of limited or non-existent communication is seldom absent. Relations got as bad as they did, declined usually beyond repair by the time they get an airing in a lawyer's office, because of lack of honest communication. An irony is that, especially with longer relationships, people can actually become closer following divorce. All the more likely if there are adult children involved to bring their 21st Century acceptance of new norms to the table. Much will depend upon the extent of animosity which creeps into their financial settlement negotiations. That in turn will be affected by the quality of advice provided to each by their lawyers and the extent to which that advice is heeded. But I have had several clients who, after years of stifling in a failing relationship, worn down by guilt over an ongoing affair or simply bored by the mundane pattern of their existence, are suddenly freed by confession, by the all round honesty which the process demands. No one has to pretend any more. Both reach the point where they accept that there is no going back, the cliff has been jumped, they have failed to achieve "The Fairy Tale".

HONESTY AT THE OUTSET OR ELSE?

A fair financial agreement is reached. Their new lives breathe the optimism of a fresh start and they can finally look at their former lover and appreciate those basic qualities which produced that first kiss. This happens when people have shared a greater intimacy. When Truth brings Pain with her the only certainty is that she will always outstay her guest. The more truthful a relationship has been the older, and so the lesser, is Pain in the face of Truth. Whilst Familiarity is reputed to nurture Contempt in Her brood, She also produces Her fair share of Security. Fresh truths, especially those whose discovery is unintended, have the sharpest bite and produce the most extreme reactions.

When I was first in practice I had a spate of clients who had either cut up their lover's ties or had their priceless lingerie drawer scissored in especially delicate places. That seemed to 'go out' as a socially acceptable demonstration of anger - or perhaps people have reduced their supply of both! Computers and mobile phones now have the lead in terms of hassle factor if they become the target of a wronged lover's ire.

Though direct physical aggression falls into a class of its own, Human Nature will feed on the vibe of His Mother's party guests and display reactions entirely out of character with his usual persona. It's a thin line between love and hate. It does seem that for anyone to produce a strong and lasting feeling of either (as opposed to a passing hour of illicit sexual deviancy or of road rage) you do have to give a shit. For someone to be able to cause you such pain as to produce an out-of-character extreme reaction, it has to matter to you. But then I guess it would matter to anyone if a complete stranger threw your treasured hifi equipment from the window of a

FAIRY TALES by Sharon Moore

fifth floor flat; sold your great Aunt's best china at a Car boot; chain sawed your caravan in half on your front drive whilst you were on holiday; rucked your best mate in your front room.... all of which I've encountered in practice.

The reaction to the original disclosure of truth, whether that disclosure be voluntary or otherwise, usually has two elements. The action caused by the reaction to the truth is not only that per se but also a provocation, a call for a further reaction from the opponent in the game which has inevitably filled the intimate's space, a 'so what yer gonna do about that then bitch, get yer lawyer to write to mine' provocation, its ugly manifestation. Childish 'tit for tat' on the surface but often a means of holding on, a means of prolonging the other person's involvement in their life. Even some acrimonious involvement is better than the prospect of none though the players in the game may be oblivious to this subconscious motivation.

People frequently display a need to feel clever. To have pulled one off on the opponent without the opponent knowing and then being able to disclose it at their whim (regardless of their lawyer's advice). There really are no clever strategies in terms of hiding monies when a settlement is being discussed. And to move monies or other assets around in such an attempt, risks the rightful wrath of the court, which can only be to your detriment. Much will clearly depend upon the quality of the opposition and their fact finding missions. What a company Accountant might value the business at can be a fraction of its value in terms of settlement but if no valuation is sought by your spouse ... ?

As during it, so at the end of it. There are no clever answers in relationships but more rests upon whether the questions

92

are asked or not and whether the answers are supplied honestly. Very short marriages are invariably based on a lie, or at least a failure to address Truth but rather sweep Her under the proverbial carpet.

Typically, in a traditional Asian marriage, representations have been made by either the bride's or the groom 's family which have induced the union; if these transpire to be at best distortions and more often blatantly fictitious, from the extent of the 'dowry' to the extent of the education possessed by one of the happily arranged, there will be trouble. The distrust and 'loss of face' which such a situation creates means that, even if the Romeo and Juliet at the play's centre are prepared to fight the odds and soldier on, the families become so entrenched in their hostilities and feelings of cultural betrayal that they make progress practically impossible.

From finding that you are poles apart in your views regarding the parenting of children (whether at all and, if so, in what way) to the discovery of a pre-existing wife and life; a child molestation charge; credit card debt… it takes a relationship well strong in other ways to survive and recover from a launch on a lie, or unspoken truth. Most won't make it.

Assuming there have been no major avoidances of disclosure, it would seem that our relationships are frequently at their most open, honest and intimate at the point of initial Commitment - whether by marriage, moving in together or whatever the point which signifies for us the taking seriously of the coupling and potentially seeing it feature in our longer term future. We are most likely to be honest at this time. The being 'in love' bit is usually around its peak and its blindness will accept just about any Truth on offer. If you choose not to be honest at a time when you absolutely know you can be honest without major repercussion, you will never be honest once Familiarity has borne her Contempt and the repercussions of disclosure may be far more serious.

If there is anything about which we cannot be honest at the outset there is a risk. It may well be that we have taken what is effectively a calculated risk, whether consciously or otherwise. A thirty-five year old woman who is desperate to have children would probably be ill-advised to share this information on a first date. It may take years for a woman to admit that she supplemented her student grant by one or other of various dubious means available to her. We are told that in surveys it is proven that men tend to over egg the pudding when it comes to relating their sexual history whilst women will 'under egg' in line with generally accepted social norms and standards. But if Honesty and thus true Intimacy is the ultimate goal, if warts an' all is the only way of achieving a secure, understanding, longevitous relationship, when should the honesty kick in? It we don't get that timing right the danger is that we inevitably find ourselves in a coupling where it is now impossible to be honest, that the Truth which should be revealed is so far from our partner's expectations or perception of us, that to reveal it now would have devastating, and likely final, results.

We become like so many of the couples I have tried to disentangle, arguing about which way round in the cutlery drawer the spoons should go. Because of the lack of real intimacy neither is able, or perhaps willing, to discuss what is bugging them and it becomes easier to argue about relative trivialities than to grapple with the important underlying issues. The spoons become the focus. The argument itself

94

becomes a power struggle, a battle of wills, a bid for who wears the trousers, and when. There is also an element of safety in the trivia argument. We are on safer ground - quite clearly we are right in putting the bowls of the spoons furthest away so that they do not get caught as the drawer opens. And, in the overall scheme of things we know it is not really important, not life threatening, not relationship threatening. If a relationship is perfect in every other way would women really bitch about the fact that he leaves the lid off the toothpaste or leaves the toilet seat up? It usually represents the tip of a much deeper iceberg (and anyway shouldn't totally equitable toilet etiquette dictate that everyone completely closes the lid on the toilet?!)

For the thousands of people I have seen who are intent on carrying the spoon arguments into the lawyer's office and ultimately, the court room, it ceases to become an argument about spoons but rather, a way of ultimately proving who is right, of course having entrenched themselves in their unquestionably vitriolic corner. The important underlying issues are harder to tackle, greyer, more difficult to feel self assured about before you do battle. Real issues between partners are seldom black and white.

Years in family law teaches you that there are always two sides to an argument and sadly, had the people involved in them been able to properly explain where they were coming from, they may well have avoided any argument completely. Whilst I agree with those relationship psychologists who contend that a good argument can actually vacuum the stuff from under the rug and clear the air, it is also important to realise that we rarely directly raise the big underlying issue. Rows about who is supposed to take the children to school

95

on a particular day might really be about the division of labour within the household, the attitude of one to responsibility, the fear that the person refusing has a more pressing engagement …. An argument as to why the gas bill hasn't been paid might really be about the larger financial issues between the pair, the fact that one feels that the other is not equally contributing, is being frivolous with their money, is never responsible enough to remember things whilst the other feels like a walking, talking diary and events organiser…

What undoubtedly does happen in an argument, is that emotions and adrenalin run high. Reason loses Her strength in the force of Passion as She is unleashed. People lose their rational guard and say things which they may have only thought within the secrets of the windmills in their mind. Even if it is just a 'spoons in the drawer' argument, there has been a clearing of the air by the Honesty which Passion has elicited. Ironically, that may make us feel closer to our partner. Once the 'red mist' has cleared, the force of the Intimacy created by the frank exchange, having aired issues which may have been niggling for a long time, can be as strong as the force which facilitated the argument. And how many millions of us have experienced the passion of making up. Sex may not be everything but it's a powerful tool to bridge gaps, to cement the power of a spent argument, to signal the entrance of Forgiveness.

Despite having spent the entirety of my professional life embroiled in litigation I, like so many of us, do not enjoy confrontation. But reasoned passionate discussion within a relationship about sensitive issues can rapidly decline into a 'heart led' exchange of angry words. It is part of our self-defense mechanism when we feel that we are under attack. It is also a healthy sign. People who fear that they may be physically attacked by expressing an opinion, stop expressing any contrary opinions. Couples who are terrified to express contrary opinions because this might scrape at the fragile and carefully contrived surface of their relationships, never argue. If we ask ourselves what issues we would never want to raise, or be raised, in an argument with our partner, that may well give us an insight into the extent of the Honesty which we have achieved. If the 'no go' areas relate to significant things then it is likely that we did not start being open and honest about those things as early as we should have, when they were smaller, easier to be honest about.

Of course there are always the exceptions, people who are so socially and morally inept, the man on top of the Clapham omnibus wouldn't have endured five minutes with them never mind a substantial chunk of his adult life! People who use their fists to compensate for their inadequate mouths, are not capable of engaging in opinion exchange. People who are totally adamant that their position is the right one making them blind and deaf to any alternative suggestions, are not capable of reaching a required compromise, even if it is to agree to disagree.

Another inhibitor invariably raising its head in the argument circus is the overwhelming need to apportion blame ; the feeling that this is essential before any further progress can be made.

"It was/ is/ will be his/ her fault that …"

I have seldom had a client who has not spoken those words. Again it is part of our self-defense mechanism; it attempts to put into black and white what is innately grey. Complex arguments polished and practiced by adults over a period of time equally seldom have a single perpetrator.

> "For the sake of the argument, let's say it was all my fault. You contributed to what is in dispute not a jot. The end result is the end result. What do we want to do about it? Can we, and if so how do we want to, move on from here?"

I could count on two fingers how often that has been said! Whilst that may not be surprising within my four walls, it is within their own.

So many couples seem unable to move beyond the blame apportionment stage. The first, or even the fifth, time this happens will rarely signal 'The End' but those unfinished arguments will fester and niggle whether they have been swept conveniently under the parlour carpet or the kitchen rug. Everything in life has a price.

The BBC ran a documentary a while back looking at love and the ways we might preserve it. It showed various long term couples who were each shown photographs of their partner, some of which had been enhanced to set off better features and minimise the worst. Those choosing the enhanced image as best representing their partner were found to have a positive attitude to their relationship. Those relationships in which there was difficulty and conflict chose the unenhanced image as the most accurate representation.

When a brain activity analysis was carried out it quite literally showed that whilst the 'joy' part was turned on, the 'rationale' part was switched off. Infatuation does make us blind and the fact that it does makes it easier to fall in love. It airbrushes out the warts and enhances the image of our partner which we see, both physically and mentally. From Mother Nature's point of view, the 'love factor' is important for the future health of us as an animal and for our procreation.

If we manage our relationships and actually work on them, it can be easier to stay in love than we might think. It was suggested that there are four dangerous signs to look out for, a kind of blue print for the stages of love breakdown. All relate to the extent to which and the way in which we communicate with our partner. When that starts to decline, there is a withdrawal by one or both with brief, if any, answers given to the other's questions. This state then escalates, one or both becoming negative and inflexible. This in turn produces negative interpretations, the 'you've never loved me' accusations. Finally the arguments lead to invalidation and one or both will actually attack the other, at least verbally if not physically.

We have to find a way within our couplings to talk about sensitive issues without fighting. In this way we can turn things around to enhance the present and the likelihood of a future rather than always dwelling on the past and trying to apportion blame. We have to properly deal with issues and put them behind us, managing our conflicts. There is little point in trying to do this when destructive Anger is the predominant vibe. We have to choose our moment, find a good time to discuss whichever nettle we are trying to grasp.

I later tell you about a couple who reconciled in my office - where the scene alone made it more likely that one would walk off or explode with pent up frustration. It provided a channel for straight discussion and was greatly assisted by the objective views expressed by their lawyers which set a calm scene. That was their last opportunity and both knew it and they had had the benefit of two highly paid referees. We often don't appreciate just how much we care about someone until we feel we are actually losing them. However we play an impossible game if we continually leave our 'discussions' until our relationships have hit crisis point. Sometimes, just being able to reach out and hold someone's hand is enough to diffuse an escalating mood.

At the outset of a relationship arguments between two well matched partners are almost inevitable as each jostles for position, tries to establish some ground rules and more finely tune their understanding of the other's idiosyncrasies. These are often quickly diffused since both are under the power of new love and anxious to try to make this relationship work.

As Familiarity breeds Contempt, or at least Complacency, and both feel more secure in an established relationship, there is a tendency not to make the same effort to heal any rift. When, in the early days, neither would wish to part at the end of the night with a disagreement left in the air, when we are living together it's easier to go sleep in the spare room knowing the other will be there in the morning. If rows don't get cut out naturally as the relationship develops then they certainly can be with work and attention. Quality time, communication as friends and physical contact without an overt sexual context, such as dancing or just cuddling in front of the TV, are essential.

When infatuation inevitably fizzles out, if we have ensured that we have addressed these aspects then true love begins. We have a true base on which to create a solid bonding and hold each other with genuine respect rather than belittling the other's ideas and feelings. We feel like we're both on the same side, our side.

So – when? At what stage in our relationships, do we tackle this 'warts an' all' stuff? It must depend on the extent of the 'warts'. The younger we are, the less warts we are likely to have acquired but in this 21st century we are increasingly coupling later (abortions to women in their 20s increased by 25% in 2005) and split up/divorce more often to seek out a second, third, fourth… coupling.

Children from a first relationship are often a reality. Honesty about their existence and involvement in our life goes (almost always) without saying. As an adult of twenty-five plus, our partner will expect us to have had other sexual experiences. Thankfully, Virginity as an issue is now history for the majority. As our society has changed so has our expectation of it and those in it with whom we are mostly closely involved. This, in turn, allows for greater honesty. In an age where having a child out of wedlock ended in abortion, adoption, shotgun marriages or banishment, a woman's silence fifty years ago over any such 'unfortunate incident' is, at least, understandable. And one can only assume that their necessary male counterparts stayed equally stum.

As society has enabled its individuals to be, outwardly, what they have always been, inwardly, we have acquired a freedom of choice in both our life-styles and behaviour which none would want to trade. Ask any gay man who has lived in both eras.

But, everything in Life has a price - we make our contract with Mother Nature. The 'everything' is on offer and when we accept it, She will extract her consideration, Her price.

101

Mobile phones and computers come with a price tag - they make us more transparent to Big Brother and to our partners. How must Ulrika Johnson rue the day she emailed her friend about her fantastic sex life with saucy Sven.

In my last five years in practice more adultery petitions came about because of discovered texts and emails than from any other cause. The evidence is now concrete, no longer hidden by a partner's ignorance or behind passionate denials of something which could never have been substantiated. It is harder to hide our warts and it is easier than ever before to be honest about them.

But do we want to bare our souls? Would we rather keep some mystery about our persona, our inner sanctum? The age old approach to an 'adulterous relationship' has been to say nothing and hope to remain undetected unless and until that relationship becomes more important than the existing one. Mother Nature's price tag doesn't change - to have true intimacy with another soul can only be paid for with the currency of Honesty. As it is in the beginning, so it ever shall be.

The different tenets of Honesty arise at different times. When we meet and become involved with a partner, we have our past to be honest about. Most of us instinctively know when a relationship is passing from 'fun but relatively casual' to 'potential serious future'. If our eyes were bigger than our bank balance and we've been struggling juggling, to feed the hidden debt, declare it. If we might have a child, if we may be an alcoholic, if we fancy next door's cat, speak now! There is a point at which we either speak now or forever hold our peace - and live with the unknowable consequences of that decision.

HONESTY AT THE OUTSET OR ELSE?

If we go into a relationship carrying lies or putting up with them, they will do their dirty work slowly. We can never be surprised by subsequent pain caused in that relationship by dishonesties, not knowns. Honesty about past should be the easiest. Things that we did before meeting or committing to our partner should be relatively straightforward in today's relatively taboo-free climate. Not feeling able to tell our partner about a particular aspect of our past should ring a warning bell. Whatever the issue is we know that we will be highly unlikely to feel able to discuss anything in the future which stems from the same wart.

It seems that we do generally achieve that level of Honesty in the throws of our love's lust; even ignoring a counsel of complete perfection. After all, we have less to lose. We test the compatibility of our chosen 'potential one' with snippets at first to gauge their reaction. And from that reaction we quickly learn whether it would be wise to follow that Truth path or take a rapid diversion. Rapid diversion should signal alarm bells. You can't fit a square peg in a round hole however attractive or convenient it may seem at the time.

Overall Honesty is a prerequisite of the commitment process though requiring delicate handling. To offload a lifetime's confessions may make us feel absolved but leave our hitherto sheltered partner, reeling from the implications of the information before them. Details get fed in slowly as each fresh confession is presented, wrapped in the semi-disguise of pastry parcels packed with other historical trivia, digested, lived with. Still, it is likely to surface in some subsequent disagreement where a long-standing irritation can finally be scratched, explored, legitimately.

Both the transparency and freedom of our twenty-first century call for greater honesty if our relationships are to survive. We must grasp more nettles than ever faced past generations who either had fewer or were still able to maintain secret gardens to grow them in.

To be completely honest with another soul, we have to communicate. Every single client who ever walked through my office door had one thing in common with their predecessors – lack of, or breakdown in, communication. From infidelity to the revelation of true homosexuality, the discovery of unknown debts or assets to the existence of another life within a life. Secrets unspoken. Though most of the issues do not represent insurmountable problems, they all hurt horribly and cause unfathomable damage in some cases. None would have hurt to anything like the same extent if they had been communicated honestly earlier, discussed and dealt with in whatever way possible.

Not only is the old institution of marriage declining, so is the length of our 'unsanctified' couplings. Communication is at its root. In the by gone age of our grandparents where there was no television and people made their own entertainment, communication was harder to avoid. With no internet, mobile phone or email, people were forced to communicate with a smaller support network upon which they relied all the more. They were more likely to communicate with their partners but they were also less exposed to the communication of others in a wider circle. There was possibly more communication within a relationship because there were far fewer outside distractions, fewer people with whom we could otherwise choose to communicate easily and people were much more concerned by what the neighbours might think.

CHAPTER TEN

TRUTH

If we are able to psychologically cast the idea of the Fairy Tale aside, or at least accept that it will be harder to achieve now than ever before, but we still aspire to a 'till death do us part' coupling, how might we still endeavour to realise that goal? Time breeds Communication breeds Honesty breeds Trust – if you let it. True Intimacy is the potential offspring.

The last generation used to say 'new wives need time spending on them'. The outset of many true relationships is often the time when both are most open to total communication, walking inside each others skin, building trust and telling the truth. We actually listen rather than just hearing, we give more than merely going through the motions of togetherness. If we don't start as we would like to end up we won't end up as we would have liked to at the start and we wake up, possibly years later, with a stranger.

There is one reason, and one reason only, that all people lie. It is because, at the moment of telling the lie, we are frightened of Truth, frightened of the truth's potential consequence, its impact on ourselves. Initially I'd written '…ourselves and those we care about.' The woman who has been 'unfaithful' (another interesting word) may protest that she lied about her affair with the postman because she didn't

105

want to hurt her partner, which may be part of the truth. The thief who lies to the old lady, by suggesting he is a travelling salesman rather than a criminal, does not give a shit about the old lady, though his patter may well suggest to her that he does so. But both the adulteress and the conman have self-interest at heart. If the woman had the choice to partner the postman and wanted to, she would tell the truth to her man. If she doesn't do so it is because she does not want, or cannot have, the postman.

What of the person who lies to another with apparently no self-interest, to protect that other's feelings. What of the woman who lies to her girlfriend when she asks if her boyfriend is having an affair? If she truly cares for her friend, she will tell her the truth of her knowledge if she believes her friend will ultimately be happier with that knowledge (and so she will, selfishly, have a happy friend to play with rather than a depressive one who never wants to go out). If she believes her friend will be happier without the knowledge, she lies to avoid their shared unhappiness.

Lies, for fear of Truth, bred from innate self-interest. But lies beget lies.

Of course, there is a massive difference between telling a lie and not actually disclosing the truth. During my training my Principal once said to me that my Honesty (frequent open disclosure of the truth) was my biggest strength and my biggest weakness, my best trait and yet my greatest fault. He has been proven right on countless occasions since.

Many insurance contracts require us to enter them in the 'utmost good faith' to be legally binding, from the latin 'uberrima fides' meaning overall truth, most abundant faith. Sadly, few of our relationships could stand such soul-bearing.

People can't always 'take' the truth. And if we demand it, we must be sure we can 'take' it too. Take care what we wish for! But if we can find a partner whose real truths we can take and who can really take all our truths, therein true Intimacy is born. Tall order – very few of us make it. Perhaps it's just the next Fairy Tale.

For the relationships that we have with various people in our lives, from our Mothers to the man at the paper shop, it is quite clearly not a good move to always tell the truth, the whole truth and nothing but the truth. By Almighty Mother Nature! It is not a lie, it is management of the truth. But it is only through truths that we gain Intimacy. We share many truths with our family without choice because of our joint life histories. But the man in the paper shop will, ten years later, simply be the man in the paper shop if neither he nor we volunteer any truths, show some underbelly, exchange some details of our lives. And truths do have a delightful way of snowballing. If we share a truth, however trivial, with another, we are highly likely to get a truth back which leads us to a further truth etc. It is not that we give in order to receive but rather that we stop sharing ourselves if others fail to reciprocate. Truths can make us feel vulnerable. The other person then has something 'over us' whereas, as with our best friends, there is a mutual vulnerability in our sharing of our intimate truths which creates security. In simple terms, if our mate betrays a confidence they know they run the risk of us doing the same to them.

There are those I know who do not want others to know 'their business' at all, they rarely share their truths with others or show their under bellies even if others offer their truths to them. Consequently they may have many acquaintances but they do not have any real friends, or very few, and so the knowing of some of their truths is confined to their family. This may be a safe option but it denies them the richness of a variety of friendships.

To give that whole truth to a soul mate - all of the truth, warts an' all – will lead to the deepest, most unshakeable, strongest, most full-filling, happiest and most long-lasting relationships in this Twenty-First Century Britain. And that Nirvana will only be possible if we truly know ourselves first and so we know the truths we will have to share and those future possible ones which will ultimately have to be shared.

Anyone who has lived in a relationship with someone they truly treasure but who holds a lie between them will have imagined how good it would feel if that lie wasn't there. The lie becomes the stone in the gall bladder, the sand grain in the oyster which will not produce a pearl. Ironically, I believe that the majority of relationships which do, currently, really satisfy the 'Truth, whole Truth, Nothing but the Truth' test, are between couples aged over about fifty-five. When their relationships were in their infancy, they were constrained by the strength of religious, moral and social norms which kept people together or rather, prevented them from splitting up. They have now had the benefit of years of getting to know their partners and their truths. With the freedom that the last thirty years has brought to us, those people either grasp the Twenty-First Century's freedom and escape (I conducted a high proportion of long-marriage divorces) or they have had time to grow intimate.

TRUTH

The trouble is that real intimacy, unlike the lust of being in love, takes time to grow. Truths that would not have been acceptable or tolerated in the earlier years of the relationship are now digestible, acceptable. Of course, not all couples who stay together for a lifetime have such intimacy either – children and family, money and assets, also play important roles in keeping people together, perhaps contentedly. However we now have nothing to keep us together except our own will and, more often than not, we are likely to bale out before we can achieve that level of openness.

The other reality which we have to be prepared for is that we ourselves change as we grow older and wiser through our life's experiences and the experiences of others with whom we empathise. Our needs, our priorities, our desires, our views all change with the years if we are allowed, and allow ourselves, mental freedom. I acted for several male clients who had had very lengthy marriages who had then met a woman, usually at or through work, and decided to file for divorce. Invariably their sense of guilt would prompt them, despite my legal advice, to provide extremely generous settlements to their ousted spouses.

I was impressing upon one of these clients how much lower a financial settlement I believed the court would order than the one he was instructing me to offer. He explained that he could not blame his wife in any way for the breakdown of the marriage. She had been a loving and dutiful wife and an excellent mother to their children. She had not worked since they were born because he had not wanted her to. He had wanted a homemaker, to have meals ready for him when he came home from work, to be there for the children, to decorate and adorn their home and herself.

And now he had fallen in love, in the midst of his crisis, with the kind of woman he'd never known that he wanted. She was a strong career woman with an active and varied social life, with her own opinions and ideas. He had believed he wanted a woman like his wife but had changed and now felt he wanted this other kind of woman. He could not help how he felt but it consumed him with guilt whilst his wife was consumed with her own confused desolation.

Ironically, he had helped make his wife as she was. She had become dull, boring, unstimulating to him because her life was all of these things. She was not unintelligent nor unattractive but, despite their decades together, they had stopped any real and honest communication. Its absence had been filled with other things - until the only thing he felt he could honestly communicate to her was that he didn't love her and wanted a divorce. When it has been allowed to reach that point, it is unlikely that any amount of reconciliation counseling will save the day.

A stitch in time saves nine. Had they each spoken candidly, years before, about how each felt what they wanted had changed, it may well have been saved. Communication, of itself, is not enough any more than love, of itself, is all that is needed for a long and happy partnership. For that to happen both have to be committed to actively sustaining it, committed to making it work. Once that resolve dissolves it is usually only a matter of time before the relationship dissolves. Mentally, even though those who have lost it may not be shopping elsewhere, they are open to the seduction of a striking window dressing which will eventually lure them into the shop. Prevarication excludes Commitment which requires some self-imposed blinkering, keeping our eyes on the pavement.

Compromise is the third golden 'C' word. Honest committed communication will not prevent a relationship faltering without preparedness on both sides to compromise. When one or both of the pair continually refuse to compromise, either conflict becomes unavoidable or one of us starts taking on the appearance of a doormat. How this is managed in practice will depend very much upon the particular couple and their personalities.

Compromise is not always possible because of the black and white nature of the disagreement. Whether or not we want to have children cannot be compromised, there is no middle ground to be had no matter how well we communicate our view or our commitment. One friend of mine deals with it in this way. If it is something which he does not feel strongly about but his wife does, he will let her have her way, which he does often. For example, he does not have particularly strong religious beliefs whilst his wife is a fairly staunch Catholic and so he agreed that their children should attend Catholic schools and be raised in that faith. It may have been different had he been a staunch Protestant of course.

Needing to compromise automatically means that there are two opposing points of view and the ease with which a compromise might be reached will depend on the extent of that opposition. In my friend's case, his wife concedes that her point of view is often the one which is carried and accordingly, when he does have a particularly strong view upon something, his wife will concede even though she feels strongly too. He has exchanged quantity of 'wins' for almost certainty of a 'win' when it really matters to him.

FAIRY TALES by Sharon Moore

Some issues within relationships are incapable of
compromising but there has to be a balance in the way we
concede or the Yin Yang of that relationship will start to
disintegrate. Compromise is rarely a child born of Anger and
so will rarely be achieved during the course of an argument. It
is a dish which can seldom be achieved unless served cold
since it is a rational, rather than emotional, reaction.

CHAPTER ELEVEN

HONESTY THROUGHOUT

After the flush of the outset and all the insecurities that it can highlight, Security nurtures Complacency. We forget or ignore the fact that good relationships have to be worked at, that Honesty is just as important to maintain what we sought to create as it was for its creation in the first place.

What seems to happen at some point, once a relationship has been established, is that Honesty wanes or, in some cases, ceases, on any real level. Ironically the birth of family often signals this change. The woman is naturally preoccupied by her new role and equally restricted by her new responsibilities. The man is conscious of his own greater responsibility in the world but also feels safer in his present and his future. A child brings an extent of guaranteed permanence which even the partner cannot provide. The sharing of intimate thoughts and feelings becomes marginalised. Everyday practicalities of who is cooking what for tea, who is organising the replacement fridge and when, what has happened at work or at home, take over. Especially with the arrival of children there is simply less time to indulge the true fabric of the relationship and this invariably leads to a decline in sexual activity. This isn't just because of time constraints but reflects the decline in the level of intimacy. We know an old love can never bring the excitement peculiar to a new conquest but the advantages of an old love, if it is True, far outweigh temporary titillation however gratifying the latter may be.

We reach a state of contentment with our partner and then, at some point move our sights to other things, whether it is building a business or a harem. We invest in the house and then stop making the mortgage payments - and are surprised when the property is repossessed! We take our eye off the ball. Familiarity breeds Contempt. We lose perspective in the hurly burly of our rat race lives. Then suddenly, perhaps when the children are old enough such that they can no longer provide a convenient diverting distraction, Time becomes the enemy. Two people who know practically all there is to know (they think) about the other's life find themselves strangers in the same room, looking into a long-treasured mirror and not recognising the reflection looking back at them.

In a family law department, it is as sure a fact that the 'new clients' list swells after the Christmas and summer holidays, as it is that most violence provoked injunctions walk in on a Monday morning after the weekend's 'celebrations'. Even in the absence of children, we distract ourselves with a multitude of inexhaustible tasks thrown forth by life's vicissitudes. Two week's break from that schedule not only produces time to reflect, to reprioritise, to regain perspective, it is also often the last straw, the realisation that we can no longer bear to live pulling the wool over our own eyes. That seems like the easiest way but ultimately it takes a great deal of courage to tear up all the practical comforts of our life, our friends, our family. We prefer to take the easier option until it dawns on us that it is quite the opposite. If those other relationships which we share with people in our coupled life will be jeopardised by the fallout, they were probably worth changing anyway.

One of the fundamental mistakes we seem to make in our relationships is the expectation that our partner, whether consciously recognised or not, can fulfill all our needs and desires. No-one is perfect, everyone has warts from our own perspective - and so have we.

Way down on my 'checklist', my ideal man would enjoy Scrabble, theatre, motorcycling, dancing … but the chances of meeting someone who meets all our criteria in one lifetime must be miniscule especially since age produces experience which only serves to extend the list. Some interests grow together with a relationship but what usually happens is that we use other relationships to compensate for any deficiencies. We have a mate to play squash with, we join a theatre group, we increasingly maintain outside independent interests and careers. Many of my parent's generation are horrified at the thought of their partner going away on holiday with a mate; most couples these days would expect that to occur - whether for a stag/ hen weekend or a longer break.

But in this process we often seem to see our differences as emphasising our partner's shortcomings, obscuring the other's valuable attributes. It may start as a source of irritation but it will fester. Just as we would adjust the feelings sometimes provoked by our parents' or our children's shortcomings, we need to learn to extend the same courtesy to our closest and adjust our knee-jerk reactions taking account of who that person is which may differ quite substantially from who we are ourselves. We cannot expect others always to react or behave as we would ourselves and if we do expect them to, we set ourselves up for a fall.

Something like 80% of all divorces are supported by the fact of Unreasonable Behaviour. There is only one ground for divorce which is that a marriage has 'Irretrievably broken down'. Simply stating this to be the case is insufficient and the Government's proposals for a supposedly 'no fault' divorce, though embodied in Statute, have never been brought into force despite lawyers having trained for the long awaited implementation.

However, the 'Unreasonable Behaviour' catch-all effectively allows anyone who wants a divorce to get one provided they will officially point a blaming finger ("It's his fault"). Assuming that those elusive perfect people do not actually exist, two 'angels' would be able to divorce using this Unreasonable Behaviour supporting fact. The only clients who use the 'two years separation with the consent of the other' fact, are those who choose to. Some actually don't want to point the finger or want the time to make sure they've made the right decision.

Upon learning of my profession people's comments range from:

"I bet you get to hear some juicy stories!" to "oo, no way could I do that job!"

There is an inevitable curiosity at the secrets disclosed in a divorce lawyer's office. And, of course, there are colourful details which still have the power to surprise, if not shock, and surprise if only at what an individual can grow accustomed to. When you walk into an office like mine, you have to be prepared to bare more information to one individual than you have ever shared with one person, except, in some cases only, your partner. All your financial details, all your debts, assets and income. Well you'd expect that. But, often in the raw of your emotion, you need to explain what's been going on in your marriage, who said what when, how you feel, how your children feel, when you last had sex, where you sleep, the date upon which you concluded that your marriage was over... And in the case of adultery, why you allege this, what information you have to substantiate your fears, has your partner admitted it and if so, when, where and in what words. Whether you feel certain that you want a divorce... short of stripping off naked it's a fairly grueling thing to have to go through with a complete stranger. Distress, embarrassment, anger ... and at the peak of this emotional rollercoaster you have to take in the alien legal advice given and make rational, sensible decisions whilst fearing big legal bills.

I recall a forensic pathologist, a Quincy, talking to us law students back at Liverpool University. It left a lasting impression when he volunteered that a lifetime of death-site visits couldn't numb him to the stench of death or the horror of a violent end, whether sought or not. But the violence of the colour fades with years of practice; it's all variations on a number of themes. It becomes no less sad but the remorseless inevitability of Human Nature reminds you of His Mother, unbending. If you showered Her with gifts and even became celibate because of your devotion to Her, She would not prevent Her Tsunami from sweeping you away if you happened to be in the wrong place at the wrong time..

FAIRY TALES by Sharon Moore

A woman returned to me for a second divorce having employed me, via Government funding several years before, for her first. She was what my mother would call a ' blousy girl', an expression which always seemed to have some relevance to a woman's mammary size but with something extra thrown in. A man would hardly use the expression for it is used by a woman to describe another and mildly bitch. I liked her and her frankness. On this particular day she was distraught. She and her mate had decided to model their newly purchased Ann Summers skimpies "for a laugh" when their respective partners returned from a mates-night-out 'down the pub'. The boys had suggested they should lap dance to show off their purchases. One thing lead to another and her husband ended up screwing her mate on their new settee which she was still paying for and to which he refused to contribute. Both appeared to be equally heinous crimes in her smudged panda eyes.

You experience a kind of internalized groan when such scenarios are relayed to you. Not at the particular individual but with our Nature – if it's not one thing it's another. Why don't we ever seem to learn that it really is an 'eye for an eye' where She is concerned. If you play with fire you have to be prepared to get your fingers burned - and not cry about it.

I acted for a woman whose long term husband had badgered her about getting involved in 'swingers' parties. He had a mate at work who raved about the ones he had been to. She initially refused and subsequently, reluctantly, agreed. It had become such a big issue to him that she thought one party might shut him up and send him in search of a more 'wholesome' hobby. She found that the people were not as she had expected and were in fact tolerably wholesome. After years of faithfulness, her sexual freedom had her Husband's seal of approval. She discovered the difference between men's love making. She had her first 'lesbian' experience. She loved 'the scene'. After the first flush of the excitement of several monthly parties, even travelling to Europe to indulge with networked friends, he became reluctant and ultimately refused to go. She divorced him - on the grounds of his adultery, not his unreasonable behaviour! She was currently 'involved' with a man she'd met through 'her circle' who had left his wife for her. Be careful what you wish for because She will exact her undisclosed price if you take the gamble because, according to Her law, every action produces a reaction which often cannot be predicted by the actor.

The vast majority of the divorce petitions which I prepared were sadly mundane. People run down by the rawness of their emotion which had burst out into their stifling monotony of a life of sleep, eat, work, eat, work, TV, sleep, pay bills, work, eat some more…. In the absence of the more predictable examples of behaviour unacceptable to our man in Clapham such as violence, alcoholism etc, I am left with an equally predictable list of complaints when pressing a client for potential 'Unreasonable Behaviour' allegations.

> "I want to go out and socialise while she always wants to stay at home. She isn't interested in my friends at all"

becomes:

> "though the Petitioner has made repeated and concerted efforts to involve the Respondent in social events, she refuses to participate in any such and rejects any friends which she perceives to be his alone"

and could actually mean:

> "The Petitioner is completely irresponsible with money
> and whilst the Respondent is struggling to make ends
> meet, put food on the table and money aside for bills, put
> their relationship on a stronger emotional and financial
> footing, the Petitioner just wants to go down to the pub
> with his mates. The Respondent knows the Petitioner
> complains about her to his friends and that they snigger
> over his indiscretions behind her back..."

> "We hardly ever have sex and he's always disinterested in
> the bedroom"

becomes:

> "despite the repeated efforts of the Petitioner to engage
> the Respondent in sexual relations, the Respondent has
> repeatedly rejected the Petitioner's advances and shows no
> interest in instigating or pursuing sexual intimacy"

Just like an adultery allegation or admission, the symptom not
the cause is being disclosed. The reality could be anything
from the husband having become physically unable through
to the fact that the last thing he feels like doing is shagging
what is left of her brains out because she has been a complete
bitch in other ways. It is the end result which is disclosed.
The means by which we have reached that end are largely
insignificant in the legal process, though not in life.

I shall look at the means behind the end result of adultery
elsewhere but it will now be clear that an Unreasonable
Behaviour petition is often, at best, a carefully edited version
of the truth and, at worst, down right misrepresentation.

There are always two sides to every story. The reality is that it 'takes two to tango' and if the marriage is effectively at an end, albeit as a result of a unilateral decision, it makes absolutely no difference in 99% of cases as to who divorces whom and upon what basis. To defend a Petition only serves to delay the inevitable divorce whilst increasing costs. There are lawyers who will invariably indicate an intention to defend divorce proceedings where costs have been claimed from the other spouse. The ensuing correspondence and negotiation invariably produces fees equal, if not in excess of, those fees which were originally being disputed. All that is achieved is that the parties' acrimony and the lawyers' fees, have escalated. It is common to offer no defense to even the most misrepresentative of Unreasonable Behaviour petitions; to accept the divorce but deny each and every allegation made. It makes no difference if we both want out and even a unilateral decision has to be accepted by the other, whether immediately or ultimately, following lots of wasted hundred pound notes.

Whatever the substance of the client's complaint, what the Petition really represents is a flag that communication on any real level is tenuous if not non-existent. Intimacy has been lost and so, the potential Paradise. In theory it is not too late; in practice it usually is. These relationships were not necessarily feted to fail, incapable of ever soaring the heady heights of an intimate existence. Difficulties are frequently exacerbated by those outside the partnership, family or friend, leading to division of loyalties. But just as we must ultimately carry the responsibility of our own actions, so we must take fully the responsibility of the partnerships we try to forge and the next generation which might be born of them.

FAIRY TALES by Sharon Moore

If for no reason other than to respect the care which we once held for a person, we need to communicate our truths.

There are all manner of truths hiding in the shadows of "I want to go out, she wants to stay in" not least the frank discussions which should have taken place often years before. If 'love' conquers all then even 'a lot of like' must have a great deal of power.

CHAPTER TWELVE

MEDIATION

Successful mediation by definition requires a preparedness on the part of both participants to compromise, to take their gloves off and come out of their corners.

Several years ago there was a great furore within the matrimonial field when the government, liberally caring for its subjects, decided that Mediation was the answer to all the long painful expensive legal battles used to carve up matrimonial assets or time spent with children. The fact that a significant percentage of those battles were, at least in the shorter term, funded by the Government via Legal Aid (now helpfully renamed Public Funding to impress upon the tax paying masses who pays this reaper) should not pass unnoted. It became a prerequisite, save for inevitable exceptions, for anyone potentially qualified to receive Legal Aid in the family law field, to first be referred to mediation. Of course, they could not insist upon parties voluntarily participating in adult discussion. Given that it is precisely adult discussion which will, by definition, be lacking in the vast majority of relationships referred to it, many in the field felt this had all the hallmarks of another Poll Tax white elephant. Indeed, in practice, it was extremely rare for both parties to agree to such an attendance.

There was, and has been, a very low take up and the powers that be had to console themselves by then forcing people to attend a session individually to be told what mediation was - before they could get public money to argue the legal standpoint.

For the minority who do take this final option, the result will, in my experience, seldom lead to an enduring financial agreement and, much more often, leads to an entrenchment whose consequence will be costly in time, emotion and money. It is one thing for a mediator, largely unqualified in the realities of family law, to assist parties in scheduling contact visits with children, arranging venues, resolving transport issues, dietary and medical requirements etc. It is quite another to ask such a person to assist parties in reaching a fair financial settlement. Even if the mediator has relevant legal knowledge, they are not directed to use it to assist parties in reaching a fair financial settlement. Clients will invariably return to their respective lawyers with the joyful relief of an agreement only to be advised in the strongest terms (lawyers would be negligent if they did not do so) that either the agreement reached is immensely favourable or unfavourable to them.

The NFM (National Family Mediation) specifically state that 'mediators do not give legal advice' and Relate, which claims to be 'the UK's largest provider of relationship counselling and sex therapy', has a similar caveat. I don't doubt that a neutral mediator can be helpful in getting warring parties to the talking table, acting as a referee in their disputes and facilitating calmer discussion of issues. However, to attempt to chair a debate regarding a fair and reasonable financial settlement, whether within the context of marriage or otherwise, without any reference to what the law deems as such is, in my view, a recipe for disaster. Advising clients on the steps to be taken to achieve a true value of all assets and, that information having been obtained, advising them on the most likely outcome if the matter were to go to court, is the hardest part of a family lawyers job. It takes years of experience in practice, handling hundreds of cases, to be able to confidently and accurately assess the margin of possible likely outcomes. Many family solicitors steer shy of giving such opinions and will rely on taking a barrister's advice before giving a client a clear indication of what they should be offering as a settlement. With that in mind, does it not seem bizarre that our Government is actively encouraging the use of mediators who, even if they have legal knowledge, are not allowed to share it?!

I had a lady client who had two small children. The home was not over sized for her needs nor located in a particularly expensive area. The children attended local schools and she had built up a network of friends and neighbours on whom she could rely. She came to me having attended mediation at the insistence of her husband, whom she suspected had already sought some legal advice, and because of a desire to settle as quickly as possible to minimize the disruption to the kids. After several visits together and various papers and documents having been produced to provide proof of their assets, she had reached agreement with her husband.

The house was to be sold and the proceeds divided 60% in her favour in exchange for her making no claim against his pension. There was not a lot of equity in the house and the money she was to receive would have taken her off DSS Benefits but was not enough to enable her to buy a new suitable home. She still had no idea of her husband's self-employed income. She didn't understand what his pension was worth or the extent of her claim on it. She was facing the prospect of living in rented accommodation and living off the modest lump sum until that had run out, when she would go back onto benefits and receive assistance with her rent. The husband was acquiring a Clean Break which, in simple terms, means that he did not have to pay any ongoing maintenance to his wife after the divorce though obviously he would have to pay maintenance for the kids.

This 'settlement' was woefully inadequate and significantly less than she would be awarded by a Family court. The husband, waving his 'terms of agreement' before his own lawyer was incensed that he had received a letter from me stating quite clearly that under no circumstances would his wife now agree to their home being sold. His lawyer in turn had to confirm that the 'agreement' reached had no realistic prospect of being imposed by a court without his wife's specific agreement and, indeed, the agreement reached in mediation had no binding effect whatsoever. He was enraged at his wife reneging on the agreement. He now understood from his lawyer that the house would not be sold and, if he transferred half of his pension rights over to her, he might expect to get a share of the equity in the house once his youngest child was seventeen or completed full-time education some twelve years away. Alternatively he could 'off set' her claim on his pension against his interest in the house. He was spitting feathers. It was she who had had the affair. He was told that this made no difference.

My client phoned two days later. She was beside herself. Her husband had been round the night before in a storming mood. He had woken the children with his shouting and they had become so upset that she had had to arrange for her mother to come over and collect them in the middle of the night because she could neither assuage their distress nor her husband's white anger. Her mother had urged her to phone the police but she didn't want to involve them. It was bad enough her long-standing neighbours having to hear their undignified screaming matches never mind about having the police on the doorstep. And her husband would have gone berserk. He had pulled the wire from the phone after she'd called her mom and she'd clung onto her bag containing her mobile phone, willing her new partner not to make his usual last thing goodnight call before he went to his bed. Fortunately, for whatever reason, he had not but that small smile from lady luck was mountainously overshadowed by her husband's total disbelief at the turnaround in his fortunes apparently because of me, to whom he had apparently referred with the most imaginative of terms, none of them endearing!

She had phoned the police after he'd eventually left. He had raged at her for almost three hours urging her to stick by the agreement reached in mediation and everything could be resolved quickly and amicably. He would even agree to transfer 'some' of his pension to her and would also agree to buy the kids school uniforms each year and pay for a holiday for them. He had said that if this couldn't be agreed and it was going to drag on for months, he could not afford to continue to support his own rented flat and their home and would make immediate arrangements to move back in. My client was totally distraught, at the end of her tether and not at all happy with me. After all, a week ago, everything was calm, contact was going well, the children were more settled

than they had been for months and her estranged husband
had even been helping out doing some much needed DIY
jobs around the house (ready for the sale!) And she could see
her husband's point - did I really think it was fair that he
should give her half of the pension which he had worked
hard for throughout their marriage and have his mortgage
capacity tied up in their home, potentially for the next twelve
years when her youngest would have finished his 'A' levels.

She was totally panic stricken at the thought of his moving
back in. He had also implied that if he didn't move back in, at
the very least he would stop paying the mortgage. She had
'been on to' the Benefits Agency who had advised that she
would not get any financial assistance from them for nine
months from the date of application. The mortgage couldn't
be paid and then the building society would repossess the
house. Everyone knew that they never got the best price so
she and her husband would end up worse off! She had made
up her mind that she wanted to go with the agreement
reached in mediation. She just couldn't cope with any more
stress and nor could her kids. She would not entertain the
idea of trying to secure an injunction against him since this
would further inflame the inferno of her current situation.

I tried to calm her down but she was in no state to receive
and act upon legal advice. I was fast becoming the enemy, the
breacher of her peace of mind. I finally persuaded her to
come in and see me for an hour at the end of the week
having offered her a reduced fee for the visit. When she came
in three days later she was calmer but ostensibly more
resolute. Her husband had phoned and apologised for losing
his temper and had ended up in tears on the phone. A good
family lawyer has to walk the tightrope of a relationship

breakdown, trying to keep a balance between the emotion and the practicalities whilst treading a very narrow route within the confines of the legal process. A week before my client had been blissfully ignorant as to the inadequacy of the agreement reached in mediation; I had been blissfully ignorant of her or her problems.

The simplest thing for a lawyer to do in such circumstances would be to obtain a signed letter from the client covering your back against a negligence claim at some time in the future when Logic once more reigned over Emotion. I could then just draw up the agreement in the required form of a Consent Order. From the client's point of view it would be sorted quickly and relatively cheaply. Having received his legal advice, husband would be more than aware that he had got a 'great deal'. He would be far more amicable over contact visits and the children would be affected as little as possible in the circumstances. All of these aspects are, of course, extremely important and must be weighed in the balance when looking at the route to be taken to reach financial settlement. But I think a family lawyer fails in their duty to a client if they simply take the easy route.

A client walks into a divorce lawyer's office for the first time and is frightened about how much it is all going to cost and what the outcome is going to be. They are invariably in a highly emotional state induced by a cocktail of sadness, guilt, anger, fear … A trust has to be created in which a client realises that you will do what you believe best for them. The work will not be undertaken because the lawyer wants more fees, a common suspicion, but because that trust has been established. This is not an easy vibe to create especially when the client is likely to be at their least trusting! Furthermore the client can still not buy control; there are no guarantees within the greyness of equitable family law.

My mediation client was faced with various pressing issues. I had to explain that she was unlikely to be able to prevent him moving back into their house if he chose. He was a joint owner and he was paying the mortgage. He had never been violent to her or the children nor had he ever threatened them. The last incident had not involved any physical threat and I suspected that he had been strongly tutored by his own lawyer as to the inadvisability of treading that path. He had been assiduous in heeding that advice. In 'normal' circumstances one might suggest that she reason with him as a father, pointing out the likely effect on the children of his return. But he was furious at the turnaround and the legal advice he had received and he missed his children. The Green Eyed Monster gnawed at his brain at night, imagining her in some passionate embrace with her new lover. There was basically nothing I could do if he did move back in but 'behaved' himself.

Likewise he could stop paying the mortgage. As a joint signatory to the mortgage document he had a prima facie obligation to pay it but if he didn't and the Building Society did ultimately take repossession proceedings? Well, at least the house would be sold and his dented mortgage capacity restored. He would have been told by his lawyer that a Building Society rarely starts proceedings unless the mortgage is at least three months in arrear so he could bring some pressure to bear even if he did ultimately meet the payments.

She would be entitled to maintenance for the children but the court could no longer decide on how much should be paid taking into account all the particular financial circumstances of this case ... She needed to press the CSA to get the forms out to him as quickly as possible. The payment clock would only start to tick once the forms had been posted to him. She would then have to wait until the CSA had carried out its assessment and hope that her self-employed husband would be both cooperative and honest with them. She could apply to the court for maintenance in her own right, at least until an overall settlement had been agreed, but this would take both time and money. If we were going to make application to the court we might as well put in a full application relating to the whole financial settlement. As in life, so in law - there are no guarantees. A client pays a lawyer according to the extent of their expertise and experience in dealing with cases and so having an ability to give the most educated guess as to the likely outcome. However, no-one can predict the individual attitude of an unknown judge who might well preside over the proceedings nor how the verbal evidence will come over on the day.

I made two columns on a page of A4 and on one side listed the 'agreement' terms and on the other the terms which I thought she could achieve if the matter were decided upon by a court. This didn't mean the case would actually go to court. One thing I could guarantee was that his lawyer, who I knew of old, would not take this case to a court on the basis of the offer currently being made by his client. I told her that I did not want her to be sitting wherever in five years time thinking 'I wish my lawyer had been firmer with me at the time, I wish she'd impressed on me the importance of the decisions made then which would materially effect the rest of my life'. If my client felt that she had made a fully informed decision then I guess I had done all I could.

It would be nigh on impossible to work in a field like this unless you believed in the underlying fairness of the law which you are charged with implementing. Over the years I had various new clients who said they had come to see me as I had a reputation for being formidable. I would always explain that I was not in the business of metaphorically nailing anyone's bits to the wall but I would fight for what l considered a fair and reasonable settlement on their behalf. That tenacity is what a client pays for on the back of confidence in the lawyer's legal knowledge and advice.

After a week of deliberation my client, though unnecessarily apologetic about her initial reaction to me after 'the incident', said she wanted to go ahead with the agreement. She totally understood my advice but, taking everything else into account, just wanted it over. We did manage to negotiate a few better terms but the house was sold and she did have to go into rented accommodation with her children. Had they never been to mediation which had wholly inflated the husband's expectations, I do not believe that would have been the outcome. The husband would have received realistic advice as to the likely outcome from the beginning, as would my client. The range of possibilities to be considered by them would have been much reduced and a more balanced result would have been the consequence. The husband might argue that, actually, mediation worked fine for him (!) but he would be unable to assess the way in which his children might have developed differently had they remained in their own home with a mother able to juggle her finances and secure in having some provision for her old age.

What I believe should happen is that, after both parties have produced paperwork to demonstrate their income, assets and liabilities, they should first see a neutral family law expert who could advise on the best realistic outcome for both of them, so as to at least reduce the range of disagreement between them. If the argument that each should be individually represented prevails then their respective lawyers should be bound via the court process to have a meeting to try to settle the case at the outset. At the very least they could agree what was in issue and ask any questions which had arisen from that disclosure direct. The alternative is to have experienced family lawyers conducting mediation sessions and guiding the parties around the law. But I suspect that this would be rather more expensive for the Government than paying the current mediators wages.

I also think it can help if a new client actually brings their soon-to-be-ex partner with them. A client can always ask for this to happen. Whilst I would always spend some time alone with the client, and have to impress upon both of them that my advice was directed only to the one who would be employing me, it had advantages. In terms of the petition, the spouse knows what to expect. In terms of major issues like sale of house, the spouse will know what his or her unbeloved is likely to argue. It cuts out the distrust of what exactly the other's legal advisor has said. And it gives the spouse the opportunity to meet and weigh up the lawyer. This usually doesn't happen until a formal court application has been issued and parties are attending the first hearing!

Family lawyers are criticised for not supporting or encouraging mediation but, in matters of finance at least, the pitfalls, in my view, are obvious.

CHAPTER THIRTEEN

SUPPORT EARLY ON

Is it unrealistic to suggest that, in the same way that we are increasingly looking for help in locating a partner in our hectic twenty-first century lives, we could become socially accustomed to actually being proactive in terms of preserving our relationships and nurturing them?

Whilst we do have 'Relate' (formerly the marriage Guidance Counsel) and various private practitioners offering a similar service, couples only tend to attend such meetings as a last ditch attempt to rescue their relationships which are already on the rocks.

The reality of life seems to be that, if we cannot learn to modernise our relationships by ourselves, society should be bound to provide support. If any practical help is to be supplied by society for the greater good of that society, it needs to happen much earlier than following a referral from a family lawyer when the milk is spilt and the tears have started. It is an important and separate issue to provide help and support to couples, practical 'relationship techniques', a referee in some cases.

A rare opportunity arose whilst I was in practice. The husband came to see me seeking a divorce from his long-standing wife. I talked to him about the reasons for his decision, how he felt and the conversations he had had with his wife. I was used to hearing these stories. To have reached the point that you have come to sit in my office, it is invariably the case that your relationship really has "irretrievably broken down."

Having received my standard advice at the first meeting, having gone away to mull over it, he confirmed that he wished to go ahead. For some reason I truly felt that this marriage was not at an end, that both of them had backed themselves into a corner and, because they had stopped communicating with each other, they didn't know how the other really felt. When you ask a client the reasons for which they feel their relationship is over, they will list a series of complaints and problems. When you ask them how much of what they have just said they have communicated to their partner, the majority has not been specifically relayed and that which has, has usually been conveyed in the extreme of emotion - anger or distress.

It was also pure chance that I knew the wife had instructed a very good and sincere male family lawyer whom I knew, liked and respected. I decided to give him a call. This was somewhat unorthodox since my client's clear instructions were that he did not wish to go to a Relate meeting and that he wanted divorce papers issued as soon as possible. My male counterpart confirmed that his instructions matched mine. I said that I felt that it wasn't really what my client wanted, despite what he had specifically said to me. To my relief my counterpart confirmed that be had felt exactly the same way about his client, despite her similar specific instructions.

We agreed to try to persuade our respective clients to attend a round the table meeting with us all present, at least to try to agree the financial settlement between them, which was not particularly complicated. They each agreed. We were squashed into my cramped office around my disk. Neither of us lawyers had any training in mediation nor were we quite sure how to 'play' this one. After some initial mundane discussions about the law, I came clean. I explained how I felt about the case and that I had spoken to the wife's lawyer who had felt the same. I explained that I had never been moved to do this on any other occasion in my career.

They asked if they could talk on their own. We lawyers hung around in the waiting room, like kids waiting for a detention, wondering whether we had done the right thing and whether there would be an explosion from within my office at any moment. After about fifty minutes, I decided to go back in. They were smiling. They had done more proper talking to each other in that time than they had in years. They left together and subsequently confirmed that they both wished to withdraw their instructions as they were reconciled.

Had they not happened to choose to visit the lawyers they did, had I not made that call, had we not agreed to act somewhat unprofessionally but for the right motives, they would probably have been divorced. This is not to blow my own trumpet but rather to illustrate how the present system does nothing to really help couples backed in corners, needing some outside positive input.

Ten years ago my mother was horrified that I felt the need to join a dating agency. Today, some of the most 'executive' of my friends attend Speed Dating entirely unabashed, though frequently disappointed, and belong to online dating agencies. Is it so unrealistic to suggest that we could become socially accustomed to actually being proactive in terms of preserving our relationships? One might tease the Americans that they have replaced their best friend with 'a quack' with whom they can share all their secrets but many modern western societies face similar problems.

The influence of both the family structure and the Church have declined dramatically in the past fifty years. It is a rarity for non-Asian Brits to live within the extended family. Half a century ago, even if parents weren't living in the same house, they usually lived around the corner. People had more children and these larger families centered their social lives around their family. Family participation in our relationships was unavoidable. The effect of the decline of the influence of religious mores on our social groups has also been dramatic. It has produced a never-before-experienced freedom to live simply by the laws of this enlightened land but without any other constraint. The law has hitherto been the bottom line. Increasingly it is the only line.

Just as it was for the Dating Agency only ten years ago which carried a stigma and was viewed by those who had coupled unaided as a kind of admission of failure, such washing of one's dirty lingerie and inadequacies in public, via relationship support agencies, is deemed an embarrassing and 'unseemly' thing to do, particularly to a Brit. Look what happened when Jerry Springer tried to bring his show to the UK. No-one would come forward with the kind of I-divorced-my-husband-to-marrry-his-father revelations that the Americans appear elated to share. I recall that the best we could offer were identical twins who had to admit to their respective boyfriends that they worked as lap dancers – and that was probably a publicity stunt on their part.

137

The admission that any help might be required at all, in the realms of our personal relationship, can only be justified by the sheer overwhelming reality of our increasingly brief liaisons. We are not good at it, no matter how much we think we do OK. It was little over twenty-five years ago when there was only one girl we knew of, in a year of 90 students, whose parents were divorced. If there were more they did not let it be known. What percentage of children in a class today would have parents who have ever been married or indeed live together now? And, how are they going to fare when it comes time for them to forge their own couplings. Can we rely on the pendulum theory that might optimistically propose that that generation will be better adapted to twenty-first century life, better able to preserve their relationships? Or will the 'sins' of their 'fathers' be visited upon the 'sons' tenfold?

Not only is every Englishman's home his castle, it is also fortressed to keep in his secrets and personal life in all its intimacy. The old stiff upper lip is still evident; it seems we would rather watch our relationships dissolve under our feet than seek help. If and when we do, we almost always do it when it is too late. If one or other or both people are not good at expressing feelings, or feel so enraged by whatever-it-might-be that sensible objective adult discussion degenerates into a 'slanging match' and banged doors at best, should we not provide easily accessible non-judgmental support. If 'it never seemed like a good time', 'we were so busy with other things', shouldn't there be a realistic social support which works. It is at that stage that we could often do with some outside help and objectivity, that point at which some oiling of the wheels of our discussions can prevent a seizure further down the line. Should we not consider a change in our attitude to such outside involvement? A stitch in time saves nine.

We can use our families to attempt to assume this role - or they assume it unbidden - but they have their own blood born subjectivity which prejudices their approach - whether towards or against their blood. Mutual friends caught in the midst of such crossfire are likely to regret the experience. Is it right that the most likely time for someone being referred to 'anger management' classes is when they are trying to persuade the court that they are to be trusted to have unsupervised contact with their children or in arguing against being prevented from living in their own home? If we don't address our warts before they cause serious problems we continue a complacent attitude to our relationships which is evidently not working.

For those of us who have experienced the tremendous good fortune of having two loving parents in our lives from birth, many of us go through a pathway of enlightenment in our understanding of our parents and our relationship with them. As a young girl, my father was second only to someone I'd never met and wasn't at all sure about despite Sunday school. He knew everything, he would always be able to protect me and anyone who contradicted him must be wrong. As I grew older I realised he was not perfect, he made mistakes, he got it wrong sometimes - from the gestation period of an elephant (my biology teacher could not be told it was ten years!) to the way he lived his life in a more general sense. In the early years of this realisation I felt angry, cheated, lied to (as I did when they told me about Santa Claus). I resented my father for his failings, his shortcomings. After that dawned the realisation that of course he had flaws, eccentricities, skeletons - as did I - and that was part of what I loved about him. People in glass houses should neither throw stones nor peak in the reflections. And finally you realise that what makes your love so intimate is the very knowing and accepting of the faults. Love, warts an' all.

It appears that we often commence our sexual relationships in the same way. Despite being older and more experienced, more tainted by life's realities, we want to believe in the perfect qualities of our new beau or belle. It is how we react when they fail us, when one of their frailties or warts surface that sets the tone. Do we allow the same latitude as we would our parent, are we afforded the same latitude by our mate? Do we often reach the point of intimately knowing our partner, loving them despite their warts or at least loving them more because of our intimacy with their insecurities and faults, a shared understanding that makes what we share unique and therefore invaluable and therefore irreplaceable?

CHAPTER FOUREEN

SEX, SEXUAL FREEDOM AND ADULTERY

If we have a nicotine or alcohol addiction we will always find the time and money to purchase our props. If we have a good sexual relationship with our partner, we will always find the time and energy to make love however jumping-off-the-top-of-the-wardrobe it is not.

We all have a libido, our sexual drive, and our desire to have sex, what kind, with whom and with what frequency will undoubtedly play its part in the success of our unions and the amount about which we need to be honest. There are a million and one reasons why the frequency with which we would have sex if stranded on a desert island with our mate would differ from that in our busy lives at home, with jobs, mortgage, kids, frayed tempers and disrupted sleeping patterns. But when we suggest that we don't have the time or inclination because of such things, we fool ourselves. Sex can be a very easy way of communicating without the awkwardness of carefully chosen words in the fall out of an argument which has lasted hours or a disagreement which has lasted days or weeks. Ultimately actions do speak louder than words and a few gentle caresses or two hours of sweaty combat can say more than a book full of words and create a springboard for less heated discussion.

Who can't hear must feel. The couple who fail to communicate with, and listen to, each other will undoubtedly fail in their declared shared goal of a lasting relationship. The same applies to sexual attention to each other. The bonus tends to be that one leads to the other - sex and communication, communication and sex. The passion of a one-night stand or a fortnight in Hedonism I (like Rocky there is now a II and III — why are we not surprised!) draws on our earthly baseness rather than our emotional spirituality. However wide or lurid our particular sexual experiences may be, most of us would say that our 'all round' most satisfying sexual experience (though not necessarily the best sex) was with someone to whom we felt, at that moment, physically attracted, whom we cared strongly about and felt cared for by and the intimacy felt 'warts an' all' encompassing. With that woven into our fabric we seek a mate for the longer term.

Sex is like Bridge - we can play the game for years but always have something new to learn. An ongoing sexual relationship bears its rewards and reflects the level of input and understanding. It can create a bed rock, a shared safe haven and underpin all the other complexities of our adult relationship. If we can be sexually free and open about our needs and desires, a key is provided for the pathway to true intimacy and a relationship in which no masks are worn, no games are played and the party comers are all very welcome. Self-doubt, Insecurity, Selfishness will hang their heads at the gate. There is no place for them at the warts an' all party.

That is not to suggest for one moment that couples who have irregular sex are doomed to an ultimately broken relationship or that couples who have it five times a week will be 'sailing by' at sixty. The importance lies in the fact that we are matched in our physical, as well as mental, needs and that we are able to properly talk to each other when things go awry. People exhausted by a hectic twenty-first century lifestyle cannot feel sexy and horny on demand. But we can ensure we make time for each other and seriously invest our attention into our relationships rather than taking the easier option of collapsing in front of the T.V. or the computer or having a few mind-numbing drinks at the pub. Nothing's for nothing and with all that our relationships are now exposed to, they need more effort than ever to keep them together and on track.

I heard a recent straw poll on the radio in Bournemouth in which 70% of the male callers who were in relationships said they would like more sex, in response to that specific question. The implication was that a minimum of 70% of similarly placed women would not agree. I doubt that to be the case, suspecting that the women in those relationships might well also answer that they would like more sex. We avoid talking about such issues because they might expose our own vulnerabilities and inadequacies. The less we address them the more they become thorny. I have seen many clients who have spent years in sexless relationships or ones in which 'the act' was reserved for high days and holidays. This was rarely because neither party wanted sex.

When a client last had sexual relations and the frequency over the past six months served as a crude but effective litmus test for me in gauging the extent of the 'breakdown' upon which I was to advise. Sex may not be everything but it's absence or rarity usually flags other underlying problems. Invariably one party will have tried to instigate 'relations' only to be rejected by the other. This might have been because of tiredness, because one was withholding what they knew the other wanted as a punishment or a means of gaining control, because they were upset …but when such rejection is repeated, sooner or later the other will cease making advances for fear of further rejection. It is now harder for the rejector to make a first move and so couples find themselves locked into a pattern of behaviour they find it impossible to reverse. When one party moves out of the joint bed because of his snoring, her need for a harder mattress, their need not to disturb each other when they go out to work, it is invariably the start of a slippery slope. Just as the vast majority of people who have a 'trial separation' never move back in together, so people who get out of the bed for any reason other than a head cold, rarely resume slumber together.

I had clients who had spent years sleeping on the settee or in the spare room. One poor chap was even made to sleep on the wooden dining room floor when he had a cold sore 'to prevent the infection spreading to the rest of the house'! However painful or difficult it might have been to discuss the state of their sex lives when they were still sharing a bed that would be as nothing compared to the nigh on impossibility of getting the two back into it after years of a settee or spare room. Without sex then the best that can be achieved is friendship and eventually one or both will want more and go looking. If we are married, the end result may be an adultery petition.

To start at the end and work backwards, an adultery petition usually requires a consensus between the pair. They have usually taken legal advice and appreciate that it will make no material difference who divorces whom and on what ground. The process takes the same amount of time and costs largely the same - around £800 including court fees, solicitor's costs and VAT. Costs are often used as an incentive. 'Provide a confession statement to facilitate the issue of the proceedings and we'll only claim half of fixed costs from you. If you don't, we'll have to draft an Unreasonable Behaviour petition and will claim all of the costs 'to be taxed if not agreed' i.e. put before the court for its approval involving additional costs to be borne potentially by the disputing party.

I invariably explained to a new client that to pursue an adultery petition you need a confession statement which traditionally runs along the lines of "I blah of blah confirm that I have had sexual intercourse in various places with a person, whose identity I do not wish to disclose, since blah date and such adultery is continuing. I understand that this statement is to be used by my spouse within the course of divorce proceedings". I would often add "and I agree to pay a contribution of £x towards costs, a cheque for the same being enclosed" so that that issue could be put to bed early on.

The only real alternative to a confession statement is clear evidence which suggests that, on a balance of probabilities, sexual intercourse has taken place. I once had a petition bounced by a District Judge when the adulterers were living together since I could not prove they were actually having sex. I didn't make that mistake again.

Colloquially I tended to say 'unless you've got Polaroid's of your partner in the act, if they are denying it then forget it'. I suppose today we would use our digital camera or the one on our mobile phone. Even with such handy technology, I have yet to meet the cuckolded who has had the foresight to break into the marital bedroom, in fabled 'home early darling' style, and take pictures of the cuckholder in action. But I know there must be at least one matrimonial lawyer out there who has been faced with such explicit evidence.

Those cases with which I have dealt and had to prove an adultery petition, defended by the other side, are non-existent. You don't issue an adultery petition unless you can prove it or it's admitted. Frequently it is strongly suspected and later uncovered but without cooperation those petitions become ones of Unreasonable Behaviour or expensively pursued white rabbits. I have had a couple of clients who have admitted to adultery, which l strongly suspected had never occurred, because they wanted to avoid being confronted with a black and white list of behaviour outlining why their formerly beloved purportedly can't stand them.

In one case I acted for an older gentleman. His wife was some twenty years younger and he suspected an affair though she adamantly denied one. Unbeknownst to her, he spent hours trying different 'educated guess' combinations on her briefcase to be 'rewarded' ultimately with a click of the lock and several letters clearly alluding to sexual relations as well as several full-frontal photographs of his dear lady and her younger gentleman in a somewhat sparse hotel room, even more sparsely attired (though not both on the same photo).

Correspondence was dispatched to her representative, a familiar colleague in the family law field, alluring to the nature of the evidence, written and pictorial. From all that I knew of the background circumstances of the case, the marriage was well over. But, for some reason not fully disclosed to me, the issue of an adultery allegation was a hot one. On his "client's clear instructions" - a phrase often used by solicitors to indicate that although they may have advised differently, this is what their client is saying - the letter in response indicated that any adultery petition would be "vigorously defended". This is another stock phrase used by us vainly intended to put fear in the mind of the opponent that 'a win' is not a guaranteed outcome. If right is on your side, that sort of goes without saying!

I foresaw a ridiculous amount of costs ensuing for absolutely no good purpose. My client was increasingly adamant, in the face of his wife's continuing and vigorous denials, that he wanted a divorce based on her adultery "regardless of cost." As a pensioner of insubstantial wealth, I recognised the smell of Principle's stranglehold on Reason. Equally, it seemed his wife's clear statement to both her lawyer and husband, was that her legs had remained dutifully shut. Perhaps it is at such times that the farcical over-importance of a singular physical act screams out its full irony.

Popular public opinion would suggest that this kind of scenario would herald joy to a solicitor's bank balance - lots of increased fees legitimately incurred upon the basis of a client's clear instructions. The reality is that, aside from the fact that you have to give a shit about your clients to do the job, you also want a sound settlement achieved as quickly as possible with the clients' trauma levels and bank balance hit as little as possible. It is simple business sense. l did not have a shortage of clients; time is costed by the hour; ten hours costs the same if it is spent on one file or ten but by spreading it across those ten, the variety makes the work more enjoyable and your costs are likely to be recovered more quickly if their burden falls on several shoulders.

A client's priorities normally feature speed and minimum cost fairly high on the wish list. If I were to conduct a file so as to lengthen the process and increase costs, my client would become increasingly and understandably frustrated. There is no-one he can justifiably take that out on more than me and his estranged, normally in that order. Disgusted clients do not tell their friends about you in such terms as would encourage them to use your services. In short, they make for bad business. Hence there really is no incentive for a lawyer in demand to intentionally run up costs. Now I can put that soap box away!

I telephoned the lawyer. My older client, who had been married for more than two decades, was completely devastated by the fact of his wife's adultery. Nothing in the preceding stretch of years had apparently prepared him for it. His Pain fought his Anger and his Upbringing fuelled his Outrage. However, my 'clear instructions' from the second visit when he had disclosed his 'finds' were that their precise nature and content should not be disclosed unless absolutely necessary.

These instructions arose from two main drives. The first was that, after such a period together, my client still did not wish to embarrass his wife with the disclosure to third parties of clearly, highly personal, written and visual images. The second was that he had carefully duplicated the letters and photos, returning the originals to the briefcase, no doubt rewhirling the code numbers. Wife was entirely unaware of the nature of his evidence and the extent of his betrayal of her privacy. She had remained confident that she had carefully concealed any evidence which might give him what he wanted, Truth. His preference was to remain the injured party; he who harbours no blame should throw the first stone. He had been betrayed by his wife but still felt he had betrayed her by looking in her private place for the evidence of it. Two wrongs do not a right make but, in the circumstances….?

Her solicitor stated that he had spoken with his client at length and she continued to deny a sexual relationship with anyone (my client having understandably lost his appetite at this stage). I suggested that I fax over copies of the actual 'evidence' itself given that the only other option appeared to be the issue of proceedings annexing copies of that evidence.

My client had stated that if there was no other option, I could disclose. To me the option of disclosing to the greater court staff a full frontal of a lady weathering well but past her prime, a respectable member of the community whose only 'sin' was to stray from an ill and aging husband to a younger and doubtless 'perkier' man, smacked of hypocritical witch hunting. There should be no need to put people, already having an emotional nightmare, in that position. Neither did I relish the consternations of my home-town judges at the professionalism I had applied in reaching the need for such exhibits. My client's sensitivity to the basic shame overrode even his strong desire to keep the precise nature of the evidence, and so his own deeds, a confidentiality with me alone. Both would have been overridden had we not agreed an adultery petition with the wife.

Her solicitor, as nonchalantly as any harangued and busy family lawyer can be, confirmed that he would take a look at this 'evidence' if I faxed it over. His client's confidence, and his belief in it, was reflected in his attitude. I strongly suggested that he stand at the fax machine to prevent the secretarial pool having first gaupe. Had that lawyer trusted in my judgment the faxing would have been unnecessary but perhaps he was curious too! He called about half an hour later and confirmed that an adultery petition would be admitted provided that the 'third party' was not named and husband paid the costs of the divorce. The 'third party, 'man number two', was clearly married - she wanted her divorce but she had not wanted to embroil him any further in fear of chasing him away. My hunch only.

Rewind first interview with this client. General discussion on divorce, not really his desired result at that time. Advise issue Unreasonable Behaviour petition. Adultery only suspected and strongly denied. Explain need for clear evidence if no written admission. Advise no point. Lead to further antagonism and costs; financial settlement unaffected by who starts the divorce and on what basis. Had that advice been heeded he would never have had to face the impact of the contents of the briefcase on himself, let alone its, and his own, disclosure of treachery to complete strangers. Costs and acrimony would have been reduced. But he would never have known the full Truth if he hadn't taken his chosen route and, having discovered it, could and would never again delude himself. She does have a way of balancing things out.

Another client with a similarly long marriage and very much still in love with his wife, came to see me. He had a property development business primarily run by his wife whilst he pursued a professional career. The longstanding carpenter, who was closely involved with all their projects he suspected of having an affair with his wife. Again I explained the basics of starting a divorce. We talked about Unreasonable Behaviour. It wasn't that he wanted a divorce but he had to address his suspicions, he had to know The Truth.

He was a truly gentle man - honourable, principled - and I met him at his lowest emotional ebb with no-one to talk things through with, reason, bounce thoughts. So he used me. I explained that a lot of the time he wanted from me was not what he should be paying me for i.e. my legal expertise, and it wouldn't 'further his case' by my knowing as much detail as he wanted to share with me. He said he fully understood that but he needed me to listen, to give him an objective ear. He told me later that he cried with me that day for the first time since he was a boy. This was after he'd pursued his own need for the Truth and arrived in my office clearly distressed and with a resigned sadness in his eyes. He had fitted voice-activated recorders into his wife's car, under the seats.

He had previously discussed a more elaborate plan. They had recently purchased an investment flat and he knew that his wife and carpenter were due to inspect it on a particular morning. He would secrete video recorders in the bedroom and living room (the most likely hot spots). I pleaded with him, for his own sake, to avoid such a course. By now I was equally convinced that, despite her adamant and continual denials, she was 'doing' the carpenter and could see no possible benefit to my client, nor indeed anyone else, in his watching inadvertently home-made porn starring his beloved.

The only reason that this shudderingly painful plan was not pursued was because the car's voice activated microphones did the job first - and perhaps, hopefully, because he listened to my advice. He insisted that I listen to a tape. It was too big for my office machine so I had to sit in my car in the office car park. His mature wife's voice was clear as a bell on the tape. She was at first giggly, high on the sexual frisson which, from the contents of their conversation, was clearly passing between them, even down a phone line. But the conversation became serious as they discussed my client's continuing suspicions of them. His wife grew increasingly anxious. It was clear that she loved her husband, knew him well enough to know that he could not withstand the Truth and continue on their expected path, and was desperate for their liaison to remain concealed, both from her husband and from her lover's wife. This man was not only pivotal to their business of 'doing up' older houses, he had also become a friend to my Client, as well as his wife, and was often at their house, drinking tea in the morning before work commenced etc thus the breach of trust was especially vile.

This was probably our fifth meeting and only now did he instruct me to instigate divorce proceedings. I tried one last time. By then I had a great deal of respect for my client, I liked him and I believed that he and his wife still loved each-other and could grow from this disclosure and go on. My first tac was an oft-used one. 'In all these years have you never been unfaithful, done nothing which you have intentionally concealed from your wife because you did not want to hurt her?' Even if a client denies it to my face, the unexpectedness of the question usually undresses the Truth, just for an instant, in their face. It might plant a seed for further reflection when alone with his secrets in his castle. Unusually, the answer was an unequivocal "no, never". Having started l had to press on. Whilst his wife's denials piled on lies and hurt, the underlying 'opening of the legs' to obtain a cherry as well as the cake wasn't the real issue. The act was far outweighed by the flagrant abuse of trust.

Sitting in an office listening to people from all walks of life for numerous years produces a gradual realisation that our Human Nature, our animal instinct, when pitched against the mores of any society, will always triumph. The less those mores are enforced and upheld, the truer this will be.

He was now firmly resolved to proceed with a divorce based upon her adultery. A confession clearly was not going to be forthcoming and so the evidence of the tapes would have to be disclosed to 'encourage' such a confession. My client did not wish to do this. Like my client who had discovered the photos of his wife by spending hours trying different combinations on her briefcase, this client did not want his own treachery disclosed. So his next plan was to listen until he knew where they would be meeting next, through the car bug, and then unexpectedly come across them, as if by chance.

They usually had their assignations in one of the properties which was being transformed by the carpenter and his team. He had keys to their properties and the last thing I wanted him to do was walk in on them 'in the act'. Even his original plan to put voice activated cameras in the property would at least be less destroying than the live show, especially for a man who was already so traumatised. But he really did still love his wife so much that he almost needed to rub his own nose in it to have the strength to divorce her.

In the event, they did not turn up at the allotted time. Despite the fact that he had spent the weeks since his discovery trying to behave as nonchalantly as possible, he was so emotionally crumbled inside, it showed on the outside without him having had to utter a word. It was clear from the tape that I had listened to, that the lovers were spooked, treading on eggshells to prevent any unintended disclosure. There were other tapes which my client had which referred in much greater detail to the sexual activities in which they had clearly been indulging. Strange that even after all that she had put him through, he was determined not to have to disclose these to me, let alone the wider public of the County Court, out of deference to his wife (and perhaps because her knowledge of his own deception might diminish her own). When he confronted her and ultimately extracted her admission she remained ignorant of the tapes or the extent of his knowledge.

They clearly loved each other. His wife's disclosure having followed his, she had remained clear in her wish to preserve their marriage. My client did not feel any need for revenge, for retribution, to make her squirm. How could he when he still held so much love for her, in spite of himself. He was only very sad. I urged him. Could he not forgive, if not forget, and preserve the applecart which they had stacked together for their old age? He had thought about this at considerable and repeated length. He foresaw that whenever his wife left the house to go wherever - shopping, appointments - he would be haunted by ghosts of possibilities. He would want to know where she was going. He would want to know why she was late having earlier wanted to know what time she would be home. He had never treated her like that and he could not start now, however able or willing his wife might have been to do so (for the present at least). For him there were no choices and to be true to himself he had to cut the cord in full knowledge of the pain which would flow from it.

This need to make oneself's head rule one's heart has been repeatedly rehearsed with me over the years. As technology improves and becomes increasingly accessible to, and affordable by, the public, I can only see that this kind of surveillance of partner's will sadly become increasingly common as we police our relationships. Many people still don't realise that messages sent by them on their mobile phones are stored in 'sent items' and computer hard drives store many a secret which the user thought had been deleted.

An exacerbating factor for this client was the period of time over which he feared the deception had continued. Wife and carpenter had had a long association. The carpenter had been a regular visitor to the matrimonial home which housed their office. He wanted my opinion, which did accord with her own protestations - no mature, intelligent business woman giggles like a schoolgirl unless the iron's relatively fresh in the fire. This was not a sexual relationship which had been going on very long in my view.

In relation to his case, my client received the kind of all round support service that many clients need but can't afford. By paying me highly by the hour to, for example, sit in my car with his tape, he enabled me to give him that service. Understandably most clients do not want to pay me six months road tax for an half hour conversation with their lawyer about emotional views and discussions rather than legal ones. They often need it, resent it when the lawyer does not then have the same intimacy with their feelings but often cannot afford to pay for it. Bearing in mind that everything which motivated me to do the job benefits from a client who is pleased with the service provided, however much he regrets that he was ever in need of it, a balance has to be made between the effects of escalating costs and need for emotional support. By definition, at the time, the client is rarely capable of making that decision but may well bemoan the consequence at a later, less traumatised, date.

FAIRY TALES by Sharon Moore

So why, looping back to evidence collected for adultery, do people expose themselves to such hurt? Why go so far as having to face a full frontal photo of your wife's lover or a video of wife and lover inspecting the credentials of each other rather than a flat?

A couple who became dear friends of mine shared their intimacies with me. Time has healed the sharpness of the emotion and they are able to laugh about it now. They are both extremely attractive people, in their chalk and cheese personalities even more than physically. They have both lead colourful sexual lives both prior to their meeting and long after they had established their relationship. He was fairly frequently unfaithful to her. 'Live by the sword, die by the sword' as he once said to me, when he discovered Jill out in a swordfight.

The 'burn' that this particular played-with fire may inflict, is that we actually build a deep emotional attachment to someone outside the relationship which becomes, or may seem to become, bigger than that which is being threatened. We never know Mother Nature's price in advance. They were able to tolerate, understand, accept each others indiscretions because they were usually no more than that. Their security in their ongoing relationship was not threatened. But Jill now believed she loved her lover more.

However the suspicion was raised in Jack's mind, he determined to pursue The Truth, and something more. He set up a bug on the telephone line which recorded conversations throughout the day. As this was some considerable years ago, it also involved secreting a tape recorder under the settee! He would return from work most evenings and ask about her day of shopping with her mom, visiting girlfriends, walking the dogs ... After she had gone to bed he would listen to her conversations with her friends about her lover, how she felt about him and conversations with her lover making arrangements for a liaison which might well have happened that very day.

There are significant differences between his situation and that of my client who had used the voice-activated microphones. Firstly, Jack was a lad unlike my client who could therefore throw stones and stare square-shouldered into the reflections of the greenhouse. He did choose to do the latter and not the former to his credit. Secondly, Jack was not driven by a need to know what he already suspected. He knew Jill, he knew about the sex in his mind but he wanted to know about the real threat, the extent of the emotional infidelity. That is something which one rarely extracts via the confessional – more information than you need to know. And once he knew, from his late night vigil of her day, that her heart was turning against him, he needed to make himself hate her enough to turn his own heart and make himself walk away. The depth of their love and the extent of their understanding and accepting of one another, warts an' all, needed a mechanical digger not a mere spade to even attempt to dig at its roots.

So he listened nearly every week day for three months. It took that long to hate her enough from what he heard, to begin to accept that their marriage was over. The problem with this was that, when speaking with her lover, she would be influenced in what she said by what she knew he did, or didn't, want to hear. Jack did not get at the real truth by listening to Jill's conversations with her lover.

They had been together ten years, the last two married. There was the inevitable 'scene' and it was agreed that Jill would move out. A suitable house was found in the area and it was not until the eve of the day for contract exchange that they looked at each other across their lounge, both in tears. The enormity of what was about to happen hit them both. The anger, hurt and intransigence of the last few months had waned by its familiarity. Jack said "I don't want you to go" Jill said "I don't want to go". Jack phoned the vendor of Jill's new house and gave her his good news which was her bad news. One man's meat is another man's poison.

Jack always said that the surface of their relationship, as seen by colleagues and acquaintances, appeared an idyllic one. This is true of many relationships which are only seen outside their own front door. Those friends and family who were privileged to see behind the closed door, knew of the deceptions and indiscretions, the face value games and lies which had peppered their time together. But underneath there was a bedrock which I doubt anyone or anything could crack. The extent of their true intimacy built that. Survival of this crisis ultimately strengthened their bond.

The more a relationship is tested and survives, the stronger it grows. People with untested safe relationships run the risk of finding that they are left with a superficial emotionally empty and unfulfilling bond, a shell wherein no snail dwells. Human Nature coverts a prize which has been fought for, worked for - be it a Beamer or a partner. Ironically such 'relationship trauma' also reestablishes our bonds and strengthens them. The psych seems to be - our relationship hit a crisis, if my partner was prepared to fight as hard as I was to find a resolution then in fact her emotional attachment to me has been reendorsed, I am more secure, I feel more whole by being able to be myself and to truly know my partner. No masks.

It never rains but it pores. It is uncanny the number of times when people are facing crisis in their relationships that there is crisis in other areas of their lives. Perhaps it is the added pressure which often means that a problem at home becomes the straw that broke the camel's back.

One client for whom I acted for a considerable time in relation to his divorce was clearly of foreign origin but this had never been pertinent to my instructions. It wasn't until at least our third meeting that he had unexpectedly asked me if I had realised his origins. In fact, his was the underlying culture which we have recently 'freed' by blowing ten bells out of the country's infrastructure and killing and maiming thousands of innocent people of all origins - friendly fire in a deadly guise. Two wrongs do not a right make: Twin Towers; the square in which we watched repeated footage of Saddam's great statue toppling to a 'heil Hitler' salute's position. This was followed by the cringingly stark image of the Americans – equaling the euphoria of the Iraqis pogo-ing, arms akimbo – shrouding Saddam's head with the Stars and Stripes. An American victory over Saddam? A feeling of warped revenge for 9.11? The human connection, like those weapons of mass Destruction, remains elusive. He who can keep his head when all about him have lost theirs. With the world's media recording, the red, green, black and white of the Iraqi flag quickly replaced the American's Stars and Stripes prior to the statue's decent to a bent horizontal. The motivation was obviously different and arguably better intended but the emotion pelting us from our screens was of the kind which put one in mind of a witch hunt, a hanging by the 'mob'. The reason of the moment was lost in mob euphoria of the kind possibly only otherwise inducible by magic mushrooms.

This client was the only Iraqi I have ever got to know on anything other than a polite-salutations-to-fellow-travellers level. He instructed me when we were on the brink of war and all of his family members were in Iraq, for whom he feared on a daily basis. He had not known how I might react or my views on the situation. Our arrangement did not include general discussion on 'current affairs' only the one specific affair. Once I knew this it explained why he had seemed to be under such incredible pressure throughout his instruction of me. If he is representative then, if it is possible, my horror at his homeland's suffering can only deepen. But it is also a good illustration of the way in which, as I practiced over the years, I realised that if I did not hit on all relevant questions, I could miss pertinent facts. The lawyer, just likethe client, is often unaware of the entire picture.

CHAPTER FIFTEEN

INFIDELITY AND LIES

Mankind has always needed a sexual outlet, a pressure valve - we need only look at the most inhibited rule-run societies to find the greatest sexual deviancy. We no longer even treat as revolutionary the reply to 'What news from Rome?'!

The infamous Molly Luft, purportedly 'the fattest whore in Germany' said, in a recent interview in Bizarre Magasine, "I see men every day, most are married. Every day in Berlin, thousands of men visit a whorehouse and betray their wives. All those guys and their lies. You get hard. And deadened to other people. But you remain extremely vulnerable." For as much as Human Nature is beautiful so it is ugly.

Why do we 'cheat' on each other sexually? And why, given that many of us do, do the repercussions have to be so dramatic notwithstanding what we all know. Of course, there are a minefield of reasons as to why we 'cheat' many of which have been responsible for visitations by members of the public to my office and friends to my home. Sexual mismatching, drink, unexpected irresistible opportunity, boredom, mid-life crises, flattery, greed, revenge ... the list is endless. But if we take one step back from that, all have one common element which, when we move to the next stage, produces the problem. Every action has a reaction, a consequence. We reap what we sew. Everything in life has a price. Everything. That is what maintains the balance, the Yin vs the Yang.

Invariably women - and increasingly more men than might be expected - admit that the really damaging issue is not actually the sexual act incumbent upon a referral to infidelity but the lies and surrounding details and corrosion of trust which that produces. People talk about trusting their partner. 'Do you trust him?' actually translates to 'Would you expect him to suppress all animal urges in whatever situation because he loves you and would never want to lose you?'

In my book, 'Do you trust your partner?' should mean 'Do you believe that you have formed a partnership of such intimacy that if anything happened of import, sexual or otherwise, they will tell you, share it with you in complete detail if you wished them to (as I would but not all do). In my experience, those relationships which have worked best, at their best and at their worst, have been those which had that kind of trust, that kind of honesty.

The more truth that is already known, the less painful any new truths will be. And truth has to be communicated - we still await the day when Woollies sells crystal balls. It has to be told and it is the pain which such truths can cause that causes that same animal in us to lash out and destroy all we have or all we might once have had. We smart from the pain of lies upon lies and our own anger - as much with ourselves as with the perpetrator. Anger that we could be so foolish, so unschooled, so self-imposed blinkered, so naïve, so trusting.

Looking back at that list which fell off the top of my head:

Sexual mismatching covers a wide spectrum of ills from a homosexual suffocating in a heterosexual relationship (lots of lies upon lies, lots of pretending) to basic differences in libido and sexuality (to wit, more anon). These can be the most difficult to communicate to our partner because they relate to a condition which will not change and present the most difficult to affiliate with an ongoing relationship.

Drink gives us 'spunk' (leave the wings to the Red Bull) in the metaphorical sense, almost always, and in the literal sense, depending on your karma that night! When we become inebriated we let down barriers, we say and do things which we would not have the 'balls' or perhaps even the inclination to do, sober. Women suffer from 'beer goggles' just as much as men. People can seem increasingly physically and mentally stimulating as the glasses glug down. If this leads to a sexual encounter it is self delusion to have an I-can-look-at-myself-in-the-mirror-and-not-feel-guilty-because-it-wasn't-really-me expression and ignore it as a memory (to be visited occasionally, alone, in secret). Whilst it may well be true that such incidents would be much more infrequent without alcohol they reveal a predilection which is not alcohol induced. We tell ourselves that we need not disclose such incidents – 'what's the point, it didn't really mean anything, it doesn't change anything'. No, but the sharing of it could do - for the better - and even enhance the relationship in a way that would not have been possible if it had never happened. A 'positive' can come out of a 'negative' if we want it to.

Tales of the 'Unexpected irresistible opportunity' are usually wonderful at highlighting our true nature (and often make for a good yarn). I have listened to many examples in my office over the years, from a woman who was discovered with the

FAIRY TALES by Sharon Moore

cable fitter to a bloke who was 'treated' by his work mates
who paid for 'extras' in a topless bar. But my traveller's tale
of an Ozzy I met in South East Asia must be one of the best
and is both heartily sickening and sickeningly heartening in its
reality.

He had worked in London for a number of years and there
met, and fallen 'in love' with, a fine English girl. They became
very close and engaged. Both were potential high flyers
working in The City. He had an opportunity of three months
work in Sydney. It was a hard won opportunity to return to
his homeland and forge a link of experience which might
have been invaluable in years to come. It's not what you
know but who you know. She was locked into the ladder of
her own career, ambitious and wanting to match the success
of her young husband to be. It was only three months, it
would fly by, it would do them good. Everything is relative.
We have to have experienced hunger to truly appreciate a
good meal. They parted at a London airport. One of the
luxuries of time is an ability to observe and whilst I don't
have it in me to be a train spotter, I could stand at the arrivals
section of Birmingham airport - irritating the hell out of the
electric doors as I dart in and out to avoid the cold and drag
on my fag – for hours! So many joyous reunions - pure
emotion, unmasked honesty. People-watching can become a
drug!

My Ozzy left amid a great deal of hugging and kissing,
unsupressable tears, all the usual outward symptoms of great
affection, selfish loss, and fear. They promised each other
regular communication. All was as it should be according to
the gospel of our reasonable man going giddy in Clapham.

164

INFIDELITY AND LIES

He got on the plane, settled himself in with overhead storage canisters suitably secured - money, phone, passport, book, munchies all in easy reach. The frozen grin girls were gesticulating in automatic pilot synchronicity, impressing upon their blatantly ambivalent wards the necessities of understanding fall-down oxygen masks and inflatable lifejackets secreted beneath the seats. As King explores in 'From a Buick 8', although mankind has an indomitable ability to get used to the impossible at the same time we block out the possible by reference to percentage probabilities. It always happens to someone else. Well, in my Ozzy's case, it happened to him.

He got politely chatting to the girl in the adjoining seat who would be his travelling companion for the next twenty-four hours or so. Travelling does encourage us to form relationships with the people we meet more quickly than in 'normal' life primarily because we have much more time en bloc with others. What you do, where you live, where you socialise … becomes of far less importance than who you are and how you came to be there. Faces get left by the home door and, unaccompanied by family or friends with whom we are used to wearing an appropriate mask, we become much more who we are. It is that which made this particular story happen.

They got chatting for some hours, distracting each other from the plane food and seen-before onboard movie. The cabin crew turned the lights down having fed and watered their charge. She fell asleep on his shoulder; he fell asleep aware of her on his shoulder and enjoying the stolen intimate experience of the body contact. He tucked the blankets around their legs and arms. He woke up to a warm familiar stirring. Her face was pressed into his lap. In that wonderful middle earth between sleeping and waking his mind luxuriated in the fiery excitement in his loins as the warm wetness of her mouth worked expertly on his shaft. He felt as though he would explode at any moment. The excitement of the 'tabooness' of the situation was overwhelming. She looked up at him only once. Their eyes locked for a few seconds and she smiled at him before returning to his lap. It was one of the most exciting and yet most guilt provoking memories which he treasured. It wasn't looked for, it wasn't planned, it wasn't even a vague male fantasy in the young-man-in-love's mind when he boarded the plane.

Now the hard part. So what? Firstly we have to answer a question with complete candour. Is there not a part of us which, if we found ourselves in a similar situation, wouldn't want to ride that tide, hit the 'fuck it' button. Do we really want to stop the obliging young lady before the crescendo and protest our undying love for another. Whilst the female anatomy makes an equivalent unobvious occurrence practically impossible, I would hazard that there are few males (under the age of 50 or at all?) who would not allow the action to achieve its obvious conclusion. Added into this particular equation, which is hardly a part of everyday life, was the knowledge that no-one could see, no-one would ever know and they would never see each other again. Even in every day situations, 'the choice' can raise its Id driven head at the most unexpected of moments. Human nature can be warm, unselfish, caring, empathetic … but sooner or later, so many such plane rides down the road, Nature will out.

So what did he do, my Ozzy. He shared it with me because it was so relevant to what we were discussing, we were miles from home and I would never see him again either- or his now wife! To that point at least, he had told no other. He loved his wife, it made entirely no difference but it was a lovely forbidden place to go to when he was all alone in his head. It's around about here that I personally appear to slip off the norm of human reactions. If I had been the fiancé and Ozzy had subsequently called me and told me what had happened, I would have been pleased. Very few of us share such things. Everyone dissembles for the greater good. No-one spills so completely unless they are completely intimate with their partner or completely in careless contempt. It is a thin line between love and hate.

It can be so much easier to be 'economic' with the truth, which we feel better about than telling a lie. If Ozzy doesn't tell his fiancé about the unexpected irresistible opportunity he won't have to go through the tears, renewed guilt, heavy debates over 'why?' (because it felt good!) Additional questions following business trips, hassle he could do without. No-one will ever find out. A few anxious paranoid nights spent inwardly debating the likelihood of his being contacted once the secret films of the cabin had been reviewed by the airline. But he told himself that that sort of thing probably happened far more frequently than the airlines had resource to reprimand after the event. Father Time's healing abilities allowed Guilt to slide out of view.

It's as though we all know the truth but don't want to look at it. In our world of mobile phones, email, internet, speed dating, newspapers' 'perfect partners', we have access. Access that our parents never knew let alone our grandparents. My grandmother lived with her neighbours and people from the surrounds who came into the garage she operated, marrying

167

the man who years before played her husband in a school play. She played a Mary but was quite uncontrary.

We have continued to raise our children on this outmoded inapplicable fantasy. Still! After all we know! You grow up, you fall in love, you get married, you have children, you raise them and you retire to your bungalow with roses round the door and to the sunny days of your memories and grandchildren. Firstly, do we now believe this is possible or indeed desirable? Secondly, do we want to do something to calibrate the equilibrium? There is something animal and basic in us which requires that we pass on our genes. Survival of the fittest. Natural selection. Think of all those generations of our genes which have fought to survive from prehistoric man to the present, through wars, famine and disease. Whilst whites have had centuries to rape and pillage, farm and industrialise, the slave trade really sorted out the black men from the boys. They survived through strength and wit, two of the most powerful aphrodisiacs known to Womankind and doesn't She ultimately make the world go round. Gene selection got a forward thrust through slavery which only The Enterprise could have convinced us of. Every cloud … Yin and Yang. But this natural selection had nothing to do with how 'good' a person was, how religious, how honest and upstanding. It is just one of a trillion examples of Mother Nature exacting her unbending rules. If only the 'bad' died young.

So we raised our girls to expect an all-protecting all-caring all-consumed father figure, the lesson being further distorted by the lack of sexual involvement (in the majority of cases at least). And they sit in my office and cry. And yes, it still hurts. After years of observing, voyeuring a person broken down by the inevitable reality of life, the expectations dashed on the rocks of fantasy island. It could never be so. We built you up for a horrendous fall. Like the lie of Father Christmas. We did it knowingly, knowing it wasn't so, it would never be so. Hoping it might be…?

Do we keep the Fairy Tale alive because we desperately want it to be true? We want our offspring to enjoy the Shangri-La that evaded our own lives. Or is there a cold place in ourselves where we would rather not look that takes satisfaction from it being the same for everyone else, even our children. No pot of gold. No triumphant lap of the ground. No easy fix answer.

People, like children, play with fire until we get our fingers burned. It doesn't necessarily stop us but it teaches us the consequence. Action: reaction. People push boundaries often unaware of the eventual consequence but thirsty to sate our curiosity for knowledge of it. And that takes a certain level of arrogance especially when it relates to our relationship, a belief that what we have with our life's partner is unbreakable, insurmountable, guaranteed. How do you get there? Are any of us that secure? Are any of our relationships? Who can know whether another human being will be there for them 'come hell or high water'.

Men and women broke down in my office because the dream let them down. It doesn't work out that way. They can't match their parents - but what do their parents' stories mask? If those same citizens had been raised with realism, with the reality that life is short, often shorter than we anticipate. 'It won't happen to me'. Life is hard. Money doesn't buy you out of that either and life is what you make it - hard, painful, soul searching, mental and something to grasp with both hands, note its surprises and appreciate life all the more for giving them to you. People can only grow through life's experiences. Everything is relative. No-one becomes wise spending their lives in a cardboard box.

One marriage which became infamous in the last century was that between the writers Vita Sackville-West and Harold Nicolson. Their relationship lasted over fifty years despite the fact that both were openly unfaithful and she had several 'love affairs' with women, the most notorious being that with Virginia Woolf. When Vita died in 1962 she left behind a detailed autobiography recording much of her early life and her loves. Their son, Nigel Nicolson, having waited over a decade until some of the main players were also deceased, then published his book 'Portrait of a Marriage'.

The book flap explains;

> 'It was one of the happiest and strangest marriages there has ever been ... Both Vita and Harold were constantly in love with other people, and each gave the other full liberty "without enquiry or reproach" knowing that their love for each other would be unaffected and even strengthened by the crises which it survived ... It was based upon a 'trust' of a totally different kind from what that word implies in most marriages ... She believed, in 1920, that one day society would accept that women can love women, men can love men, and that a marriage as deeply rooted as hers could survive and actually be enriched by infidelity ... A marriage successful beyond their dreams, because it was based on mutual respect and tolerance, and enduring love'

Vita described their relationship thus:

"To love me whatever I do. To believe my motives are not mean. Not to credit tales without hearing my own version. To give up everything and everybody for me in the last resort"

And her son says

"It was one of the strangest and most successful unions that two gifted people have ever enjoyed"

If our relationships are to involve adultery it seems that this model is one which should be aspired to though we must ask ourselves whether it is vaguely possible within the confines of our particular union.

CHAPTER SIXTEEN

WHY DO WE DO IT?

We have seen the end result of infidelity and the consequential legal process. So how does this whole adultery business start and why are many people increasingly secretly sexually unfaithful? What is the effect? Do we want it to stop? Can it be stopped?

The only thing which ostensibly differentiates a 'mate' from a mate is sexual contact (and then not always but that's a separate issue). Sex is fundamental to the vast majority of couplings. As an issue it remains a thorny one, not only influenced by thousands of years of religious teachings but also by millions of years of evolution. It is no surprise that sexual relations with third parties usually arise as a symptom, rather than a cause, of relationship difficulty. I am not suggesting that a blissfully intimate and apparently ideal coupling will stamp out any susceptibility to sexual misadventure. The reality is that just to hold hands with a relative stranger can be more sexually exciting than an hour's worth of foreplay with a familiar partner – and there is always the possibility of an Ozzy situation.

Why do we do it? One reason for adultery's frequency seems to stem from another delightful facet of Human Nature. We may find ourselves living in a strange house with a strange woman and a strange life and we ask ourselves, how did we get here? But we prefer the devil we know, we have a natural basic fear of the unknown, the thought of going out single again in the big world, starting all over again with family histories and life-changing recollections, sexual fumblings and relearnings. But we are then in a phase of potential availability. We're not really looking but if something came along we might consider it. And if a mere sexual distraction came along which might at least take our mind off the strangeness at home, well…

Few people have relationships which are not, in some way or other, on the rebound. Whatever time has elapsed since the last one we will try to take our lessons and conclusions from the previous relationship into the next. Few choose to face the reality of a failed relationship and sever the ties without first ensuring that at least someone is potentially waiting in the wings. These potential rope ladders are strung out before we jump the cliff, often left dangling there for years, non-practicing 'couples' who are each other's rope ladders, insurance policies.

Everyone will draw their own conclusions but if we accept that the most honest, open and truthful relationships are the most intimate and so most strong, it follows that a stronger bond can be wrought from the adultery, if it occurs. The blister which is left from the burning of our fires will heal and can become a stepping stone to that state of intimacy. It may not be the case that a person wanted to jeopardise their life at home but are somehow thrown into their lovers arms by the deception.

The lover knows that her man or his woman is married. The lover often assists in the subterfuge, reminding the spouse of the hour and the need to return 'home', making liaison arrangements, listening to the lover's outpourings about the intimacies of his other relationship, listening to their lover lie to their spouse on the telephone. The very fact of the lie which is being perpetuated by the adultery, weakens the first relationship and strengthens the second. The level of true intimacy, warts an' all, becomes higher in the adulterous relationship than it is in the pre-existing one. The lover knows we are sleeping with someone else (the permanent partner). There can be far fewer deceptions. Because we instinctively recognise that such a level of intimacy is good we may find ourselves living with an even stranger woman in a stranger house wondering ... how did I get here?!

There is also a peculiar trust born of an elicit relationship where both are involved elsewhere and don't want that to change. Both are putting their stability on the line, both are reliant on the other not to disclose the relationship to their permanent other. Both are equally vulnerable and the secret-shared pact creates another tangle in the web we weave.

This is just one of the ways in which the relationship born out of an affair can rapidly become more intimate than the one at home which has taken possibly decades to create. Another is the sex itself. I have heard men complain, all over the globe, that a woman will often do things with her lover that she wouldn't dream of doing with her long-term partner - presumably this was born out of their experience of both. One friend, a highly sexual woman herself, once suggested that having sex with her husband was like having sex with her father in as much as she felt that she couldn't let go, she couldn't behave like a complete and utter slut in the bedroom, she would be judged. Unless someone is generally shy about sex or about their body, both genders can find themselves to be more experimental and abandoned in an emotionally shallow relationship where they care less what the other thinks.

Though we run the gauntlet of a deeper emotional attachment, many affairs start out as a primarily sexual thing. People are often in their 'safe' relationships and are not looking to get out of them. Factors like 'where are we going to live', 'do we want children', even 'how much money do you earn', are non-issues. The aim is to have a good time and not get caught. Sex may not be everything but in such a relationship it plays a major part. Men and women can be freer sexually. Men can find it easier to have passionate sex with another woman and have fewer mental boundaries particularly once their significant other has become the mother of their child; Women may be able to behave more 'like a whore' in the bedroom, or even the hotel toilet, and not care so much, if at all, what their transient partner thinks of them for it.

If some guy at Edinburgh University can prove that around twice as much sperm will be produced by a male ejaculating into a new lover rather than a regularly serviced familiar wife, then surely the drive which is created by that biological fact, will play its part. People grow together in their sexual habits. Some people may love their lover to 'talk dirty' in bed, but this is something which, generally, has to be done from the outset and may not come easily particularly if our partner is not used to such conduct which makes it harder for us to instigate - perhaps 'dirty words' are more appropriate from a 'dirty lover'. If it turns us on, it creates an intimacy in sex which we have never shared with our permanent partner - men's affairs with 'slappers', straight men's affairs with gay men. If we start doing it with our partner now it will seem suspicious - and so the gap widens. It is easier to ask a relative acquaintance to 'suck my cock... harder, faster ... yes, you dirty bitch' than the mother of the two apples of our eye. If the lover comes up trumps and there are sufficient other coupling factors in place to make the relationship feasible, the pull that the intimacy of this sexual honesty creates can be decisive. Equally, the lover who holds and strokes his lover post coital, who bathes her and washes her hair, who kisses her at impromptu moments because he wants to, who pats her bum when she's passing, who hugs her to him as soon as he sees her, can brew a powerful drug. Having found new enjoyment this only serves to highlight its absence at home and comparisons can be cruel in their starkness.

The sheer monotony of our working lives can be enough. A bit of excitement helps to remind us that we are alive, we have choices, though we've joined the race there's many a path for the rat to take. The term 'midlife crisis' is often banded about to cover a multitude of sins. When 'mid life' precisely occurs these days is a subject for dispute in itself and, obviously, the older we get, the older 'mid life' becomes. 'Middle aged' is such a dull term that no-one wants to be associated with it. But there comes a point in everyone's life when we see doors closing. 'The world is your oyster' attitude of younger days is replaced by a growing certainty that certain things, if not done now, will never be done. When we know we can no longer easily go out and pull an eighteen year old, the writing's on the wall (regardless of whether that particular dish any longer appeals).

My Dad says that a peculiar thing happens to men as they grow older (only the one?!) As a fit and physically attractive

man, playing sport regularly throughout his life, being blessed
with good basic materials, I have no doubt that he has elicited
his fair share of female interest throughout the years. He has
been with my mother for almost half a century but
maintained an arguably healthy flirtation with the opposite
sex. This is outwardly tolerated by my mother who will do
some eye-rolling and smirky looks from time to time but
there is an element of her that inwardly appreciates the
attention which he may get. But, for him, there was an
indefinable time when he ceased to be a 'bit-of a lad' and
metamorphosed into 'a dirty old man'. Words and actions can
be exactly the same but such behaviour towards the opposite
sex, and especially the younger ones, is no longer appreciated
but rather, at best, humorously tolerated. It seems that, as a
society, there is a respectable age beyond which both men
and women have been expected to settle down, behave and
not exhibit so freely the sexuality which was considered
'normal' in the age before. If such behaviour gets a green
light response then the possibly ensuing affair is almost a self
validification. There's life in the old dog yet. People don't just
have affairs for sex any more than people just have sex to
cum.

Prevention is better than cure. If we don't stray sexually from
our chosen partner we won't have to deal with the
consequences. Or is that too simplistic, impractical or
unrealistic in this Twenty First Century? Mother Nature's
enforced and inescapable consequences, from pregnancy and
sexual disease to the sheer emotional turmoil upon a
relationship unprepared for the event, help to keep our Ids in
check. If we want to escape any consequences, we have to
fantasise about taking certain actions without consequence.
Perhaps the nature of fantasy.

FAIRY TALES by Sharon Moore

On-line chat rooms provide an almost virtual reality where people can represent themselves in whatever way we may choose, change appearance, social circumstances and even gender. But once we cross the line into hard reality we are fools to ourselves if we believe we will escape all consequence. Whether we delude ourselves in believing we are invincible or whether we recognise it as a calculated risk, we make an irreversible choice. Having made our beds we have to lie in them; if we have chosen to lie then we cannot be surprised when the hurt created for ourselves and those we love far outweighs the pleasure which we first chose to take.

CHAPTER SEVENTEEN

IS IGNORANCE BLISS?

Beware the blistering fires bred of blissful ignorance. If and when, when and if. We deceive ourselves in the answers to those submerged questions. At the peak of the 'moment' the 'If' they find out is an unthinkable impossibility and so the 'When' need not concern ourselves. But in the initial aftermath for a novice player, when guilt is at its greatest, the 'if' becomes a certainty and the 'when' becomes the brain's sole topic of recreation.

Having been unfaithful for whatever reason, do we put our cards on our home team's table? Generally not. We struggle to fit the reality of who we are - warts an' all - into the framework of society's monogamous demands. What they don't know wont hurt them - or me. There is nothing to know. My indiscretions don't affect my feelings for my partner. Why cause pain to someone I care about when that can be easily avoided by my belated discretion. It is inconsequential. They will never know.

Whether a 'one-off' or the commencement of further relations, almost invariably it is not intended to become the commencement of anything serious but is rather a case of sexual desire overwhelming any rationalised thoughts about the wisdom of the act which is about to follow. Men have said to me that, unlike many women, if an attached man goes out - whether it is on the town with his mates with a view to meeting a new stranger or to meet a specific acquaintance - he will have decided in advance whether he wants to have sex if the opportunity arises. Women, men have suggested, do not usually intend to stray, or at least not go the whole way, but nevertheless find themselves in that position. Perhaps men are more honest with themselves about their true intentions, their nature, even though they may be less honest with their partners about them. But when we look at who we are unfaithful with, the completely detached stranger scenario is relatively rare. Not many of us get the equivalent of an unsolicited blowjob on a plane! The sting in the viper's tail is that the majority of people have affairs with people they know, often well, and (now here's the rub) whom their partner knows.

It is one thing to discover that your man has been screwing his secretary for six months (men will be men, she obviously led him on, she's left now anyway ...) and quite another to find he has been bangin' your best mate, plotting behind your back, in your house, when they'd both lied to you about what each was doing that day. The difference is in the emotional attachment associated with each scenario. You know your best friend is fantastic, that's why she's your best friend and you know your partner well enough to know that his relationship with her is not merely physical. The threat of losing the one you thought you loved is so much greater and the pummeling that this gives your ego, self-confidence and self-respect is excruciating. If you have to shit, don't do it on your own doorstep! The problem is that we are often far more tempted by familiar doorsteps.

There is the scenario of the 'one-off'. It may be such because we are abroad, on a business trip, will never meet the person again in our 'normal' life and we press the 'fuck it' button because we can. Or we get so pissed we escape our usual constraints and wouldn't want to touch that person with a bargepole, in the cold harsh exacting reality of daylight with a clear head, again. Pussy on a plate can be irresistible especially when served with reason numbing alcohol. Cock on a cocktail stick can be equally attractive.

So it's a 'one off'. No damage done. No apparent disclosure. No facing of facts nor necessarily your own Judge and Jury. Time is not only a great healer; He also makes fast work of today's news. Contemptuous disdain for the guilt we felt before the deed's fact becomes a familiarity, dares to creep into our recollections. And we want to recollect. Even our guilt is fathered by an instinctive 'do unto others as you would be done unto' and 'what goes around comes around'. A selfish fear. How would we feel if the tables were turned? Not just at 'The Act' but the lies which will almost necessarily have accompanied it, at best a lack of disclosure of the truth which may have continued for a considerable period by the time of disclosure or discovery.

Credibility becomes an essential factor; just as it does in a court of Law. We all behave differently towards those whom we believe are open and straightforward with us rather than those whose motives we find ourselves questioning, whose lies we suspect. If a Judge patently believes what a client is saying, which should support the argument which that client would hope to promote, that client will have won the Judge's lenience whatever the other circumstances. If we are revealed in a lie before the Judge then clearly the opposite will apply. It is not only the material fact over which we have lied but the fact that we have revealed a character trait, an ability and preparedness to distort or misrepresent facts, even in the presence of the eyes of the law. In revealing such disrespect for the law, the remainder of our evidence becomes circumspect and far more permissibly open to scrutiny. So when we are discovered in a lie we have to prepare for the doubt which will be cast on even our greatest honesties.

Worst case scenario, we get found out. The means of our partner's discovery may affect the end result. Revelations in public at large social friends and family functions are, in particular, to be avoided at all cost. The bride who finds her groom banging her chief bridesmaid must be the extreme of the example but such a scenario has arisen several times in my practice. Perhaps that could be seen as a cry for help, the last chance to blot his copybook so horrifyingly that any further talk of matrimony can be discounted. Or is it a final rash act before the expected monogamy of matrimonial bliss? Either way I've seen the abominable fall out which inevitably ensues. Man's inhumanity to man!

To say to another human being that you want to share the rest of your life with them, and forsake all others, is a massive and often terrifying proposition, not least because we doubt our ability to meet society's, and our mate's, expectations.

However the prelude might be introduced, the music then has to be faced. Our fete depends on how we handle ourselves from then on in and how strong are the ties that we have already laid. To contemplate more lies involves more risk. We can't be sure what they know already (by voice activated micro recorders or by accident, makes no odds). The further detailing of the truth will potentially create further hurt but if given rather than taken, volunteered rather than extracted, the mere fact of the truth will be balming. If lies are allowed to beget lies then the greater the abyss we create for our relationships.

Best case scenario, no-one gets herpes, a need for a pregnancy test or to know. We've got away with it. The price? It will rarely be a 'one off'. That sexual-faithfulness-to-our-chosen-partner bit lies deep in our psych. It is something which people who achieve it hold up like a trophy, a self recognition of integrity. Once it is breached, Pandora's possibility-filled box will have been opened for good. We can't lose our virginity twice. The 'one off' becomes a 'ten off' 'or the 'one offs' increase in intensity and frequency. Like serial murderers, the first time is the hardest but once the taboo has been broken we often seem to adopt an 'in for a penny, in for a pound' mentality.

The 'ten off' is potentially most dangerous. For any relationship to move forwards requires both participants wanting to find a way forward and seeing this as a realistic possibility. If the relationship with the 'mistress' grows stronger in its clandestine intimacies than with the 'wife' and the increasingly gaping gap tears between the man she knows and the man as he exists in his own head, he may reach a point where he practically doesn't care what wife thinks. He's already reached the cliff edge by the time she discovers they're even going for a walk.

A 'mistress' feeds the lies by facilitating them whilst savouring the juices of the Truth for herself. That combination is often capable of administering the fatal blow to any long-term prospect of the first relationship surviving. The serial 'one offer' may be like the 'ten offer' who keeps a prostitute or a

183

longstanding 'friend' with whom neither see a realistic future 'together' but fill in the other's 'gaps'. The replacement 'all rounder' factor is reduced. In the case of the serial 'one-offer' so is our health and safety but the deception can be equally as corrosive. What would anyone involved in a happy fulfilling sexual relationship want with 'one offers' or 'fuck buddies' as the Americans so quaintly like to refer to them? Sex outside a regimented understanding.

As we get to know our partners we become habitualised. The whole Act becomes a personalised mating-dance routine. There may be those odd three hour sessions on a Sunday afternoon when something rattles our sex cages but generally, we know what to expect. Typically we go to bed. A particular way of touching or cuddling will signal the desire of one, the unspoken question, the offer. The responding touch of the other signals willingness, the acceptance. Each stimulates the other to make the Act a physical possibility. It may be that she climbs on board and subsequently vocalises the summit of her pleasure, his signal to roll her over and ride his own pleasures home. There will be variations on the theme but the bread and butter is the same most times whatever 'unique' format ours takes. Some will incorporate oral stimulation as a norm whilst others will preserve this as a 'treat'. Unless the couple's intimacy allows them to touch on every sexual fantasy or inclination without embarrassment or fear of instant discommunication, it is likely that there will be 'shortcomings' on both sides.

Pandora's possibilities may have bred one off realities which have hitherto been outside the remit of the stable relationship. If we throw our partner of five years around the room calling them a dirty b... when we have never used such behaviour with them, expect an inquisition or hilarity. Sex is mental.

This may seem an extreme, our domestic reality may be far less dramatic in its content. A 'one offer' presents a solution but creates a problem. Unless the new experience, and the excitement which it has brought, can be discussed and our own relationship grown as a result, the danger is that the mother relationship suffers far more from the effects of the other's undisclosed experiences. The adulterer's attitude to our partner will also change, at least and in so far as it relates to our sexual relationship. The core relationship either needs to be able to stand alone, unsupported by the compensations of another or it needs to embrace the benefits which outside experience can bring, learning from it to achieve a higher level of intimacy. The only middle ground is to lie.

'Cherry on the cake' sex, where the cake of the main relationship is fine and the extra is an added titillation, can be quite livable with and can enrich the cake by its sharing. Perhaps a part of the male psych which resists disclosure even of the cherry in such circumstances springs from an underlying fear that what's good for the goose is what the gander is getting. Because of the way in which they are grown, men are far better at giving it than taking it when it comes to sexual indiscretions and has roots in their ability to respect themselves when their woman has traded elsewhere for her needs.

But Ignorance? Is superficial bliss hiding a multitude of inadequacies or areas with room for improvement which will never see the light of day whilst their existence remains hidden from our nearest and dearest on the deluded pretext of not wanting to hurt them - or ourselves? We are left having to delude both them and ourselves further about the quality and extent of what we've actually got and the weathering of time which it will withstand.

From all that I have witnessed it seems the odds of someone who has strayed outside the relationship straying again are about the same as those applying to domestic violence, having another go at a later date. We break the psychological barriers which society has tried to instill in us and once a taboo has been broken ... The deadly sins grow deadlier the more often they are committed and yet the ease with which they are repeated equally grows with the repetition. Familiarity breeds Contempt.

Setting aside the multitude of 'one off' fantasy scenarios that we could all contribute to, the reality is that we tend to 'stray' with people we know, often well. Invariably our significant other knows them too, often well. Even 'one offs' with such socially close people can cause incredible pain and disruption if not distinction of a number of close relationships. If such liaisons have continued for some time they inevitably involve many betrayals and deceptions outside the actual sexual act itself. These are the hardest infidelities to recover from because they involve an emotional as well as physical involvement. It is hard for the partner to remain secure in their arrogance when the fact that they have been consistently deceived is slapping them in the face.

The better part of Valour is Discretion [not abstinence, nor honesty]. Does being discreet really require the most courage? If it were easiest to simply tell the truth, wouldn't everyone be honest about their 'tendencies', their affairs and passing triflings. I have heard the argument that it is easier to admit to an affair, to assuage one's own guilt by pouring all forth, leaving our partner to deal with it and move on. But that is the accusation of the wronged not the testimony of the wrongdoer.

Forgive if not forget? But if it were the easiest course of action wouldn't everyone take it? The simple reality is that it is easiest to say nothing, not to upset the apple cart, not to have to face unforeseen consequences and hope that we don't get found out. We tell ourselves that we are cleverer, more discreet, than all those other people we hear of who are found out in an affair. We flatter ourselves with our unique ability to have and eat cake. And we do, invariably, get away with it.

Great Healer Time blurs the memory of the guilt we felt at our deception. It becomes a nothing, inconsequential, and easier to do again because we got away with it before. It may be again, with the same partner the same week or it may be again, with someone new, years later. Guilt subsides lulled by cultivated Self-justification.

Many will never be discovered. 80%? Secrets taken to the grave. And those of us who ultimately stay together to that end would doubtless turn in them if it were suggested that any other course might have been preferable. Why be completely honest when my long-term partner will always be oblivious to it. Is that what we want? Is that what our long-term partners deserve? Had my parents been entirely honest with each other throughout their fifty years together they may not have made it for so long. Does the end justify the means? Or is any talk of something more intimate than that simply idealistic poppy cock?

CHAPTER EIGHTEEN

MONEY

Money is of different significance and means different things to different people and what any of us would do if we had 'a lot' of it varies hugely between ages, culture, geography ... Most of us earn our money through working and our ability to earn 'good money' is often directly related to our access to education. Within the context of our relationship, managing finances during it and dividing finances at the end of it can present a seemingly insurmountable problem for many.

In the UK to have a good disposable income usually means that if you're out looking for nothing in particular and see something you really like, you know you can buy it, within reason and dependant upon how much you've got. Personally, I'm talking on a new pair of shoes or furniture for the house scale rather than a new XK8 Jag. If someone asks you to go out socially the decision rests on whether you want to rather than whether you can afford it. Money also provides the security blanket of knowing, wherever you are in the world, if it is possible to buy a ride home to a hospital, you can. In my case the former is the kind of luxury I persuaded myself was my reward for years of study, hard work and long hours. The latter is part of why it is such a difficult reward to give up. Most people I know who earn 'good money' work hard and long hours and so the likelihood of needing a flight home from a distant land is substantially reduced!

Lawyers, and family lawyers in particular, have a much maligned reputation with the public, fat cat moneygrubbers who charge the cost of a meal out to write a letter, people more intent on diarising when they might next bill us rather than taking any real care over our predicament. They provide a service driven by need not desire. Very few people consult a lawyer with relish unless they are labouring under some misapprehension that they will be able to achieve what has deluded them and, metaphorically speaking, ensure that someone else's balls are nailed to the wall.

Narrowing my remarks to those in my particular 'family law' fraternity with whom I am most familiar, I would ask you to seriously examine that preconception of 'the lawyer'. Money makes the world go round. Money opens doors of power, influence and experience. No doubt about it, money is not what makes us happy but most people would prefer to be unhappy and moneyed rather than unhappy and scraping round to make ends meet.

Anyone who ever chooses a particular job path will have considered the financial rewards which may be achievable. As dedicated as many of them are, I suspect we would suffer a dire shortage of nursing staff if the going rate was 12k pa. Similarly, if it were 32k, we might well be inundated with prospective carers. In most cases, lawyers are no more money driven than the next man - though clearly the likelihood of their achieving higher salaries is greater. Money motivates us all to a greater or lesser extent. A qualified solicitor of some 5 years plus experience and following in any given field is likely to earn around 30/35k – outside London (the London to which one goes 'up' notwithstanding its geographical location both grammatically and in terms of salary).

It takes a minimum of six years to qualify as a solicitor in England and Wales: usually three years at Uni studying a Law Degree; a year at Law College to secure your Solicitors Finals; two years training in an office on a current Law Society recommended minimum of £17,110 in inner London and £15,332 for the rest of England and Wales. Different rules apply to the rest of the U.K. This is six years whilst your piers are starting to buy cars and holidays, make roots. The Government's financial support has fallen to an all-time low - at least my uni fees were paid even though my parents funded the Government's recommended living allowance. Had they not been in a position to do so, the taxpayer would have contributed to my future. I still left Law College with a 3k loan in 1986. That figure has typically increased more than tenfold for the average student today leaving uni and excluding Law College. It seems that flies in the face of what our society needs. Money makes money but also keeps money as it helps open the university door which now slams in the face of a penniless intender with anything other than total confidence in their ability to succeed or a scholarship.

True, there were students who spent a high proportion of the taxpayers money on 'whiskey and beer' just like the infamous Irish prodigal son, students who rarely attended lectures and usually managed to scrape through with some kind of Degree (even if they had had to convert to Sociology to achieve it!) Some tax payers were understandably up in arms at the student excesses which they saw on their Liverpudlian streets whilst they worked hard to raise the funds. What if we gave a student ten years to become a higher rate taxpayer at which time any student loan for fees would be written off on the basis that they were then more than putting their fair share back in? Or does that simply drive the wheel of capitalism when we ought to be seeking a more spiritual existence? It would certainly discriminate against women who are less likely and/or will take longer to become a higher rate taxpayer if they also serve society by popping at least one sprog into the workplace. Whatever the answer, it is a travesty to the U.K.'s education system that men and women who often had the benefit of a private education from the springboard of their own fortune of birth, and almost without exception received assistance with the cost of their tertiary education, have now largely abandoned such assistance for the next generation.

If we do not do something to address the funding of tertiary education by society, rather than the individual, the moneyed will get more moneyed whilst those without will have a far harder climb. We will be left in a Victorian era without even a Fairy Tale. Ask an engineer who has worked his way through the ranks of apprenticeships, who finds he has reached a level but is competing against relative novices to the practicalities of the job but who hold a degree. If society is intent on continuing to use the currency of a degree to allocate the better paid jobs then shame on it if, at the same time, it effectively excludes the poorer in our society to access that channel in the first place.

I wonder if the conservatives will still be falling out about the merits of Academy Schools and Grammar Schools if and when this book ever gets published. I fear so.

The potential damage to our Society of 'the classes' being further divided by their access to or exclusion from education may be far greater than the inequities which that inflicts on individual members of our youth. Education in its truest form is teaching others to question, opening the mind to unexplored possibilities or alternatives. Until we reach the point where we can say, this is where we all want to be, this is the Promised Land, don't fix it if it aint broke, society will always strive to improve, develop, progress. This takes more than a group of people who have learnt the particular tools of the trade. Our ability to reason is supposedly what separates us from the Bonobos but full reasoning only comes with the benefit of exposure to the facts, or those which are known. If people are exposed only to others who are of similar backgrounds, similar opinions, similar prejudices, we end up with the small town views which produce a Laissez Faire mentality, a stagnation of development and a narrow-minded life and outlook.

I am not implying that if anyone attends university they will automatically be broadminded, liberal and entrepreneurial nor indeed that anyone who does not attend won't be those things. Many arrive already too brainwashed - give me the child till he's seven and I'll show you the man. But at least it is one means of placing a load of young people, all of whom have achieved a certain level of education and thus an ability to reason productively, in one place where they are relatively secure and accommodated. Again, today's financial pressure often means students remain in the nearest university town so they can live at home and save on board and lodging. They lose the benefits of living in a different town in a different part of the country. The melting pot of ideas and opinions which is thereby produced is the real education.

Exposure is the key. If a young adult doesn't have the mental agility required by traditional book learning they can gain just as much life knowledge by being exposed to experience. 'Blissful' ignorance or, worse, indifference to the others in our society causes partition, dissemination and ultimately its breakdown. True tolerance can only be born of an informed mind whether the source of that information comes from verbal or written communication. Either way it requires us to try to walk around in someone else's shoes. To listen. To take account of the particular nature of the other and how it has been nurtured.

I spent four months in St Tropez when I was 21. That was an education. None of us had any money. And I mean no money other than what we were able to earn that day, no fallback bank account. One of the guys in our beach gang - I was cutting hair, he was selling cold cans from an icebox - was twenty-six then and one of the oldest working the beach. He was a little muscular guy with a Leprechaun grin, dirty chuckle and bleached curls to his shoulders. He'd been sitting in his local somewhere in Catholic Ireland when a mate had called in and asked if he fancied keeping him company on a truck delivery to Southern France. Having nothing particular to do he had agreed and ultimately stayed on to work the beach for the summer. Whatever our varied experiences, that group of around twenty-five young people who shared the cornucopia of the Blue Coast's pearls that summer, discovered a new experience of lifestyles thrown together by instinct's defense to being in a strange environment, with a different language, a long way from home, who became very close fathered by our need for each other.

FAIRY TALES by Sharon Moore

At the end of four glorious beach bumming months several of us headed for the October Fest in Munchen. As people gradually disappeared at the end of the season there were tearful goodbyes and details exchanged. My Irish friend said there was no point in swapping details. If his family knew he had spent the entire summer with a group of 'Prossies' they would literally, seriously, excommunicate him. He added, with a tear in his eye, 'and four months ago, if that had been my own cousin, I would have done the same thing to him'. He just hugged us a lot. Travel, experience, time to communicate, just 'getting' someone else's perspective, permanently changes people. If only our own home-grown 'Seven Seveners' had spent a summer on a beach with a bunch of assorted bums.

Human Beings are innately the same all over the world. The more limited our experiences or the stronger our outside influences such as religion or social mores, the more narrow minded we will be. We must learn to see people in context and realise, when we are faced with the likes of the Irish cousin or a Seven Sevener, there for the grace of our particular nurturing, go all of us. That doesn't provide an answer but it does lead to far greater understanding of those around us with whom we have relations be they members of another nationality/ religion or the person we want to build our life with.

As a partner in a busy practice I earnt 'good money'. That avenue was only possible because of my ability to access education. The huge restrictions upon that access which our current potential students face are criminal and only serve to broaden the gap between rich and poor. Though it may seem that I have digressed I felt it important to stress that there are many forms of education but although our lessons through life's experience can be invaluable, they do not pay the mortgage!

For money to be truly appreciated we have to experience being poor, at least indirectly. Everything is relative. Yin and Yang.

As I have travelled I have increasingly understood what poverty really means, firsthand, in my face. Certain images can never be eradicated from my memory. Sitting in a restaurant in Delhi, glazed from the footway outside but otherwise goldfish bowled to the world and his wife. Whilst we sat and ate our meal several children, undressed in rags, standing on the dusty pavement, made eating motions to us just inches away from our goody-loaded plates. Holding their left hands below their chins like a saucer, they were sweeping their right hands from the saucer to their lips, fingers bunched together as though holding food, their small mouths opening to receive the ghostly sustenance. In your face.

Further back, nearly thirty years ago, holidaying with my parents in Italy, the stark image of bundles of women on church steps, the babies and toddlers in their arms intentionally crippled to increase their pathos and thus, their money pulling power as, with downcast eyes, they held out their grubby palms to the passersby who were seeking out Caravaggios and other riches of the Italian culture. For it is better to have lived, albeit maimed, than to have died all but a babe in arms.

Thin skeletons of men on the beaten mud pavements in Calcutta, their arms and legs twisted, their heads buried in the earth to increase the worlds sympathy. We had been warned that many of the children were 'employed' to beg and had to hand their coined rewards to their adult overseers whilst receiving a meager 'wage'. A girlfriend and I bought as many bananas as we could carry and started handing them out. Children ran to us from all directions as word spread on the street of the fortuitous behaviour of these strange white girls. The sightless men wrapped their fingers around the fruit.

Fifteen years ago, Aborigines in the Northern Territory of Oz, torn from a way of life developed over centuries and put in camps, metal fenced from the rest of the town, housing mobile homes on struts. They were given dole money which bought alcohol for, displaced from their traditionally nomadic social order, they had nothing else to do. Biologically they lack the Caucasian's ability to process alcohol in the same way which meant they rapidly became inebriated and their alcohol-induced Id-driven behaviour spilled out onto the streets of Darwin. They could be seen, bolshy and loud, amorously sexually amoral or downright violent. They had been given food, shelter and even four-wheel drives but they had been robbed, a proud people reduced to the lowest echelons of their new society. They were poor from the heritage they were losing without being generally equipped with the tools, which come of lifelong exposure to 'western' culture, necessary to do something about it. 'Progress' is inevitable to us all but the scales were severely imbalanced. They were left lost and forcibly rooted upon their own land which they had wandered, tended and worshipped for longer than their white 'beneficiaries' had even laid eyes on it.

The man who haggles hard over a sale because his family's supper depends on it is only truly seen by those of us from more privileged circumstances after the event, when we are removed from it. Bartering over a purchase is often as alien to those of us from the UK as discovering at the 'checkout' that the price is not the price because varying percentages of sales tax then have to be added when shopping in the US. But, when in Rome. We become part of that man's reality and haggle back, often as vehemently. After many occasions of returning home and feeling the guilt of a hard argued but brilliant bargain, I now engage in the bartering but, to the bewildered surprise of the vendor, then hand him extra, after his game of haggling has been played to both our satisfactions.

We can clearly be poor in all sorts of ways but the bottom line is that, if you don't have the means of survival - clean drinking water, a balanced diet, disease free accommodation - the other poverties are irrelevant. It is easy to lose sight of the fact that two thirds of the world's children do not regularly have clean drinking water in our consumer, capitalist-driven little enclave. As individuals we might only be motivated to do something about this as a result of our direct personal experience combined with an ability to seize recognised opportunities. Travel broadens the mind but increasingly those who do not travel are unable to claim ignorance as the world gets smaller and appears in our living room via the television or the computer screen.

Everything is relative; 'poor' gives meaning to 'rich'. I once asked a client, so incredulous I couldn't help myself, why she had married a man who, in anyone's book, had behaved like an utter bastard from the outset of their relationship and ultimately beaten her within an inch of her life in front of her two young children. She said, without malice or anger but rather a resigned patience with a question she had clearly been asked before, 'you have never lived in a high-rise with

197

two young children surrounded by drugs and discarded needles, lifts that don't work and stairways the urinary odour of which sting your eyes, where sleepless nights are prompted by worries surrounding money and your ability to provide properly for your kids'. In such circumstances a well-stocked, heated and fully-functioning three-bed semi in suburbia can appear a fair exchange for verbal and physical abuse. Take care how we judge others when we have never stood in their shoes. Her drive to protect and provide for her children had outweighed her natural instinct to protect herself even though, as it turned out, there was a real risk of her children being orphaned. Perhaps it was a calculated risk since, in the urgent domestic violence proceedings which followed our interview, he was given alternative accommodation at Her Majesty's pleasure and subsequently, in the ensuing divorce, she was awarded the house!

If we manage to reach an understanding in relation to our respective sexual beings, be it that we both remain 'faithful' or otherwise, or we 'get away with' those 'indiscretions'; if we manage to form a union in which one party isn't driven to knocking ten bells out of the other, whether mentally or physically: the other great trouble maker can be money. Anyone who has been financially secure would agree that it alone does not make for happiness but it does help make life more comfortable.

In the context of our sexual relationships, money cannot be ignored since it can have an immense impact on their success or otherwise, whether we have 'enough' or not. Of course, 'poor' in the UK is 'very comfortable' in say Jamaica. There, many people are literally living on the bread line. If they don't earn money that day they don't eat. There is no uniform social security or pensions system, there are no loans available without asset security and even then, interest rates are phenomenal, their extended family often has no money, there are no savings for a rainy day. Doctors, dentists, lawyers have to be funded. Poor in the UK usually means we are provided a home in which the obligatory TV and fridge will be housed, if not a computer and a DVD player, we have a certain regular income which will continue until we die, credit and loans are available and the NHS will try to ensure our medical needs are dealt with. I recall one of my legally aided clients once proudly confirming to me that he was 'fifth generation unemployed'. Of course, the taxpayer funded his successful application to have contact with his children - presumably so that he could expound the advantages of that way of life to a sixth generation. .

Too little money produces pressures within a relationship usually centred around what the little money which is available ought to be used for. But having to struggle together to make ends meet can also be a great relationship strengthener. If we've faced deprivation together and got through it, that in itself somehow revalidates the bond and makes it harder to give up. Many people's relationships were actually happier before they acquired a certain level of comfortable income. Money buys choices but those choices of themselves create potential for friction and stress. A self-made man's wife once complained to me that he had reached a point where he felt he could buy anything and anybody (which invariably he could) but with the consequence that he failed to really appreciate the family and friends around him who would crave his company not because of what he'd got but for who he was, or had been.

FAIRY TALES by Sharon Moore

Many Jamaicans living in Jamaica do not stay single for long because to live on your own with one wage is all but impossible there. It takes two to fund rent, services and food alone. People become much more relaxed about the fact that, as one relationship breaks down, couples within the same village, or even living across the street, simply exchange partners. Everyone needs eachother too much to go looking for a fight, in the majority of cases. Like a strict religion or strong cultural morality, money can be a very strong factor in keeping people together as well as being capable of being responsible for the opposite.

If someone's personality is such that they are selfish or greedy they will be selfish or greedy with money: the stereotyped man of the last century who would blow his wages in the pub on a Friday evening whilst his twelve children at home were barefooted bundles of rags; the father who will buy his son a McDonalds but not buy one for his partner's son who is also with them; the husband who happily spends his money on smart suits, nice watch, cool car, gadgets but resents his wife's spending on anything but essentials. None of that is about Money but about Selfishness - an antithesis of self-less love.

If money is not the root of all evil, it certainly plays its part in cohabitational strife. Everyone has a different attitude to money from 'the world owes me a living and I could be dead tomorrow' through all the shades of greys to 'I must work and save as hard as I can and keep the best china for special occasions'.

Having a similar attitude to money certainly helps but is not a prerequisite to marital bliss. Our last three generations have seen a massive change in the attitude of society to the issue of money between the sexes. In my great-grandfather's day he was expected to provide financially for his family and he expected it of himself. If my great-grandmother could have earned 'pin money' - which was hard with six children - it would have been considered a bonus, an unexpected extra. From the freedom to work and to be treated equally in the workplace, born from the ashes of World War II, women are now expected to work, expected to provide such income as it is reasonable, within the confines of their abilities and responsibilities, to expect.

Within the context of divorce law, a District Judge will generally concede a woman's prerogative to be a full-time carer for her children under the age of ten or twelve. Thereafter, and dependant upon any unusual circumstances, she will generally be expected to work part-time. If she refuses to contemplate this a District Judge may well decide a case on the basis of a theoretical income she might reasonably be expected to achieve. The government has only recently announced that women receiving Income Support whilst looking after their children will no longer be able to do so until the youngest child is sixteen. In 2008 that age will be reduced to twelve with the intention of bringing it down to seven by 2010. After that age the woman will not be able to claim an inability to work due to her carer responsibilities and so will switch to Job Seekers Allowance thereby losing many fringe benefits. And so it seems that women are not only expected to work, which has to be right in any society in search of an egalitarian approach with equal rights and opportunities for all, but mothers will be expected to do some work once their youngest is seven. This may also be right within the context of this century but what a world away from my grandmother's day.

FAIRY TALES by Sharon Moore

I do not think this 'progress' is a bad thing. I am an egalitarian; I want things to be fair. The point is that the expectations of each party of the other, financially, have altered dramatically over just three generations and so our age will have a major impact on our attitude to money within our relationship. Age will also affect the employment paths available to us and ultimately the extent to which we can meet our own, and our partners, expectations. Since it is employment which usually generates our money, there must be few black or white households in the UK today where both parties would not expect their able-bodied sound-minded other, to work.

There are still huge cultural differences and, again according to Government statistics, in 2004 seven out of every ten Bangladeshi and Pakistani women of working age were neither working nor seeking work. Compare this with the quarter of white British/Irish and Black Caribbean women who were neither working nor seeking work. Culturally Bangladeshi and Pakistani women are not expected to work; it is as it was in my great-grandmother's day. And look at how many more children those women have and had.

Men, across all cultures, are primarily expected to work, or at least produce an income, unless there has been a role reversal and dad stays at home with the children whilst mom becomes the earner. In 2004 only 5% of white British and Irish men of working age were unemployed. The highest percentage was amongst black Caribbean's at 14% followed closely by black Africans who had 13 % unemployment as did the Mixed and Bangladeshi groups. Whilst we can all think of a hundred reasons why those figures might be distorted, unemployment leads to financial stress leads to friction within a relationship without careful management.

The secret use of money - from a fairly modest credit card debt to a gambling habit which ultimately bankrupts the family — can be one of the most trust shattering discoveries to rival infidelity itself. The issue at both ends of that scale is again Trust. What creates the damage is the distrust which the actions create far more than the pounds, shillings and/or pennies which have been lost. What we feel, ultimately, only matters to us but what we do affects everyone around us. Lost Trust can be very, very hard to rebuild. Remember my client who clearly dearly loved his wife who loved him too but was unable to forgive and forget and move on. Knowing that every time she walked out the door he would torment himself and anytime she walked in the door later than expected he would torment her. He could not put either of them through that. The trust was gone and he felt it was irrebuildable.

One of my colleagues was pouring through a pile of documents disclosed by the husband's solicitor as part of the process pursued when working towards a financial deal on divorce. The wife had said she did not understand where all his money went. From the disclosed bank statements - which frighteningly reflect our lives - a clear pattern emerged. From a cash point in an area of Birmingham notorious for its provision of buyable female flesh, regular withdrawals of £10 to £50 had been made. It seemed that he allowed himself a blowjob on a Monday and worked up to whatever £50 might buy you by Friday. She had to compose a carefully worded query for his solicitor upon the utilisation of the cash withdrawals and prepare herself, to prepare her unsuspecting client, for what might inevitably be revealed. The case was resolved shortly after that. The husband did not want to face the shame of the truth and also knew that such revelations were likely to lose him credibility should the matter proceed to court. The wife had seen my colleague's query but never made the connection regarding the area. It was not my colleague's place to share her educated guess and the wife was divorced in ignorance.

My client's secret gambler husband did not set out to be a gambler nor did he set out to wreck his marriage and his life. But he did make a decision very early on which set him on his path of destruction. He didn't tell his wife. When he went with his mates that first night and got a taste for the chase, felt the allure of the illusion, he didn't tell his wife. When he found himself returning, and returning and then returning again, he didn't tell his wife. When he started to run up credit card debts he couldn't service, he didn't tell her. And by the time she found out, which, other than a lottery-like turn of the gambling tables, could never have been avoided, all was lost. The lies which had formed like layers to cover his habit had eaten away the fabric of his once happy relationship.

No man, nor woman, is an island. The vast majority of us need our fellow beings to retain our sanity but we also rely upon them to reflect what mirrors cannot. 'I wish to God the gift he g'e us, to see ourselves as others see us' was one of my Nan's sayings. Our close friends and relatives do this for us, often unknowingly. We often judge our own actions by the reactions of others to them such that they form part of our conscience, our Super Ego. And we are frail creatures with our weaknesses, insecurities, phobias and idiosyncrasies. There are those rarely matched couples who together add up to more than the total of their separate parts. The strengths of the one create different strengths in the other. The weaknesses don't go away but they are faced, understood, dealt with.

The husband didn't tell his wife of the first gambling visit because he knew she would be disapproving which would reflect a part of what he himself felt, creating shame. That would have been so even had he come home with a windfall (though that may well have softened the blow!) But had he told her, had they built that level of Intimacy in their relationship, she might not only have had a greater understanding but she would also have then become involved in what escalated into a severe weakness for which he required trained help. Had she known she would, naturally, have made every endeavour to help by encouraging him to attend counseling etc. All might still not have been perfect but he would not have ended up bankrupt being despised by his wife.

When we choose to hide financial information from our nearest and dearest we have to bear in mind that we are also cutting ourselves off from the benefits which only they can or will provide. The very people who most give a shit about us and our financial security (for they usually have a vested interest themselves), the ones who will give us that more objective reflection of ourselves, will not be there for us when the occasional flutter becomes a gambling habit or when we can no longer service our credit cards, no more than they will be there for us when our one-night stand becomes a love affair. They may be there in ignorance but are therefore unable to be there for us in our weakness, be it induced by blind greed or blind passion. If they know from the start, the flutter can't become a habit because it will be dealt with before it gets that far just as the screw won't become the lovemaking which seriously endangers the future of a relationship because the issue is nipped in the bud, one way or the other. At least our female flesh purchaser isolates the issue and ensures he keeps himself safer from the risk of feeling seriously and uncontrollably involved. It is far easier to keep detached from a business transaction.

Of course much of my life has been spent arguing about people's money and assets once a relationship has broken down. Suddenly those who tried to manage their joint finances for mutual benefit find themselves embroiled in arguments about who should have what and why. In marriages where there are insufficient assets to make two independent homes out of one broken one this can cause the greatest dilemma and hardship. However, the leap in equity which many have experienced over the past five years or so does at least mean that we are rarely faced with the negative equity nightmare of the mid 90's. If we don't own property then both are likely to continue in rented accommodation but in separate places!

But none of this is the kind of information which you're likely to take in and want to discuss at the height of emotion. Over the years I have refused to act for several clients who I could see were effectively unable to provide proper instructions. They were perfectly sane and cogent in their instructions but it was blatantly clear that these were prompted by feelings of guilt or pain but most of all, just an over powering desire to have the whole thing over with. To stop the pain of the prolonged operation of separation, the sleepless nights and anxiety that the feeling of being in limbo brings; the never ending lawyers requests for instructions, documentary evidence and money.

Many clients obviously settle their finances at a lesser amount than they might achieve if they pursued their arguments ultimately to a fully contested hearing before a Judge in the County Court. The latter scenario will often arise when there is a 'spoon' argument going on driven by a need to be proven 'right' and to 'win' by one or both of them.

Invariably compromise is the far better choice. The cost of the alternative must be measured in far more than money. For many of us, our relationships and emotional health are paramount. Though human beings are incredibly and amazingly able to deal with what life may throw at us, around a third of my clients were taking some form of anti-depressant whilst many of the remainder hit the most fabled turncoat of them all, alcohol. From the multicoloured acid trips of the 1960's, the common drugs of this century are becoming more available, more chemical, more powerful and they are no longer the privilege of the rock stars, the rich and the famous. The future must surely hold mind-bending drugs beyond our imagination, unknown channels of future escapism from the reality of broken relationships as well as the sheer pressure, speed and daily technical advances of modern life.

Compromising a fair financial agreement, which has to be the best possible outcome for all, can only be achieved if both people are level headed in their approach and honest about what they have. This can be a tall order for anyone who is feeling emotionally at sea. The family lawyer is there to ensure that full disclosure has been given and the reasonable arguments as to why a particular settlement is just, according to the prevailing laws, are fully taken into account. Of course that costs money and so the warring couple end up spending the very thing which they are trying to preserve for themselves.

What makes the whole process eminently more difficult is that there is rarely much trust left between the parties and, combined with the breakdown in communications which almost inevitably follows, both parties fill in the gaps of their actual knowledge.

CHAPTER NINETEEN

THE DANGERS OF FILLING IN THE GAPS

How many times have we gone over a disgruntlement or disagreement in our heads, totally persuading ourselves that the other person meant this or planned that only to find, when the red mist has cleared and we're able to talk about it, that we had totally sent ourselves barking up the wrong tree?

At eighteen and in my first year at uni I went with a fellow under graduate girlfriend to stay in Dublin with her friend and friend's mom who lived there. We stayed around a week before hitching across to Galway and on to the lovely isolation of Inis Bofin. In Dublin we went to a Sin Fein meeting with these friends, not particularly because we were sympathisers with their cause but because the mother was well known for being strongly outspoken upon issues affecting women's rights. The women of this group met in an out-of-the-way-little-back-street-room and on this occasion they described how they were strip-searched, sometimes up to three times a day, standing in a room with the female guards surrounding them. Even when menstrual, they were made to stand and drip whilst the warders took the piss out of their bodies. This happened even when they had had no visitors, the means by which anything forbidden was usually acquired, since the last humiliation. It was all part of the psychological warfare to subjugate the will of the prisoner. As young women and not being totally naive we felt sympathy, anger and ignorance, not necessarily in that order.

On top of their TV set they had a big piece of opaque white plastic with a gravelly surface and a gentle point at one end. It stood around eight inches tall and four inches wide. It was made of white opaque plastic and densely solid. When they answered my curiosity advising that it was a 'rubber bullet' I learnt a lesson which has stayed with me and goes beyond the realisation, expounded by Mr. Geldof, the 'don't believe what you read' reality. We attach a visual image to a word through our own familiarity with what we suppose it means. I doubt that many in England, Scotland or Wales, so familiar with the 'British soldiers firing rubber bullets' reports only a few decades ago upon our brethren of the Emerald Isle, imagined anything other than regular sized bullets made of a really spongy rubbery stuff which warned but didn't really hurt. This fecker would have downed you in agony at best and broken your spine at worst.

I was transported back to that Dublin sitting on a Continental flight over twenty years later, from New York's coldness – where the sub-zero temperatures ensured that the pampered pooches piss was freezing as it hit the pavement - to Montego Bay. The plane had to be washed with hot soapy steaming jetted water wielded by a man in an elevated box which could have come from Trumpton, before we could take off. Having packed my coat in my case in what I'd thought to be a clever anticipation of arrival in tropical climes, I reached for a blanket. I hoped that the earthquaked Iranians were getting more from that word that I'd recently heard in the inventory of aid arriving, than the thin navy manmade fibred square to which the airline attributed the same word 'blanket'. We should never presume adjectives on an unknown noun though we do it all the time. When we assume knowledge by implication we imbed an ignorance beyond mere speculation.

In the case of a rubber bullet it is highly likely that we have no other pre-existing information. We haven't seen one, we haven't read anything about them save that they were used by the British troops in Northern Ireland. Our mind automatically fills in the gaps, as intelligently as it can, giving meaning to the phrase by applying what we already know about 'rubber' and about 'bullets'. We on the mainland were probably further cajoled into a false sense of understanding by the manner in which our media reported their use, a sort of humanistic compromise in times of combat, much better for the body than their metal-made cousins. Even a cluster bomb or a landmine can sound 'gentler' until someone, like Sir Bob or Lady Di, makes sure we know differently.

In the case of the blanket, this is a more familiar term and, deprived of any additional detail, I imagine the soft and strong, warm and fluffy variety that used to make up my bed on top of the sheet before the marvelous adoption of the duvet. My grand mother was actually tested at school upon her bed-making abilities. Duvets have killed the art and I can only guess what might be in vogue if I ever see my 90's (let alone what they will be teaching our grandchildren, not bed making I suspect). Notwithstanding my lifetime's numerous flights I am still disappointed by the real article as defined by the airlines (I know... space/ cleaning...)

Emotionally we are prone to the same thing. We learn a fact or, worse still, we think we know a fact and make presumptions, jump to conclusions. Within a relationship, or indeed at the end of it, this can be a carcinogenic. There is no point in one person trying to spend time in honest communication if the other isn't really listening, or is making presumptions about the words we are using. We often hear what we want to hear or, in our own subsequent rerun of our version of the memory, we bring all our prejudgments to the table. We find it particularly hard to listen when we already know that we are right or, almost more importantly, the other is wrong. 'Who can't hear mus' feel' and 'he who feels it knows it' as the Jamaicans say.

It is not only a question of listening to what we hear but then interpreting what we hear. When such potentially crucial discussions arise it is likely that we are in an emotional state. Though we feel ourselves it is only with hindsight that we can see we were not ourselves. A bit like getting drunk, misbehaving and then facing the remembrances which follow the first moments of waking memory loss the next morning and slowly cringing memory descends. The couple arguing about the spoons fails miserably. They don't quite get to the stage of who paid for the cutlery drawer and so who should have the ultimate choice, but they get close.

The particular couple from whom my spoon analogy originally came were locked in a struggle which related to their own insecurities. Theirs had been a relatively traditional marriage and, once the children were grown and flown, she had re-trained. She had taken a part-time job for 'pin money'. She had been well received in the job market and promoted. She had been offered a full-time job with training and great prospects. He did not want her to take it - she was too old, she didn't need to work. He was the provider. She would only get into potential mischief with the colleagues whom he already resented intruding into their lives with early evening calls or jolly references in unguarded conversation. She was sick of feeling he always had his own way. For years he had held the purse strings and so ultimately she was beholden to him. His not-always-so-veiled insinuations about her own morality in the face of a proffered office affair were ridiculous.

The spoon thing had actually arisen when she was in a rush with the rest of her reality. But it had provoked such an oversized reaction from him that she had continued to err; it had become her stand. A convenient 'spoon focus' was actually easier to argue about than discussing the feelings of insecurity and apprehension which he had and the feelings of dominated claustrophobia and need for self-exploration outside of the box, which she had. His slurs on her ability niggled away at her newfound self-confidence making her fight all the harder to maintain it. People don't always say what they mean for the very reason that they do not always or immediately know precisely what is making them behave in such a way or feel such extremes of certain emotions.

At thirty my doctor told me I had to make some serious decisions since, if I was still on the pill and smoking by the age of 35, my risk of heart disease and associated illnesses would 'go through the roof'. I came off the pill immediately and spent some considerable time reliant upon the delights of condom-man. I was then offered an injection which consisted solely of progesterone. The pill also contains oestrogen and it is that which creates the risky side effects when nicotine combined. The injection had originally been developed for those suffering with Downs Syndrome as they are generally highly sexed but can't be relied upon to remember to take the contraceptive pill daily.

The effect on me was devastating. After twelve years of no
recognisable side effects from the pill, I became an emotional,
highly strung and rather depressed shadow of my former self.
Not totally, overtly, but I was prone to burst into tears when
I might otherwise have bitten someone's head off! I had to
wait three months for the drug to be out of my system after
which I came home to myself, head biting and all! Obviously,
this was a man-made chemical emotional reaction creating an
imbalance for my particular make up. But emotion itself and
all of the huge range of feelings which we go through when a
once-treasured relationship is being plundered, has the same
effect. We are not ourselves but it is often difficult for us to
truly recognise it since the emotions are our emotions and the
reactions are our reactions. The other person is likely to be in
a similar state and accordingly, for either to fully know what
they feel or want, let alone communicate that to the
empathetic listener in their partner, is remote. Not only do we
fill in the gaps but our whole perception of what the gaps are
can become distorted.

Into this quagmire of emotion walks the lawyer, generally an
unwanted and expensive necessary. Oh to be in a service
industry driven by want rather than unwanted need. The
lawyer can advise, cajole and encourage reason. The better
the lawyer the better the quality of the advice and the cajoling
but ultimately the lawyer must act on the client's instructions
or refuse to act. If not very careful, the lawyer simply
becomes a well honed tool via which the spoon argument can
reach new heights, the postbox lawyer who simply provides
the means for one party to spar with the other.

Into this equation add guilt, the perception by one party that
they are more to blame for the failed relationship and the

pain which it is causing others. This not only applies to the partner but the children and the family and friends who are caught up in the ripple effect of relationship breakdown. The law rarely has an interest in their perceived guilt (unless it is criminal) since it would take a week of the court's crushed timetable to decipher the real nature of guilt and 'responsibility' on a balance of probabilities. Despite the fact that we find it almost irresistible to apportion blame, the law gracefully bows out of such a fractious area.

A case which recently reached the Court of Appeal and sent shockwaves through the family law fraternity suggested that a wealthy playboy should suffer financially because of his 'blame' in the marriage breakdown due to his philandering ways. This is a very dangerous course to be avoided at all cost. Fortunately, The House of Lords agreed with me and many of my colleagues in the field. There is provision for behaviour to be taken into account when considering a fair financial settlement but it has to be gross and extreme. The man who beats his wife every Friday night for twenty years, after leaving his mates at the pub, might run the risk of a pecuniary penalty but to introduce infidelity as a reason to adjust that settlement is littered with horrendous problems of cause and effect. Woe betide us if Big Brother starts apportioning blame in our relationships.

CHAPTER TWENTY

MEN AND WOMEN

From the day we are born our gender dictates how we will behave in all aspects of our life. Not only are we differently genetically programmed but, from the moment we take our first breath till our last, all of those around us reinforce and perpetuate our differences.

In another of my mother's O.U. programmes babies were dressed in pink or blue and a group of mothers were asked to sit in a room and play with them. The girls were not necessarily dressed in pink and neither were the boys necessarily dressed in blue. However, almost without exception and apparently subconsciously, the interactive play between baby and woman was seen to be markedly different according to the colour of the baby's romper. We are generally rougher with boys, we give them more liberty earlier in their lives and we endorse many prototypes without even being aware of it.

It seems we cannot ignore the innate differences between our sexes and which pervade the Human Race. Those differences have a thousand faces, some of which are familiar and others of which can still stop us in our tracks. Society increasingly accepts that there are many shades of grey between the Alpha Male and Submissive Female but wherever our particular personality places us on that graph, it is highly unlikely that our partner will be similarly placed.

The average age of people entering a first marriage in England and Wales has increased substantially over the last forty years. In 1971 the average man was 25 whilst the woman was 23. By 2003 those figures had increased to 31 and 29 respectively. Sweden has the oldest averages at 33 and 31 whilst Lithuania has the youngest averages at 27 and 24 respectively. The norm is that a woman marries two years before the man perhaps because her biological clock has always had a louder chime.

If, to achieve the Nirvana of total Intimacy, Mother Nature requires total Honesty and if the honest truth [the Truth, the whole Truth and nothing but the Truth] is that all people, for a multitude of reasons, are inclined to stray, emotionally and physically, then we all have a long way to go yet to achieve the required mental state of being to accept this. Men, through no fault of their own other than their Nurture and their Nature, have the furthest to go, the biggest change in attitude of mind to make. Our society has brainwashed them in many ways which means they may not necessarily want to see change. What's good for the gander is not always perceived to be good for the goose!

Through the ages it has been socially acceptable for an older, indeed aged, man to purchase younger pretty women and even flaunt them in public. Certainty of the purchase comes from the fact that the man will have money and the woman will want it and its benefits. Seldom will it reflect a warts an' all experience but it functions on a level of interlacing selfish desires, at least at its outset. Exceptions are rare though I do know of some exceptional ones. However it is not socially acceptable for an older, indeed aged, woman to purchase young, muscular men far less flaunt them anywhere near society's two-faced visage. It is morally reprehensible and what of those poor young men having to deal with that wrinkling flesh! As women's buying power gets stronger and the world gets smaller, older women are seeking out their own equivalents of 'the Thai bride' in poorer parts of the world. For example, women from both Europe and America visit Jamaica annually to return to a gigolo who will give them undivided attention day and night with no strings attached. Despite the fact that the women pay for everything, eating and drinking out is so relatively cheap, it's a very small price to pay. It is an entirely honest, though frequently shallow, exchange and women are free to pursue their own urges in a way that they would be unlikely to do back home.

> 'There never was a lover, male or female, who hadn't an eye on, in fact they rely on, the tricks they can try on their partner, they're hoping their lover will help them or keep them, support them, promote them. Don't blame them, you're the same.' From Andrew Lloyd Webber's Evita.

Men are having to learn to deal with the 'modern' woman, the changing face of womankind in which women are so much more physically and mentally liberated than only decades ago. From those brave ladies who, appropriately attired and not an ankle in sight, threw their bodies in front of horses to win us our often unused vote through to the first lady speaker in the House of Commons, our first female Prime Minister. Just being acknowledged as having a valid, informed and useful political opinion is so relatively recent. Generally, women have become stronger as a result of their 'liberation from servitude' where their primary role was as housewife and mother. Their intellect and therefore opinions are increasingly valued by men; their unique skills in a male workplace are recognised as invaluable and actively sought out. The very nature of the beast is proving herself. Having been given the legal opportunity to be an equal she has proven that reality. This freedom of mind, body and soul increasingly allows women's true potential to shine - and this is not limited to the workplace or the political stage. It is a huge adjustment for men to make in such a blink of our history but I believe men will rise to the challenge and see the clear advantages to them, and to all of us, in doing so. It may take another generation but it is on its way.

This is not to suggest that men and women can ever be the same, 'all men are not born equal' despite the proclamations of America's Founding Fathers, and neither are women. Though we may be moving towards true equal opportunity there will always be individuals who, with the combined forces of their nature and nurture, make the most of those opportunities. My father once suggested to me that whilst Communism is a fantastic system in theory it is an impossibility in practice; if everyone is paid the same regardless of their job, there will always be an individual who ends up with a house on the hill whilst another lies drunk in the gutter. Within the context of all our relationships we need to celebrate our differences and learn from them for the strengths of others often reveal our own weaknesses and vice versa. At the same time we need a society in which every man and woman shares the same freedoms and responsibilities.

This last generation gap has elicited major changes in women's sexual freedom and behaviour. Women of my mother's generation, who 'saved' themselves for marriage, were not giving blow-jobs at fifteen. Remember those women in my first office who didn't give head until well into their marriages. Fellatio was something one performed for one's husband out of a duty to provide pleasure to him. It was beyond the sex act, more intimate. There was even a kind of respectability in that, by its giving nature. Cunnilingus was a far harder topic to probe since it actually involved receiving pleasure. My girlfriends and I grew up in a world where the grownups still advised that sex was for marriage, later weakened to 'a serious relationship' but no-one even mentioned oral sex (except one fifth-former who momentarily convinced us that this meant talking about it). Long before we had reached the legal age of consent and found a 'serious relationship', Curiosity had led us to this playing field. From the first 'hand job' matters progressed in what seemed an entirely natural way, without breaking the unthinkable penetrative sex taboo.

Women are much more likely to know what they want, in many things, but particularly sexually, than in any age before. Cosmo's explosion of the orgasm from soft porn to High Street main stream has been followed by a much greater understanding of the basic anatomy involved, all the way through to the fabled 'G' spot. However we remain shy to vocalise our desires and many people within relationships still find it difficult to say what we do and don't like in the bedroom. Though some ex–colleagues suggested I include a diagram by way of some illumination for those men who have not had the benefit of a communicative woman or the right men's magazines, I have resisted the temptation (they actually suggested that it should be perforated and printed in luminous ink to allow under-the-covers illumination!)

As I have said, one of the frustrating things about most porn, from a woman's perspective, is that it promotes a miseducation of our men who are inclined to forget that the majority of a woman's pleasure comes from the clitoris. There are not many women who can confidently assert that they have a 'G' Spot nor men who are aware of its potential. While 'the spoon position' or 'doggy' can be extremely enjoyable it usually requires some fairly expert hand manipulation given that the clitoris is otherwise left in mid-air with nothing to create the friction to stimulate that small but vital part of the female anatomy. In the throws of his own pleasure a man is further distracted from the job in hand and either forgets about it or becomes too rough in his enthusiasm. But how many of us can say 'direct hits hurt and cause quite a sharp pain. The clitoris has its own little hood for a reason and stimulation should use that hood to rub on the clit rather than fingers probing beneath it'? And men could never learn that by watching porn.

Much porn wants to reveal genital detail and hands get in the way of camera shots. Women are seen to groan in ecstasy whilst their clits wave around in thin air. It doesn't work like that! Some women promote some men's ignorance of the art of pleasuring them by faking orgasms. For their own sakes this should be banned! Men can hardly deceive women similarly since they leave their evidence behind. At least we can be fairly certain when we have pleasured our men.

It can be difficult for a man to find the entrance to our 'love tunnel' especially if he's aiming in the dark or without watching what he is doing! Many women have experienced her amorous lover jabbing his engorged passion into the folds of her lips or even her groin. A helping hand will often save

FAIRY TALES by Sharon Moore

the day but it can get a little frustrating if the woman always has to guide her lover in. As the easily locatable anus lies in a direct line with the hole he will normally be seeking out, how easy should it be to tell him to find the folded flower of our entrance from that navigation point?! Even within the context of a loving relationship we find these things difficult to say, especially without making him feel we are criticising his abilities. Likewise with the clit – he can be so close but so far away by a matter of crucial millimetres but it is a difficult to convey that to our lover.

Many men don't realise that the time of the month is also highly likely to affect the level of a woman's horniness. For perverse reasons known only to Mother Nature Herself, many women I have spoken to have confirmed that they are most easily excitable in the days immediately prior to and during their period. It takes a substantially lesser degree of effort to make them aroused at such times and they can achieve orgasm with far less physical and mental effort. Whilst this must be hormonal, it flies in the face of what we might expect since it would seem logical for Her to make us most driven to the sexual act when we are most likely to conceive and yet these are the very times when we are at our least fertile. Perhaps She wanted us to have some fun without consequence after all!

Whilst these are just a few examples of the universal truths women struggle to convey, everyone is different and whilst generalisations can always be made, it is only through honest communication that we can really get to know both our partners and indeed ourselves, physically, mentally and sexually. Whilst one man will love his balls being practically chewed off, another man will feel physically uncomfortable if we so much as suck them! Men don't seem to share the same inhibitions in telling us which camp they fall in! One man's meat is another man's poison but since women don't have a set at all just a sentence from a man can save a huge amount of painful trial and error!

Moving swiftly on from sexual differences and preferences, one major, and necessarily generalised, difference between the genders which effects all this honesty and communication stuff is that, in general, men do not communicate as much as women. Ask a guy what one of his friends does, where they live, if they have kids, where they grew up ... you're much more likely to get a "I dunno", "I never asked him", "He'd have told me if he wanted me to know" answer than ever you would off a woman. Many men are not used to expressing their feelings in the same way that women are and all the macho 'big boys don't cry' brainwashing doesn't help. Many women still want their men to be strong, fighters in life, but at the same time let their defences down when it comes to the relationship. This is a hard shift to ask men to make and they have to want to. Intimacy can never be forced.

I recall my form teacher at school saying that if a boy sits an exam and does not really know the answer to a particular question, he will write a few lines and then move on to a more attractive question. A girl, on the other hand, will feel compelled to write several pages on largely irrelevant topics!

I heard a Radio Four programme relating to emails and the difference between those sent by men and those sent by women, the latter being longer, more flowery, more likely to be peppered with exclamation marks and ended with kisses. The gentleman interviewee suggested that men can consider that communication, in this case via email and work-related,

denotes failure. If you have to communicate something the
suggestion was that something had gone wrong. I found this
an intriguing proposition. Perhaps in the he-man world men
can see communication as a weakness, something that
shouldn't be necessary. It certainly shows our underbelly but
until we discover our telepathic tendencies it is a prerequisite
to an intimate relationship. If we avoid it with our work
colleagues we cannot afford to do so at home. Not talking
about a problem does not make it go away and it will fester
under a veil of secrecy; a problem shared really is a problem
halved even though the sharing may take a lot of guts and
create a lot of pain. Festered secrets cause many more
gangrenous problems and pains.

Though adultery has featured in many of the divorces I have
conducted over the years, there have been many
consultations to receive general matrimonial and
cohabitational advice which have not resulted in the
partnership ending. I only get to see a fraction of our society
whose members have already taken the step of seeking legal
advice, there are many more that have dealt with the
unfaithfulness issue and moved on together from it. But there
remains a marked difference in the number of women who
will deal with it, move on from it, forgive if not forget, than
compared to men.

The 'Stag/Slag' 'Stud/Slut' conditioning still influences all of
us and controls women's behaviour who are expected to
'know better'. They risk their standing in the eyes of their
social groups if they are sexually adventurous far more than
their male counterparts, even today. Women carry the
immediate burden of an unplanned pregnancy and can
become HIV infected from a man far more easily than he can

become infected by her. Women are raised as the keeper of the sexual keys. Assuming we have all the requisite body parts, girls rapidly realise that 90% of their male heterosexual piers would take them behind the bike shed if they allowed it. The other 10% are probably the men who don't wank either! The odds go down as men mature and take on responsibilities, but not that much. Because women's access to sex is probably easier than for men, they are not so flattered by a proposition. All of this can be expected due to emotional and psychological differences but it contributes to the misunderstandings which are prevalent between the sexes.

Having laboured through 'Women are from Venus...' anyone can see the strength of some of the arguments expounded. Whilst men go off to their caves to ruminate the solution to a problem, the woman is standing outside in the cold, not wanting an answer but a hug! As a strong independent woman with a keen spirit of adventure and Carpe Deum I have often felt it has been easier to relate to men. But there are fundamental differences between our genders which are inescapable. Men do seem better able to compartmentalise both their lives and their feelings. Comprehensive psychological testing has proven that women are better equipped to multi-task. By definition, that means that they think about a variety of things at the same time. That can be a very sobering ability when faced with the drunken heat of a 'one off' particularly given its likely mental interference in the act. Add to this a pre-existing committed relationship and a woman becomes less likely to send out a green light.

It is hardly surprising that men have had a hard time adapting to this new state. Britain has always been a Patriarchy and even before this land was inhabited, they carry in their genes memories of cavemen responsibilities. Infidelity has almost been their singular domain. Women have been raised through the ages with an often unspoken acceptance of a man's 'tendencies'.

Men, in their turn, are raised under the influence of the 'He's a Stag, She's a Slag' mentality which promotes a view as to what might be socially acceptable behaviour for the two sexes It also provides an implied justification that sexual promiscuity is simply part of his nature. It goes without saying that for men to have affairs, women must have affairs - or else every 'single' woman in the UK would be heavily in demand and highly satisfied! Thus it cannot simply be a facet of the male Nature alone.

Are women less prone to stray? There is the obvious biological and historical factor of their being the bearers of children. If the most basic instinct Mother Nature has given us is survival, that means not only of ourselves but of our species. Reproduction is key. As a society we have a vested interest in producing a healthy, balanced next generation. They provide rebirth of our own century-nurtured genes, of the race as a whole and as a means to maintain a level of lifestyle into our own old age.

The child is reliant on the mother for his physical birth and nourishment immediately thereafter. Men have a natural vested interest in keeping their woman to themselves. When men discover unfaithfulness on the part of their women, their reaction is almost always more extreme than when the boot is on the other foot. It is not only all the common denominators of feelings which anyone in that situation can experience but a red mist that descends. Perhaps society has made men less prepared for it or less able to deal with it. The macho pride reacts in a blind storm. Men have not been programmed to forgive if not forget, as women have in many cases. Reason has to level with Passion before real decisions can be made. And men have to prepare themselves for the full state of equality which seems as inevitable as Mother Nature herself.

With that disturbing revelation also comes the pay back. How can two people have an equal, honest, intimate, warts an' all relationship, if different rules of behaviour apply to each of them, indeed, if any 'rules', which aren't equally selected, can apply. Most people want to be liked or at least, respected. Similarly we want our friends and family to like our partner, respect our choice. We want to take pride in our partner because that also makes us take pride in ourselves. Their respect for us gives us respect in ourselves. Does it make us proud when our partner goes out with his mates every Thursday night but plays his face when we want to go out with the girls? Does the fact that we have forgiven him an indiscretion but know that he would walk away in an instant if we behaved in the same way, give us greater respect for him? The full extent of the equality which women will seek over the next thirty years has not apparently dawned on many of us yet. We may be the weaker sex but in post-industrialised Britain, women are competing for the same jobs as men and getting them. Having brawn in this technological age is of little advantage in many sectors of the workplace. 20% more women than men are obtaining Degrees. Women no longer have to rely on their partners for their daily bread. Thank Mother Nature that they do rely on them for their sperm!

Multi-cultural Britain has even bigger mountains to climb. In Muslim culture, though not in English law, a man may reasonably take four wives if he has the means to treat them all equally. Of course it would be unheard of for the women to take four husbands! Do we accept, regardless of what our law says, it is reasonable for white and black women to reach a level of true equality whilst their brown sisters, living within the same community, are denied it? I would not assume to change any of our diversely unique cultural influences in Britain but it is difficult to turn a blind eye to these inequalities, even when some of these women see no apparent problem with the arrangement. Is it an informed decision and do they have any option?

There have been several examples of so called 'honour killings' in recent times when whole houses have been set on fire whilst Muslim families slept in their beds. One was perpetrated by young Asian men, one of whom believed that a young man in the house was seeing his sister. The family was rescued via an upstairs window from their burning home; one of the young sisters never made it out. In the worst incident, an Asian father set fire to his own home killing his wife and four daughters, apparently because the wife would not obey his wish that she did not work. As one commentator put it, these are not 'honour' killings they are 'control' killings.

Though these may be extreme examples, in an age when we are endeavouring to attain equal rights and opportunities for all, how can we tolerate a culture (not a religion) which seeks to suppress women's very liberty in the heart of our own communities? Many Muslim women in the UK are not even allowed out of their own homes unless accompanied by their husband, or at least only on his say so. How can we ever achieve a truly integrated cosmopolitan society when one section of our sisterhood is so suppressed? Like 'courting' I suspect that we can only wait for this male domination to die out with a generation (or two). In the meantime it seems we can only use the base line of the law to prevent or punish the most extreme manifestations of these beliefs.

On a more general level it is interesting to consider the law's approach to men and women and, more particularly, the manner in which it will deal with a couple's assets and income on divorce. We have now inched our way from the presumptions of a 'One Third Rule' which was never a hard and fast law but urged that a woman on divorce should be left with at least a third of the parties combined incomes or otherwise be compensated with a capital sum to reflect this. This evolved in an era when marriages had usually lasted longer than the average today and in a social climate which fully accepted and expected a wife to stay home or only work if she chose to. By marrying, the man generally accepted that he was taking on financial responsibility for his wife, regardless of whether their union bore fruit. It was expected.

The whole sexual revolution thing has brought about huge changes. As we have seen from government proposals, women are expected to work as much as men. If a woman only chooses to work part-time, if at all, a Judge will 'assume' a level of income upon her which he considers she could reasonably be expected to earn. Whether she chooses to or not is her business but the responsibility of the man to produce the income has been dramatically reduced. There are exceptions to this such as when there are still young children or where a mature wife has never worked but there has been a sea-change in the law to reflect that in society. That must be right if we are truly to achieve equality. Women cannot opt for the advantages and yet shun the less attractive side of that arrangement. There has also been a much more uniformly accepted norm that, as a starting point at least, both parties will divide all assets between them equally particularly if these are sufficient to ensure that both can have a reasonable standard of living both now and in retirement. There will be some rejigging to reflect our respective income sources and earning abilities. And given the crisis this generation is facing in respect of its pension provision, even the transfer value of that percentage of a pension which was funded during marriage will be halved or 'bought off' with a lump sum from one to the other. The assets to be taken into account are those which the parties have or are likely to have in the 'reasonably foreseeable future' (about five years) but the Government specifically changed that provision for pensions such that, even a pension which will not be paid for twenty years, is taken into account. In relation to the State pension women have often not paid their full 'stamp' (National Insurance Contributions) but can elect on divorce to assume the same contributions as the husband without affecting the man's state pension. This does not happen automatically and is often overlooked but is a commonsense provision since our entire society relies upon women continuing to have children.

CHAPTER TWENTY-ONE

CHILDREN

The fall-out which broken relationships scatter upon our children is both obvious and obscured, often by those children themselves.

According to 'seven years in the lives of British families' Berthoud and Gershuny, of all the children born in 1997 to married or cohabiting couples, 70% and 36% respectively are likely to spend their entire childhood living with both parents. This doubtless reflects the greater psychological commitment which marriage continues to represent to many of us and Civil Partnerships are likely to represent in the future. Just as married couples have traditionally found it easier to adopt than cohabiting ones it seems likely that Civilly Partnered gay couples will be higher up in the pecking order in their applications to adopt.

It seems difficult to see how anyone can argue against the proposition that every child's ideal upbringing would involve two people committed to eachother and to that child. The disagreements start when we consider the point at which the harm to children of parents living together outweighs the benefit which they gain from such an ongoing scenario.

Whilst sorting through the endless amount of paperwork that seems to accumulate in my home daily, I found the following extract. In all honesty I cannot remember the particular client to which it related but I am sure it reflects the emotion of many a 'deserted' child. Its poignancy hit me when I read it and I repeat it here as it was written:

Where were you when I needed you?

You left me.

The piece of the puzzle that is missing but will always be there,

The gap missing.

I've cried a river for you, where was you?

I'm grieving, for someone that isn't even dead.

Where was you for my 16th birthday?

When I hoped before, you would pop up before it,

Wishful thinking.

Where was you when I was in hospital several times?

Where was you when I wanted you to meet my first Boyfriend?

When I first had my heart broken

You are suppose to be here for me to guide me,

Me and you against the world?

Where was you when I first started nursery, primary

CHILDREN

And lastly, secondary school?

I guess you were being there for your sons first.

But you missed out on mine.

All of mine.

I wanted you to meet my best friends, X, Y and once Z;

they've been there for me more than you have or will be.

You left me to be alone.

To not be there for me.

To say everything will be ok?

Well everything isn't.

You didn't love me enough to stay; now I'm a broken

soul on the mend.

Where was you?

I've cried silently for you many times.

I hope you're happy, you know with your happy little

Family, but couldn't give a shit about me.

You were probably the one I would have come to when I
Couldn't go to mom nor my friends.

Yet you don't even know me.

FAIRY TALES by Sharon Moore

The faint memory of when we met, like a visitor coming to see

an inmate, we were strangers to eachother.

That was 10 years ago ... I was fucking six.

God knows what we would be like now if we met.

Am I a fool to think you would come knocking at the door!

I don't even no what to call you dad or 'blah'.

I've always needed you.

If not for mom at least for me, you're first. But I guess I wasn't your last.

I prayed to God many times,

He didn't answer.

You never came for me,

You never came at all.

And for that I'm not sure whether God exists at all.

I don't ask much in life.

Would it make a difference if you came back anyway,

Would I feel happier than before?

But its ok cause I bet you will think of me when it's too

CHILDREN

Late, when I'm six foot under.

Oh well.

P.S. enjoy the word that enters out of your sons' mouths,

"DAD", cause that word went when you left.

Oh by the way, you should have met my friends,

Y's brilliant, very funny (funniest girl you would have

ever met!), loud, and great to be around, clever too.

X, again brilliant in every way, very funny, (Y's partner

in crime) Clever.

And lastly once Z, she was crazy, weirdest imagination.

Argued the most with! Clever and a good verballer.

They are all strong-minded, that what I respect them for.

Like I said I hope your happy with your little family, and

the worst thing of all you could(n't) even be bothered to

contact me.

Yet I was your first child, and your sons call you dad.

They don't even realise what a let down their dad really is,

So I hope you have a brilliant life.

Just a few words to say how I feel.

And now you entered back in u think everything will be ok,

You can't build a relationship (after) 16 years.

Emotive, angry, hurt stuff. I think it is beautifully honest and I feel sure she won't mind my repeating it here because it conveys the emotion of an abandoned child that only an abandoned child could express and elicits a stark and powerful reminder of the consequence of our actions. I can only think that her father must surely have wept when he read it, if he read it.

Children suffer the fallout of our broken relationships, often more than their adult parents who can at least apply their own understanding, in time. Children blame themselves. Children rarely have all the facts. Children don't have the knowledge which only experience can provide. They frequently become pawns in an adult game without anyone explaining the rules. Children are forced to take sides out of a sense of loyalty to the main carer, usually mom, and are then saddled with the guilt that that 'choosing' creates.

The law, as created by precedent (the outcome of cases tried in the Court of Appeal and the House of Lords), suggests that, dependant upon the particular child's intelligence, he or she will have a sufficiently independent cognitive process to have their own opinion by the age of 10 to 12. Backed by child psychologist's findings, the perceived wisdom is that, until that age, it is possible that a child's expressed views are too easily influencable by adults to be taken purely on face value. Hence the eight year old who says he wants to live with his dad is unlikely to have his wish granted unless other factors point to this being the preferable option whilst the twelve year old with the same wish is likely to see it granted, unless there are obvious reasons why this is undesirable or impractical. A six year old has no chance unless their mother is a heroine addict or an axe murderer!

The Children Act ensures that anyone charged with enforcing the law relating to kids has to put their interests first, they are of 'paramount' importance. This, of itself, is a somewhat unnatural premise since those same parents, whilst together, might have decided to move 'Up North' for his job or keep them up till two in the morning because of her family wedding, which might not objectively be deemed to be in their interests by a District Judge having to decide between two warring parents.

Culture can also play its part. I acted for a young Asian woman who, according to usual tradition, entered a largely arranged marriage and then went to live with his parents in his family home. Though she was educated to degree level, she was treated, by the mother-in-law in particular, as a scivvy being expected to clean, cook and generally look after the domestics for the entire family. This was not what she had been lead to expect by her husband-to-be who ran his own business in which she was, supposedly, to have an active role. This lead to major disagreements between both the couple and the wider family.

They had been to see their doctor on several occasions when she discovered that she was pregnant. She was clearly very down due to the oppressive situation she found herself in at home. She urged her husband to agree to their moving into their own home before the baby was born. She did love her husband and could see that the increasing friction between them would be substantially alleviated if they were able to have their own space outside the constant vigil and criticisms of his mother. He, in turn, was under pressure from his family to stay at home particularly with the first grandchild on the way. His view prevailed.

The child was born a boy, still the more treasured gender in some Asian families. From that time she became even more ostracized within the house. She was not allowed to go out with the baby on her own. Mother-in-law frequently insisted that the child sleep in her room during the night and my client even found her attempting to suckle the baby on one occasion.

My client was at the end of her tether. She did not want her marriage to fail but she was effectively a prisoner and she feared for the consequences on the child as he grew older. Very reluctantly, and with added pressure raging between her family and his regarding the extent of her 'dowry', she decided to leave. Her father had managed to buy a small house for her to use whilst at uni and her brother was now living there. His family were apparently content for her to move there but flatly refused to allow her to leave with the baby.

She came to me entirely distraught. She could not qualify for public funding because of the equity in her house but she could not, in all conscience, sell the house and evict her brother who was now pursuing a degree course himself. She managed to find my retainer and an urgent ex-parte (without notice to the father) application was made to the court to secure the return of her child. The court abridged the usual fourteen day notice period and brought the case back two days later.

Father and extended family arrived with a barrister in tow who argued that the mother was psychologically disturbed and accordingly it would be dangerous for the baby to be released to her. They referred to the visits to the doctor, to mother's depression and even suggested that she had suggested she wanted to kill herself. I impressed on the court that my client had no history of any psychosis, that she had obviously been very down because of the domestic situation she had found herself in but this was effectively a ruse on the part of the father's family to obtain residence for a baby that they would otherwise have no hope in hell of securing.

Because the court was bound under The Children Act to keep the interests of the child of paramount importance, because it had no evidence before it to support or refute the allegation as to the mother's mental health and because of the seriousness of those allegations, it ordered that the baby was to stay at father's home and adjourned for a week pending provision of medical reports by the doctor.

It was the longest week of my client's life. She was provided with a police escort to visit his house and collect her things but she was not allowed to see her baby despite the fact that she had been breast feeding. A week later we returned to court with the doctor's report, there was no suggestion of mental instability and she was finally allowed to take her new born away.

This was an exceptional situation where a mother was, albeit temporarily, parted from her baby but, in more general terms, the effective presumption that the mother is the preferred main carer and the law's inability to punish one that is uncooperative is probably the most inequitable part of the law I practiced.

What used to be called 'Custody' and was renamed 'Residence' by the Children Act, usually goes to mom unless she voluntarily agrees to a different arrangement or is clearly the less preferable responsible parent. Fathers are left having 'Contact' (previously called 'Access') and whilst there are, officially, no standard orders this usually means Friday night/Saturday morning until Sunday night, fortnightly, or one day per weekend weekly. A fortnight is like a year in a two year old's life and even if, with older children, school holidays are shared equally, dad rarely feels that he has enough time with his children.

The problem which the most sympathetic Magistrates (Magistrates Court) or a District Judge (County Court) faces is their inability to effectively pull mom into check. The only official powers at their disposal, against a mom who ignores their orders and fails to cooperate in facilitating contact, are to fine or imprison. Given that the overriding legal demand is to put the interests of the children first, a financial penalty will most likely mean that the kids don't get to go swimming and a custodial sentence takes their mother away from them for a psychologically damaging period of time.

There was a tendency, some years ago now, for Judges (generally the Mags play it straight to the letter and the court clerk's promptings) to effectively reverse Residence where mom wouldn't play ball and give it to dad whilst mom was granted the Contact which dad was supposed to be enjoying but she had denied despite the court's orders. This was apparently frowned upon from on high on the basis that the court was almost endorsing the games which alienated parents play whilst side stepping the necessity to place the children first. Many would argue that the psychological damage, which physical separation from dad creates, is far worse. In reality Dad was usually working and Mom would thus have a significant argument that the children's interests were best served by being with her throughout the day rather than a member of the extended family or a child minder.

I had many male clients over the years who were bursting with frustration at the effective 'fait accompli' which faced them when advised that to pursue Residence would only cost them financially, emotionally and to no avail. I had several who spent a considerable amount of money with me to go through the right process and obtain the right orders only to be faced with an alienated child and an uncooperative mother. You can lead a horse to water but you can't make it drink.

Another majorly inequitable factor was that many men, used to being the main bread winner during marriage, did not qualify for Public Funding (Legal Aid) whilst their wives/partners had a lesser, if any, income being the main carers for the kids, especially younger ones, so did qualify. Women were thus enabled to take matters relating to the children back to court as many times as they could persuade their lawyers may be necessary whilst the men drained their bank accounts in a bid to keep up and have their voice properly heard, properly represented.

Contact Centres provide an invaluable bridge in enabling contact to take place despite the mistrust, jealousy, anger or feelings of betrayal which the main carer harbours. They are run on a largely voluntary basis by well meaning members of the community who turn out, usually on a Saturday for two hours, to man the building and ensure no incidents occur. Though I took my turn for years being the emergency number for staff to call if there was a problem, I never received such a call.

The difficulty is that the totally alien scenario of, largely fathers, meeting in a church hall/community centre/gymnasium etc to build their bond with their offspring for two hours a week, is restrictive and unnatural. And although they are intended to be a temporary solution they can become the only means by which a father can rely on having, albeit hugely restricted, contact with his child without being accused of tardiness, verbal abuse or inappropriate activities.

'Fathers for Justice', effectively but unofficially replaced by 'Families need Fathers' (because of the bad press received by the former) was a predictable backlash to this highly unsatisfactory situation. From dressing as Spider Man and scaling Court buildings to throwing purple paint bombs at our esteemed former Prime Minister in The House of Commons, they continue to attempt to raise the profile of their cause and bring about a much needed change in attitude and law enforcement. Many Judges (who more often than not are male) have huge sympathy with their plight but their hands are tied. At present if a mother is determined, for whatever reason, to frustrate contact, she will.

Despite the law's recognition of the child psychologists' observations, it is naïve to suggest that a thirteen year old who is constantly told that his father is a complete bastard, waster, skin flint, womaniser ... will not become prejudiced against him. Especially for boys who become the only male in the household, their natural protective instincts push them further into a compunction to take sides with mom whilst girls often become their mother's confident, a best friend, to an extent that would never have been entertained whilst dad was still at home. Children have to grow up quickly when their adult supervisors split up and are forced to take on grown up decisions, roles and reasoning beyond their years and experience.

Another problem which plagues fathers is that they do not automatically acquire the same rights and responsibilities as mothers in relation to their children. If a child is born within wedlock both parents have equal rights concerning important decisions appertaining to that child such as, where a child is schooled, what religion the child is raised with and even whether a child can have a blood transfusion or give any valid consent to medical procedures. Though referred to as Parental Responsibility it effectively gives the parents the prime power over their children. That's fine when both parents have it.

However, when a child is born to unmarried parents, a growing trend, the law gives the mother total control over the extent to which the father is to have any legal say over such matters. Until 2003, no unmarried father had automatic Parental Responsibility whilst every mother did. This was thankfully amended as from 1st December 2003 such that an unmarried father named on a Birth Certificate will now automatically have Parental Responsibility. Since most people are still together at the time of a child's birth, more fathers are now automatically acquiring the same powers.

If the relationship has broken down by the time of the birth, the mother is likely to be less inclined to bestow these powers on her ex and choose to name him on the Certificate. Also, the mother in receipt of Benefits, may be better provided for both in terms of money and provision of housing, if the father is unnamed.

Mother can agree to attend with father at a local Magistrates Court to complete a simple form and bestow Parental Responsibility on him at any time. However, given that she chose not to name father at the time of birth, such agreement rarely comes quickly and without 'agro'. The alternative is for father to make an application to the court to acquire P.R. The good news is that it is extremely rare for a father to be refused P.R. by the court. Unless, for example, he has shown no interest in his child or is deemed a danger to the child, he will be granted it.

As this is the case, family lawyers have to be firm with their female clients, explain that father's success upon a court application is practically guaranteed and, excluding exceptional circumstances, urge their clients to enter a P.R. Agreement. The Judiciary has played a vital role in this and, certainly in Birmingham, takes a very robust view, unless there are clear reasons, with a mother who is denying P.R.

Contact is the right of the child not the parent. As the interests of the child are paramount and as it is generally agreed that a child will benefit from contact with both parents, it is similarly seldom denied in some form (though we have seen the problems with enforcement).

Ironically, whether a father has P.R. or not is much more of a psychological, rather than a practical, issue. If parents disagree on how and where their child is to be educated, the fact that a father has a piece of paper giving him an equal say, will not promote agreement and an application to the court is almost inevitable. Except in emergency situations, such as a

244

child requiring a blood transfusion, having P.R. has little practical impact on most fathers. But, for a father denied acknowledgement on the Birth Certificate and P.R., frustrated by the apparent autonomy of the mother, the effect on him and his child can be devastating through the friction that it creates.

When I was first in practice, a divorce petition would indicate whether the parents were to have Joint Custody or one was to have Sole Custody. The majority of couples, even those at logger-heads on financial matters, agreed to Joint Custody; it was something which was negotiated at the very outset and this was the norm. If access arrangements then proved a problem, father could apply to the court for a Defined Access Order but this was under the banner of his often Joint Custody. This is no longer the case and to obtain a Joint Residence Order under The Children Act is extremely rare. We have moved from a position where, for divorcing couples at least, no Order is made in relation to the children or, if there is a problem, one (usually mother) will be given Residence and the other (usually father) given Contact. From what I have seen in practice, this only serves to fuel friction which could be substantially relieved if the court's 'normal' order was for Joint Residence with the details of where and with whom the child was to be at any one time recorded in that Order if proven necessary.

Anything which creates further dispute between parents, creates further stress to the children and it is practically impossible to keep them out of the wranglings as they are the focus of them. The girl in my class at school was marked as different (her parents being divorced) at a time in her life when kids desperately want to fit in and belong. As our society has changed so has the sense of ostracism which once prevailed. It would now be practically impossible to walk into any classroom in the UK and find that all the kids' parents were married (to each other) and still together (unless it was an exclusively Asian school). Their parents might still be living together but kids might equally live with their mom only, with a step dad or even an uncle or grandfather. I recall my cousin 'once removed' i.e. my cousin's daughter, being given homework at junior school asking her to write about the most important man in her life (in her case her grandfather, my uncle). Now it would be wholly inappropriate to ask young kids to write about their dad for fear of compromising the child who doesn't know their dad or who has a sporadic arrangement to see him. How sad is that.

The perceived wisdom of adults these days is that one of the main problems in our society arises from children lacking respect for their elders, for public property and even for themselves. It is certainly true that the way they might speak to us on the street varies hugely from just twenty years ago. Many no longer 'mind their P's and Q's'. There are many more physical attacks by juveniles on the elderly and infirm. And how often must we be appalled by new headlines of kids killing kids. Broken homes are invariably, though not always, a backdrop.

Almost fifteen years ago in Britain, and indeed in the rest of the world where the reports were seen, there was unanimous public outcry, shock and total disbelief at the abduction, physical (and probably sexual) abuse and murder of a two year old by two ten year olds. James Bulger was a month off his third birthday when he was lured away by Robert

Thompson and Jon Venables from the doorway of a butcher's shop in Walton, Merseyside (one of the most deprived areas of Liverpool) where his mother was making a quick purchase. They had earlier tried with another toddler but had been interrupted by cries from his mother to come to her.

The world watched the video footage of the two older boys leading Jamie off in the shopping centre. He was lead around the streets in the busy mid afternoon, taken to a canal where he was dropped on his head, sustaining his initial injuries, walked some more crying much of the time and eventually taken to a railway track where he was beaten with sticks, pummeled by bricks and stones, had batteries stuffed in his mouth (and possibly elsewhere) and hit with a 22lb iron bar. From forensic evidence it seems likely that he was also sodomised before his small broken but live body was placed across the railway track. The boys had sprayed his face with blue paint, possibly dehumanising him whilst the assault took place.

Jamie was found by children searching for footballs two days later. Robert and Jon had weighed his head down with bricks but his tortured body was found split in two, his lower body lay entirely naked carried down the track by the train that had not killed him. He was still alive when they had left him there but dead before the train made impact.

A 2001 Ofsted Report had asserted "The city of Liverpool has the highest degree of deprivation in the country". Notes from an NSPCC case conference described Robert's family as 'appalling' where the seven siblings 'bit, hammered, battered, tortured each other'. It was he who was found to have used the iron bar. As one of the youngest, Robert was regularly violently attacked by his older siblings. His single parent mother was an alcoholic whilst his father, who had left the home five years earlier, was a heavy drinker who had physically and sexually abused both his wife and his children, several of whom had attempted suicide.

Jon's parents were also separated, his mother had psychiatric problems and his brother and sister attended 'special needs' schools. After his parents split Jon had become isolated and attention seeking and would bang his head on the walls in school. It seems that no effort had been made by any of those in authority to investigate the cause of his obvious distress.

None of this excuses the sheer emotional detachment with which the boys finally dispatched a defenceless innocent soul from this mortal coil. The demonic 'Chucky', star of the video 'Child Play Three', was also suggested to have influenced the thought process, if there was one, which led to such a heinous crime. There were many disadvantaged children who had seen this video but not been driven to such apparently cold and callous behaviour.

No real explanation has ever been found for the motivation behind this crime but when considering true 'Responsibility' we must be misguided if we simply blame two delinquent ten year olds, or indeed their families, without considering the wider picture. Robert and Jon, though found to be mentally 'sane' were both obviously very troubled kids from very troubled homes. The difficulties within Robert's home in particular were known to the overstretched Social Services. Both displayed very troubled behaviour at school. Both were regularly truant and on the day of the murder they walked around a busy shopping centre in school uniform being disruptive and shop lifting before hitting the streets for over two miles.

There were witnesses to them kicking and hitting the small infant whose injuries sustained at the canal were later noted by various members of the public despite the older boys having pulled his hood up to try to hide them. The 'Liverpool 38' was a phrase later coined to refer to the thirty eight witnesses who subsequently gave evidence. Few had made any attempt to intervene and those who had had not pursued it. One elderly lady asked after the distressed toddler but was told the older lads were taking him to the police station as he was lost; another lady was going to go with them to the station but her daughter was tired and a fellow enquirer said she couldn't mind the daughter because her dog didn't like children …

When the boys were identified, as a result of a friend of Robert's mother calling the police with her suspicions (they could not previously be identified despite the CCTV footage) the subsequent trial and guilty finding led to life sentences with a recommended ten years minimum to be served. The resultant public outcry, including a 300,000 strong petition from 'The Sun' readers, saw this minimum increased to fifteen. The Court of Appeal then decided that the setting of such a minimum tariff was unlawful and the Home Secretary lost the power to set minimum terms for life sentence prisoners under eighteen. That was in 1997; in 2002 he lost the power to set minimum terms for any lifers.

Robert and Jon were in fact released in June 2001, eight years after their convictions and following 'good behaviour'. There has been much speculation as to their new identities, whereabouts and even subsequent criminal activities. The injunction preventing publication of their details in England and Wales was extended on their release for fear of public reprisals. Over £4,000,000 is said to have been spent on them upon release, and the arrangements which had to be made at that time, alone. Jamie's mother received £7,500 from the Criminal Compensation Board and a divorce.

In the cold light of a day fifteen years later it seems reasonable to assert that 'the system' and our society generally, let all three boys down. Even the perpetrators were only just at an age where the law recognises them as being capable of independent cognitive thought, able to escape outside influences and form their own opinion as to which parent they should live with, let alone what criminal activities they should be wholly responsible for.

In a society of 'broken homes', in which police time is increasingly dictated by paperwork and driven by the needs of the Revenue rather than to protect and serve their communities, in which children are exposed to a whole range of influences over which parents have little control, we can no longer look the other way, draw our curtains or cross the road. If this is the way it is going to be then every member of this society needs to take responsibility for the next generation both in terms of helping it and protecting it, sometimes even from itself.

Children do need to respect their elders but respect has to be earnt. Unless we can find our way forward to a situation where the majority of parents live together in a loving relationship, properly supporting, guiding and indeed disciplining their children then we have to look to alternative solutions to ensure that those children receive the input necessary for them to develop into well rounded, decent and caring members of tomorrow's communities. And it has to be done today.

No doubt as a result of the Bulger case, and the many other cases of children killing children which have followed, there have been many innovations and systems put in place to try to flush out such potential disasters ever occurring again. We are much more aware of the consequences which bullying can bring and schools recognise and manage it far better than was ever the case even in Robert and Jon's day. But have we really changed and adapted as a society to the fact that broken or disfunctional homes often produce broken or disfunctional children and that children far more exposed to the adult world will want to emulate those adults though lacking the tools to deal with it.

In a recent Panorama documentary, many of us must have watched with incredulity the images of teenagers beating teenagers, sometimes to unconsciousness, whilst tens of others looked on, jeering and encouraging, whilst videoing the action on their mobile phones. It seems that competition is high amongst school kids who download such videos onto the net then see how many 'hits' their particular site receives. None of the resultant 'blog' from kids visiting the site expressed any concern or disapproval of what they had seen. Peer pressure can be an extremely dangerous thing and even the best of parents have an almost impossible job to counter it.

Though I feel sure that 'the Liverpool 38' would all react differently if they ever found themselves in that situation again, doubtless having had to squash the 'what ifs' from their nightmares on numerous occasions since, would a fresh bunch of thirty eight good men and women on the street in

FAIRY TALES by Sharon Moore

Birmingham or London or Manchester or any of our major cities, really react differently today? I fear not especially in this age when we are daily informed of knifings and shootings. It is far easier and safer to cross the road, chicken.

Human nature is such that we all like to push at imposed boundaries from time to time but that is never so evident as with the young who, lacking the experience to know better, will push all the harder. That is part of the way they gain their experience. And where there are no boundaries, or these have broken down in some places, they will not necessarily innately know where those boundaries should be, where not to push.

We adults have to face the consequence of our own actions in taking the freedom which the breaking of the divorce taboo has brought, which being able to live together and have children who are not shunned as bastards has brought, which mobile phones, the internet and all the wonders of our 21st Century technology has brought. There is always a price to be paid we just don't always see what it will be until we cross the bridge.

If every responsible member of our society actively and collectively took a responsible stand, we can make our society change for the better. It doesn't have to involve major changes. For example, if any child in school uniform or of school age in school hours in term time was completely banned from retail stores, from shopping centers, from amusement arcades and parks, from any public areas where they are clearly not attending a medical appointment or pursuing a sporting activity, with the full support of the whole adult community, truancy could be slashed over night. The vendors of goods or services might have to be 'encouraged' to assist, like the fines imposed on landlords

252

who allow smoking inside their establishments. Kids have a limited amount of money to spend and will still spend it on those goods or services outside school hours. Just as two good parents do, we as a community have to show a united front, zero tolerance to show where the boundaries really lie even if their parents are unable or unwilling to do so. Could we achieve that? I think so its just that we adults have to be bothered, have to be prepared to put ourselves out and have to know that we will have the full support of the others in our society to pull it off.

As it stands, we, via the Government, have spent around sixteen million pounds in the last ten years on funding police officers to track down truants in the street. The campaign group 'Action on Rights for Children' surveyed 120 local education authorities and determined that sixteen thousand police hours are spent combing town centres every year and two thirds of those thus 'tracked' turn out to have legitimate reasons such as dental appointments. This is the equivalent of one year's work for ten fulltime officers.

Whatever the stats might be it seems it has been a woefully bad investment. Around 70,000 children skip school on average every day. Two thirds of all children are believed to attend registration but skip individual lessons sometimes. This is not across the board and in September 2005 one report, looking at 146 schools, suggested that 8,000 'serial' (!) truants were responsible for a fifth of all truancy in England. The National Foundation for Educational Research suggests that if a child misses more than five weeks in a year at school this will cut their chances of getting one GCSE at 'C' grade or above by 30% and the effect has been found to be greater on boys than girls.

FAIRY TALES by Sharon Moore

The Criminal Justice and Police Act 2001 made it possible for local authorities and the Chief of Police to impose curfews on children up to the age of sixteen, the Crime and Disorder Act 1998 having made such provision for children only up to the age of ten and only for local authorities. They are often enforced in areas with a reputation for juvenile crime and disorder such that children are banned from certain streets after 9pm unless supervised by an adult. Apparently teenage curfews are widely used in The States often during school hours, to counter truancy. Our new truancy legislation targets parents and has seen 1100 plus (by the time you're reading this) families fined and one mother even being electronically tagged because of her children's truancy.

As well as the possibility of curfews being used to combat truancy Head teachers now prosecute parents if there has been no improvement in attendance within a twelve week period bearing a maximum penalty of £2,500 or even three months in a non-existent spare prison cell. The 'Fast Track to Attendance Scheme' automatically ensures that a court prosecution is triggered if there is not that twelve week improvement and there is a dedicated truancy officer to support the process.

All the time, effort and energy expended on these measures and yet how many of us would take any personal responsibility, approach unknown teenagers in the street and ask why they were not in school. Even truancy is endorsed through our own fear or apathy. As with many things, we as the individuals making our society, need to be involved in enforcing the boundaries which the law has, as democratically as it can, imposed, rather than saying how terrible it is but leaving it entirely to, next to the parents, over-stretched police forces and local authorities for which our taxpayers pay dearly.

An increasingly hot subject, which inevitably raises its head when considering the growing lack of general respect which some children display to each other and their elders, is the manner in which parents/guardians and teachers are able to discipline those in their care. A U.N. study on violence against children has called on all its members to prohibit all corporal punishment - the use of physical force intended to inflict pain but not harm - in the family, at school and everywhere else by 2009 in order to fulfill their human rights obligations. It urged that children, due to their vulnerability and dependence on adults, required more, not less, protection than them. We adults have very strict laws about using any form of physical violence on each other.

Scotland was the first region of the UK in 2003 to make it illegal for anyone to punish children by shaking, hitting on the head or using implements such as a belt, cane, slipper or wooden spoon. In July 2004 The House of Lords voted against making hitting children illegal but it is only a matter of time before the question will force itself on them again. And what do our democratically elected M.P.s think on this issue, what do we think? There is a huge difference between individual parents making an informed decision not to physically chastise their children and it being illegal for even a loving and responsible parent to slap their own child (however difficult such a law would be to police and prove).

As here so in Northern U.S., there is a rapid trend towards parents abandoning corporal punishment of their children, abandoning smacking (or 'spanking' as they are wont to say in the U.S.A.). One of their sites suggests that Conservative

FAIRY TALES by Sharon Moore

Protestants are the main supporters of the corporal
punishment of children and that The Book of Proverbs
advocates spanking as the method to discipline children.
Many of them feel that this abandonment of physical
reprimand has lead to increased lawlessness and violence, at
least when such children reach adulthood. The site suggests
that child psychologists, religious liberals and secularists
oppose such corporal punishment and helpfully goes on to
add that children tend not to be keen on it either!

In 1986 Britain outlawed the use of corporal punishment in
state run schools though the private schoolboys had to wait
until 1998 for their smackings and rulerings to stop (they
must have had a human rights issue there!). By April 2003
twenty-eight U.S. States had banned spanking in school. We
are nowhere near Sweden which, as long ago as 1979, became
the first country in the world to outlaw all corporal
punishment of children by whomever.

It can be a hard issue for a generation who themselves were
disciplined with corporal punishment from their own parents
or teachers or both. I have heard my parents and many of
their generation say 'well, it never did you any harm, you
turned out all right didn't you?' And it may well be the case
that many children whose parents used moderate force
sparingly upon them are not emotionally scarred by the
experience (how can we tell how we might have been) but
numerous studies apparently fairly conclusively show that
even moderate smacking can have devastating effects for a
minority of children, particularly males, after reaching
adulthood.

Given the huge knock on effect on society whichever camp is
right, it seems vitally important to decide which is right and, if

necessary, pass the required laws to reflect this. Unhelpfully, many of the studies carried out by the Pro-Capital-Punishment camp find that overall it has a positive result in most cases and that if we stop it completely there will be a significant increase in violence and criminal activity by the next generation of adults. But those from the Con-Capital-Punishment camp, using their studies to back their own findings, urge that, on the contrary, the complete abandonment of such forms of discipline will greatly decrease adult violence and criminal activity as well as mental illnesses, feelings of low esteem and addictions of various kinds.

As a child who was raised with smacking … my mom once pulled my pants down in front of Mark and Moody's on Stourbridge High Street and gave me 'a good hiding' for some misdemeanour which I had performed and then turned to the three older ladies who had stopped to watch and said that they obviously had nothing better to do … and does not have children of her own, it is a hard issue. I would walk round the house with a red hand mark on the back of my thighs, because 'Doctor Spoc' had told my mother that this was the best, indeed the least dangerous place, to hit a child. I was fourteen and my mother's height when she slapped me for the first and very last time across the face. I was generally a respectful child and did not cheek my elders knowingly but I can still vividly recall the room it took place in and what was said. I looked her straight in the eye and told her that if she ever did that again I would do it to her. From my recollection that was the last time either of my parents hit me.

There is absolutely no doubt in my mind that my parents loved and cherished me and that they justified such behaviour with popular public, and even medical, opinion. But they were human and such action, like swearing, can become a habit. I certainly did not always deserve my hidings and those about which I felt most aggrieved, because of their unwarrantedness, lie uppermost in my memories of them. I can remember, as a very small child, being unable to sleep and eventually, in desperation, I broke the house taboo and went downstairs to seek comfort or help (rather than shouting from the top stair as I had been told to do) only to receive a good hiding from one of my parents and being sent off to bed in distraught tears of inequity. The following night I could not sleep again and remembering that, despite the smacking, I had then been able to cry myself to sleep, I went downstairs again and actually asked them if they would smack me so that I could go to sleep. Of course they did not. We have never spoken of it, and perhaps their own defences have blocked it out of their memories, but they must have felt awful at the time.

Another admission about which I am not proud is that, whilst I have practically zero tolerance to men's violence against women, having seen its devastating effects in my office and in a court room too many times, I have, on several occasions, under the abused influence of alcohol, slapped my partners in the throws of a row (or tried to!). As they have always been big men, and I have always been a small woman, I am easily deflected or incapacitated without the need for corresponding violence. However I feel confident in asserting that if I had not been raised in a home where slapping was an acceptable behaviour towards me (never, in my knowledge, on each other), if I had not been to a school which, though never practiced on me, still dished out the cane to the particularly naughty girls, I would not as an adult try to slap my partners.

I am not blaming my parents who, as my mother repeatedly points out about smoking, took this action largely in ignorance. They were not aware that this form of discipline could have a substantial long-term effect on my life, whether or not we agree that it did. As an adult I am clearly responsible for my own actions but we are the product of our life's experience and whilst children today may not be exposed to so much direct physical violence (the 'naughty step' having replaced the slap across the legs in many households) they are exposed to a million times more indirectly through the various medias. Such exposure could be even more dangerous since violence is thus 'normalised' without children experiencing how any violence which they inflict actually feels when perpetrated against them.

Do we really need the studies which prove that people who are violently or sexually abused during childhood are more likely to abuse as adults, whether it be directed at children or adults? Or that equally, children who have received corporal punishment as children are more likely to use it on their children or use violence on other adults than those who were raised without violence? One study in the U.S. suggests that every lifer at the time of study had experienced abuse as a child, some to the point of permanent brain damage.

Putting religious teachings aside, it seems that the most reliable source we have must come from the specialist doctors who study the effect of corporal punishment on children and unanimously oppose it as doing more potential harm than any short term benefit, being immediate compliance. How can we justify living in a society which strictly punishes any adult who inflicts a blow to another adult but provides no protection if the adult in question is inflicting the blow upon the smallest, weakest and youngest member of that society? Or is it just a question of degree … should every spouse be able to slap their other without consequence?

If the majority view is that we should permanently cease all physical violence against all other humans in our society regardless of their age, we might be a step closer to permanently ceasing violence against all other humans on the planet. However a balance must be maintained between the power of the parent to discipline and control a child and the power of a child to complain and be heard when that discipline has passed over a certain line. Many parents have complained to me that the 'I'll phone Childline' threat has become all too familiar. The NSPCC which recently took on this mantle does of course have a high profile aim to stop all violence against children 'full stop' but an unfortunate side effect of such an unfortunately necessary service is that parents can be left feeling impotent in enforcing full and proper discipline on their offspring whilst lacking the skills to find alternatives to physical rebukes.

Over the past couple of years we have been inundated with programmes such as 'The House of Tiny Tearaways' and been quite shocked that the skills of those like Dr. Tanya Byron are able, within a matter of weeks, to turn naughty behaviour around. If parents should no longer employ the 'cuff round the ear' approach then they have to be taught alternative proven methods of discipline. As those programmes seemed to prove, the naughty behaviour of a small child is almost always a reflection of a failing on the parent's part, however good their intentions. Surely this is something which should be taught in all our schools.

CHILDREN

In 'The Games People Play' Burne asserts that a child raised by an alcoholic parent is likely to either become an alcoholic themselves or will subconsciously seek out a partner who suffers a similar condition because in some bizarre way they feel more comfortable with that. They may have had a role model in their mother for caring and coping with an alcoholic or abusive father which is a thus familiar role compared with a relationship which is loving, placid and sober.

I had a female client for whom I acted on several occasions over the years both for divorce and in relation to her children. She had been sexually abused as a child and it seems likely that many of the relationship problems she experienced in her later life stemmed from this experience. She came to see me one Friday afternoon. Her eldest daughter from her first marriage at fourteen still lived with her and her, soon-to-be ex, new husband. The daughter had made an allegation that her stepfather was sexually abusing her and asked to be taken into care. My client was furious with her and said that this was only because she had two girlfriends who had also been taken into care and, because of the limited resources available, were presently being housed in a local pub/hotel. They were accordingly free to stay out until whatever time of the night whilst my client's daughter still had a reasonable curfew imposed by her and her husband. This, she alleged was the reason for her daughter's request.

We ended up making an urgent application to the court, having first made an urgent application for public funding, on a Friday afternoon. I had telephoned the court in advance to say that we would be on our way. The problem was that, as in many professions, judges tend to slope off early on a Friday afternoon whether it be to the golf course or their favoured

261

drinking hole. By the time we had hot-rodded it into Brum, all of the County Court judges had escaped and we were directed over to the crown court (where criminals are dealt with) to have our application heard. We were met by an extremely irritated judge who clearly did not appreciate having been forced to suspend the beginning of his own weekend. I opened by explaining that this was an application under Section 8 of the Children Act, the most commonly used section familiar to all judges in the County Court hearing family applications. This unfamiliar judge, clearly used to spending his days dealing with 'hardened' criminals, equally clearly had no idea what I was talking about. He admonished me in the strongest terms, for having brought no books with me. Something called 'The Red Book' has become the bible for all those involved with family work but it is rare for us to cart this heavy tome around when making a standard application. I did my best to avail him of the relevant law. He was impatient and cut my introductory submissions short, demanding that we just get on with it and ordering my distraught client into the witness box. This is an unheard of procedure within the County Court where everything usually occurs within the District Judge's chambers being a relatively small room able to house little more than a chaired desk around which everyone sits and says their piece. The proceedings are conducted in private, no one wears any legal garb and the atmosphere is intentionally relatively relaxed.

He started to cross-examine my client in a way which simply never happens in a County Court. He questioned her answers continually, barking out his queries, listening impatiently to her spluttered responses. I was fuming at the way in which my client was being treated and mentally berating a system which could condone an entirely inexperienced old man hearing such a sensitive and vital application.

And then my client folded. To my total disbelief, she finally admitted that she knew her husband was sexually abusing her daughter but that she loved him and forgave him. I could not believe my ears! The judge shot me a glance of contempt and dismissed the application. I walked out of the court room feeling totally crumbled, totally disillusioned by my own ability to suss out my client and my belief that I had been doing the right thing. I could not even look at my client let alone speak to her. I could not understand how a woman who had experienced the devastation of sexual abuse had effectively attempted to condone the same treatment of her own flesh and blood.

And the huge irony was that I knew, had it been a Thursday afternoon when she had happened into my office, we would have seen an appropriate County Court judge and the high likelihood would have been that the truth would never have come out. Something inside me literally felt like it had died and my overwhelming belief in the system within which I worked and the people for whom I did my very best, hit an all time low. But most of all, I felt completely despondent about the nature of human nature and the system's ability to adjudicate over it.

CHAPTER TWENTY-TWO

THE END OF MARRIAGE AS WE KNOW IT?

Does the Civil Partnership Act herald a sea-change in the way we are to view our relationships in the future and the manner in which Big Brother will regulate them?

For the last few years debates have raged on both sides of the Atlantic as to the ability of same sex couples to 'marry'. Currently Massachusetts is the only US State which has legalised same-sex marriage and homosexuality itself has only technically been lawful in the US since 2003 when the US Supreme Court overturned the existing law. At the other extreme, in Canada, those living as 'common law' partners obtain the same benefits as married couples after a year, with no option to evade this.

Here in the UK 'we' bit the bullet by giving the Civil Partnership Act Royal Assent (no less) on the 18th November 2004. Twelve months later, people, papers and the all important technology having been readied, it came into force and the first 'standard procedure' homosexual couples walked down the registering office's corridor on 21st December 2005. What a brave new world!

In many ways these partnerships bear close similarity with 'conventional' weddings. Bans must be posted, others can object, there is a cool off period (though only 15 days!) between registering and signing, and the legal effects if and when it all goes wrong are almost identical.

The Government propounds that the purpose of the Act is 'to enable same-sex couples to obtain legal recognition of their relationships by registering a civil partnership' upon signature of the necessary document by the second.

The participants must be two in number, of the same sex, not already married or partnershipped, not incestuous and, over sixteen, with necessary consents if under eighteen.

The Act sets out the legal consequences, rights and responsibilities of those who have partnered, different sections dealing with England and Wales, Scotland and Northern Ireland separately. As with marriage, the partnership can only end upon death, annulment or formal dissolution (just like divorce). The basis upon which the latter is achieved is identical to divorce i.e. a claim of irretrievable breakdown backed by evidence of adultery, unreasonable behaviour, two years desertion or separation with consent or five years separation. The financial implications regarding tax, social security, inheritance and workplace benefits are parallel to those enjoyed by their wedded counterparts. In all but name, homosexuals can now get married.

Ironically, they are now the best protected sector of our coupled society. Though I have, for many years, been called upon to prepare 'pre-nuptial agreements' by couples, at least one of whom wished to protect their pre-acquired wealth, the validity of such documents has always been limited. There used to be a general feeling that the Judiciary did not approve of them. For people raised in a society where it was much more common to marry early and young, perhaps we can understand their reticence at allowing one party to pre empt what might be considered fair and reasonable in all the circumstances of the case at the untimely demise of a marriage. As people increasingly marry later or for the second, third … time we are increasingly prepared to face the distasteful topic of 'what should happen if this doesn't work out' at the beginning of that relationship. In the days when the majority of couples built their good or bad fortunes together the issue was of much less significance.

Though latterly the courts have promoted an open mind when asked to consider pre-nuptial agreements at the time of dealing with divorce, they are of persuasive authority only, helpfully indicating the intentions of the parties at the outset but doing no more than that. The longer the marriage and the presence of children will usually blow big holes in the original agreement. However, solicitors and barristers alike are now offering pre-civil partnership agreements. These are claimed to have greater value than their pre-nuptial agreement cousins because there could be no argument that they were violating the sanctity of the holy union of marriage, the enemy of the pre-nuptial. There are also much less likely to be children. So, provided each party has been encouraged to take independent legal advice and both have been honest about their worth, the gay couple can fairly confidently rely upon the validity of their outset agreement.

Since the legislation is so new, gay people contemplating a civil partnership and its effects are reading and being told about the financial implications. When is a soon-to-be-married heterosexual couple ever tutored upon the financial effects of divorce? Of course the information is available for the curious but it is not a part of the process as it has become with civil partnerships, particularly as pre-civil partnership agreements are being so widely promoted within the gay community. How could the Church possibly condone any discussion as to who should have what if the marriage failed when an inherent part of its teaching was that divorce was bad and a true marriage was for life. So those civilly partnered are better informed and better able to manage their own affairs.

The cohabiting heterosexual couple have no legally binding way of embracing the protections and responsibilities of either their civil partnershipped or married fellow countrymen, without getting married. This absurd situation has been the subject of a recent 'cohabitation: the financial consequences of relationship breakdown' report by the Law Commission. It recommends that heterosexual couples who have children or who have lived together for a prescribed period (2 to 5 years) should be subject to pre-set financial remedies. It would require a positive action to opt out of these automatic provisions. The courts would acquire the right to determine whether one party had suffered an 'economic disadvantage' or a 'retained benefit' and, from that outcome, make orders for lump sums, property transfer, pension sharing etc. Though it proposes that it could not order maintenance for a girlfriend as such, it could still order regular payments if there is a child requiring child care. Big Brother is looking to regulate our lives wherever possible holding forth the banner of 'giving people certainty' in exchange for their free will and a belief in us as individuals to have the ability to regulate our own affairs. That in turn takes away individual responsibility because a law can be relied upon to find a result rather than each of us, in our individual circumstances, having to address what is really fair in our particular unique situation.

There are a growing number of road safety experts who believe that automatic road signals, telling us 'green to go' and 'red to stop', take away our individual responsibility. When people hit a cross-roads where each vehicle is signed to 'stop' and each must check that the road is clear before proceeding, people actually drive more safely because they are aware of their individual responsibility. The same with zebra crossings rather than red/green pedestrian crossings.

The time has come, in this increasingly anti-marriage heterosexual society, for us to ask ourselves the extent to which we wish to kow-tow to a Nanny State, which conveniently removes our individual responsibility to those we have involved in our lives both emotionally and financially. The alternative is not easy because it requires us to be fair and reasonable in a situation in which we are likely to be angry and hurt but do we really want a situation in which we are frightened to set up home with anyone for fear of our financial arrangements being dictated to us by the State? The immense danger which comes from a Big Brother mentality, is that we abandon any sense of personal responsibility or even morality, and adopt a 'such is life' stance both from a personal perspective and towards society as a whole.

Presently there is no real difference between the gay or heterosexual couple who choose to live without any legally binding document. In both cases each would own what they had in their own names and would share joint property. Any deviations from that assumption can be recorded in a Will or, to cover a during life demise of the relationship, a Living Together Agreement. Because of the sex discrimination laws these can be of equal value regardless of gender but they also need to be given a sturdier legal basis. The gay or heterosexual couple who do wish to have their union governed by automatic effects and obligations can opt for the civil partnership / marriage route. A rose by any other name would smell as sweet. The problem for the cohabiting heterosexual is that we rarely understand our existing legal situation and the concept of marriage triggers a myriad of butterfly conceptions far beyond its financial effect.

The clear difficulty is that the whole basis of marriage is, and forever has been, religious around which our laws have been built. As all the Great Books unanimously demand opposing genders for joining the institution, a religious marriage of same sex people is a contradiction in terms.

Does the modern man sitting in his convertible in Clapham want 'marriage' as in 'a religious recognition of his unity with another, a receiving of whichever God's blessing for the choices he has made'?

No-one needs statistics to be told that Christian church attendance has continued its rapid decline and their clergy is in crisis - and not all of its own making. Many choose to avoid the hypocrisy of a church wedding, when deliberations upon a God are largely absent from their lives, even less a visit to His House.

The Registry Office offers a cheaper alternative and deals with the legalisation and registration without the religion. Society has largely grown to accept this, though not an inconsiderable number of mother-in-laws will never forgive! A church marriage combines both. Asians, who need to register and legalise but whose religious needs cannot be provided for by a Christian church, have to have a separate 'religious wedding'. Both ways achieve the same end. But the Registry Office 'marriage' attempts to exclude religion. It is a contradiction in terms if one accepts that the concept of marriage is fundamentally religious.

In my view marriage should be confined to those who undergo a religious ceremony of some kind – a Christian in a church, a Muslim in a mosque etc. It should deal with the individual's spiritual requirements and beliefs. It should never have been related to the legal implications of choosing to register a union.

Of course, the layers of history which flow under the feet of the twenty-first century Christian church inevitably evolved in that intertwined way, when the church was rich and powerful and Henry VIII ruled his green and pleasant land and wished to behead and divorce those wives who had displeased him. In our twenty-first century, religion will not be forced down gagging throats. We are left with a confusion of marriage but where a registration alone will automatically put in place certain rights and obligations. That has become the 'effect' of marriage - tax breaks, additional allowances, death rights etc

If signing up, registering a union, means the automatic imposition of control over our resources, of ultimate dictation via a court order if the union ends, we need to be able to make an informed decision. This registration should be available to all who wish to regulate their relationship of whatever sexual persuasion they may be. I see no reason why three or four people couldn't make such a registration together if that was their individual and joint desire. Mother Nature would see that the majority were couples. Muslim's could register their four wives and ensure that all are equally provided for in accordance with his religious beliefs. All would be party to the same agreement and accordingly know the implication of its terms. A second 'wife' of a Muslim would no longer be thrown upon the mercy of the first 'legal' wife and her family, upon their mutual 'husband's' death.

There would have to be a matter of choice at the outset as to the legal effect of that registration. We should, before registering, be provided with information as to that effect. We should be able to access legal advice upon the possibilities available to us in regulating our respective financial resources, both now and in the future, and our agreement as to what should occur if the relationship fails. Not something that we have been used to dealing with at the outset of our commitment but far easier than at the time of its demise.

A financial registration could be amended by mutual agreement but would otherwise be binding. Those with children who had not dealt with relevant provision within their agreement would be thrown back onto the standard law and provisions currently practiced, just as the current position regarding a Will. If we don't have one, 'fall back' laws automatically apply dealing with all that we leave behind and channelling it to appropriate close relations in preordained percentages. By making a Will we take control over our own affairs; we could apply quite this principle to financial registrations.

If the parties disagreed upon the validity of the original agreement or the manner in which it should be changed, the court system would apply its 'reasonableness'. However there would be a strong presumption in favour of the validity of the registered agreement. The usual rules in relation to duress, mental capacity etc would clearly have to apply.

People do want to have control over their own lives. We do get frustrated and upset and even aggressive when faced with predetermined laws which we perceive to be unfair. This only breeds animosity and increases the pain of the deregistration, animosity towards the other member of the union as well as to the judicial system as a whole. The huge level of costs which can be incurred under the current system would be significantly reduced.

My view is that law and the rules which govern all of us should be completely separate from any religious beliefs or moralities. We live in a multicultural multireligious society. Marriage should signify a religious union under whatever persuasion but have no legal effect without a registration. We may or may not choose to legally register our unions but whether we are white, brown, black or blue, bisexual, lesbian, heterosexual, fat-arsed, green-eyed, red-headed, level-headed, mean and selfish and totally over bearing, we should be able to regulate our affairs as we choose. It is so on death.

Now that same sex couples can marry, it follows that 'unmarried' heterosexual couples will also want the choice of registering in some way. 'Living together Agreements' are the only current way and are considered persuasive by the courts but far from binding. This whole blurring of the strict boundaries previously set must signal the death toll of marriage as we currently perceive it. I believe in long term relationships but not the hypocrisy of the notion of marriage as seen through the eyes of a particular religion.

I also believe that two people should be able to choose to live together without the Nanny State automatically interfering with the legal, and therefore the financial, relationship between them except when there are children to be provided for (as happens with the cohabiting heterosexual couple at present). As I have been writing this book the Civil Partnership Act has been passed and has come into effect. As I write now the Government is openly discussing embodying an automatic legal effect of heterosexuals living together into Statute. This could be disastrous.

Over the many years that I practiced Legal Aid work the question of whether two people were 'cohabiting' was often a hot one for those receiving Benefits. The DSS guidelines indicated that they would be deemed as such if they spent four or more nights together on average each week and the amount of money they received would then be detrimentally effected. Consequently a couple would each secure their Council house (and sometimes even sublet one) whilst actually living together in one of them. Many cohabiting couples do so because they can do so without legal effect, they can dip their toes in the stream without being washed into the sea of financial consequence. If automatic financial consequences ensue as is being proposed, people will be more reluctant to actually live together, the number of single person households will increase and the already buckling supply of housing will break. There will be more people bringing up children with a part time partner and the strain on local authority resources generally will be unaffordable without further increases in Council tax etc. No-one should be forced to have their living together financially regulated by the State; everyone should have the option to register the way in which their living together should effect the financial position between them.

FAIRY TALES by Sharon Moore

Browsing the web America already has a site 'The Institute for 21st Century Relationships'. Typically, it has a mission statement, which reads as follows:

'Attaining a satisfactory level of love and companionship through intimate relations is an unalterable, fundamental need of all human beings. The Institute for 21st Century Relationships exists to facilitate the fulfillment of the human potential for relating and to support the freedom of consenting adults to discover and practice the intimate relationship structure that best suits their emotional and human needs. We champion the basic human right to do so free of government, societal or institutional coercion or favouritism.'

And they add:

'We seek, through education, research and support to create a climate in which all forms of ethical, consensual and fulfilling relationship styles are broadly understood and are equally respected and honoured as legitimate choices.'

It seems that if our society, through its government, continues to try to legislate for different sections of its members on a piecemeal basis producing a patchwork of relevant rules and regulations, it will be peppered with inequities and inbuilt prejudices. It will not have any inherent flexibility to adjust to what the people of this 21st Century actually want and choose for themselves.

CHAPTER TWENTY-THREE

SO WHAT IS THE SHAPE OF THE FUTURE?

It seems somewhat poetic that, as a result of the tremendous advances in technology, life has become much more transparent. That transparency is forcing us into greater honesty in all our relationships and greater intimacy in our couplings in particular. The twenty-first century must accept that unless it becomes far more open and candid in its 'life-long' relationships the only alternative is that such things will become as common as a field of four leaved clovers.

To be honest with our partner we have first to be honest with ourselves and to do that we must know ourselves. In this helter skelter life that the majority of us increasingly lead, do we allow ourselves enough time to evaluate, analyse and attempt conclusions which will turn the shape of the rest of our time here? Do we reflect upon the meaning of our particular lives now that we are safely on our track?

Of two things we can be certain — we are born and we die and we have no control over when either occurs, excepting suicide. The meaning of life for each one of us must relate to how we learn and grow as individuals in the time between those two dates and the effect we have as individuals on the greater picture, society as a whole and the individuals who compose it. We have the opportunity of making our mark on the world after we have gone, whether as Spike Milligan liberalising the boundaries of what we are allowed to laugh at; being a champion of a cause which others will learn are innately 'right' (Gandhi, Martin Luther King, Nelson Mandela, Steve Bicot...) or by nurturing a child who will go on to be the populace of tomorrow long after our own death.

Love is the greatest gift Mother Nature gave us but the Fairy Tale of a happy and fulfilling partnership for life, like Santa Claus, turns out to be not what it seemed. It is elusive; it requires dedication and an openness of mind which allows us to compromise. It feeds on Intimacy, Understanding and Acceptance. To achieve true Intimacy we need to be loved warts an' all, we need to share such a degree of honesty with those with whom we form our closest relationships that, even if that intimacy and that relationship does not last throughout our lives, we reach a level of understanding between each other which will then spread faster than a virus on our p.c.'s, and effect the way each of us conducts ourselves in that space between birth and death.

To look to the future we must learn from the past and put that into the perspective of a society where divorce is increasing and marriage and long-term relationships are decreasing. The family structure is increasingly fractured by the ready availability of travel, contraceptives, mobile phones and the net. There is far greater transience in where we live and work. Globalisation presents a real possibility of world harmony, world peace but in opening so many different doors to people-interaction, it requires our most important relationships to be stronger, more intimate and firmly built on solid foundations. The whole idea of marriage may become unfashionable, outdated or even legally impossible in the terms that we know it but the basic human desire to share our particular 'movie' with others will never go. Few men are able to live on a metaphoric island.

We Brits are a dichotomy of emotions. It is always said (mainly by the British!) that we are too polite and complain too little and yet we are a highly critical nation - it is easier to destroy than to build. This trait seems to go beyond the usual 'nationalism' which every society around the world feels. It is not only charity that begins at home. Perhaps we carry this trait into our couplings and whilst criticism can be constructive it can also be very destructive if not balanced.

As a child growing up in the Black Country I did not know any blacks. On collecting me from a birthday party at age seven my mother remarked that I hadn't mentioned my friend was "a little Indian girl". Apparently my instant response, which mortified her, was "I didn't notice". As adults it is often easier to pick out our differences rather than seeing our similarities, to concentrate on the weaknesses within a relationship rather than on its strengths.

What will the effects of this global consciousness be on our little society? In his Richard Dimbleby Lecture in 2001 Bill Clinton presented a well planned, well constructed and well delivered speech entitled 'The Struggle for the Soul of the 21st Century'. Though we had been titillated in the media by the Whitehouse titbits - how Monica choked on her own cock-sucking whilst he achieved it with pretzels - they were irrelevant, though relished for their entertainment value. His speech outlined the need for a different way of thinking. Out of evil always comes good. September 11th may have been the catalyst the world needed to shock America out of its political narcissum, as the world's greatest power, and the world out of its segmentation.

Clinton was not blessed with our hindsight but he suggested that, having 'secured' the immediate threat of the terrorist networks (yeah right!) we must make those who follow in their footsteps our allies and not our enemies. The only way to achieve this was by spreading the wealth that exists and which is generated in the future, the wealth of knowledge in health developments and technology. Whenever I am completely at my wits end with a call centre in Bombay, I remind myself that this phenomenon is a step towards that goal. If we continue to hoard the riches for ourselves then those without will try to obtain them, ultimately by using force. We can no longer lock ourselves in a golden cage atop ivory towers.

This will not be possible unless the poorer countries change themselves - to simply provide the 'wealth' to those at the top of the structure, whose wheels are oiled with baksheesh, will simply create a greater divide of wealth and impoverishment within those countries. The final key to world peace he opined was "a fully global consciousness".

Whatever your thoughts on the man, it is difficult to fault his logic.

And what will the effects of this global consciousness be upon our individual relationships. It is no longer imperative to put our packs on our backs and sit with the Sadus in Varanasi to get a feel for the spiritualism which overwhelms even the most hard-hearted traveller in India, we can see it on a screen. But it's not the same. It is no longer imperative to take those same packs trekking in Thailand to get a feel for a potential bride, we can do it online. But it's not the same. All the massive leaps forward in the dating game which technology has brought us open up a fantastic arena for really finding our 'match'. It is much more time efficient than hanging out at our favourite pub or club every Saturday night hoping the love of our life might just be unattached, attracted to us and coming there tonight.

But however we may find our lover, we have to be realistic. We can no longer hump around the expectations of our grandparents, or indeed our parents, without having to endure a rude awakening and a lot of hurt. As relationships have become more transient, in danger of bearing a sell-by date, our danger is that we instead hump around our previous hurt which strengthens our self defences and makes honest open communication even harder to achieve. I hope the people of this century will actually start throwing stones in our little glass houses, shatter our illusions and see ourselves and eachother for what we really are, not what we have been brainwashed into thinking we are. And learn to love what we see.

EPILOGUE

I finally left my Partnership in 2005 following the most horrendous legal battle of my life. Two years later my house is finished, this book is written but, not for the want of trying, there is still no baby. 'My Fairy Tale' will be the title of my next book though, as I write this, I have no idea how it will end!

THE DIRECTOR

Demeanour:	Direct and Self-contained
Pace:	Fast
Priority:	The task
Focus:	Results
Irritation:	Wasting Time
For Decisions:	Give options and probable outcomes
Question:	What and when
Speciality:	Being in control
For security:	Relies on being in control
For Acceptance:	Depends on his or her leadership skills
Measures Personal Worth By:	Results, track record

Behavioural Characteristics:

Decisive actions and decisions

Likes control

Dislikes inaction

Prefers maximum freedom to manage himself/herself and others

Cool, independent, and competitive with others

Low tolerance for feelings, attitudes, and advice of others

Works quickly and impressively by himself/herself

Seeks esteem and self-actualisation

Good administrative Skills

Environmental Clues:

Desk may appear busy - lots of work, projects, and materials

Walls may contain achievement awards or large planning sheet or calendar

Decorated to suggest power and control

Seating arrangement closed, formal, non-contact, and positioned for power

Theme: Notice my accomplishments

RELATIONSHIP STRATEGIES FOR THE DIRECTOR

Strengths

The strengths of the Director are directness and ability to get the job done quickly. The Director is blunt and quite assertive and, therefore, gets fast results. They can generalise from details rather fast and see the big picture and the bottom line.

Weaknesses

The weaknesses of the Director grow out of the strengths in that they can appear abrasive, insensitive to other people, and not concerned about details.

General Strategies

Support their goals and objectives.
Keep your relationship businesslike
If you disagree, argue facts, not personal feelings
Give recognition to ideas - not the person.
To influence decisions, provide alternative actions and probabilities of their success.
Be precise, efficient, time disciplined and well-organised.

When Selling To Them:

PLAN to be prepared and organised, fast paced and to the point.

MEET them in such a way that you get to the point quickly, keep things professional and businesslike.

STUDY their goals and objectives, what they want to accomplish, what is happening now and how **they** would like to see it changed.

PROPOSE solutions with clearly defined consequences and rewards that relate specifically to the Director's goals.

CLOSE by providing two to three options and let them make the decision.

ASSURE them that their time will not be wasted. After the sale confirm that -the proposals you suggested did in fact provide the bottom line results expected.

When Managing Them:

TO MOTIVATE - provide them with options and clearly describe the probabilities of success in achieving the Director's goals. They like to be winners.

TO COMPLIMENT - compliment what they have accomplished rather than complimenting them as a person.

TO COUNSEL - stick to the facts. Draw them out by talking about the desired results and discuss their concerns. Remember, they are much more task oriented than relationship oriented so they'll focus on things more than feelings.

TO CORRECT - describe what results were desired. Show them the gap between actual and desired . Suggest clearly the improvement that is needed and establish a time when they will get back to you, Don't hover over them when they are working on a task.

TO DELEGATE - give them the bottom line and then get out of their way so that they, can be more efficient, give them parameters and guidelines to go by.

Above all be: Efficient and competent.

ANNEX

THE EXPRESSIVE

Demeanour:	Open and direct
Pace:	Fast
Priority:	Relationships
Focus:	Interaction
Irritation:	Boring tasks and being alone
For Decisions:	Give Incentives and Testimonials
Question:	Who
Speciality:	Socialising
For Security:	Relies on his or her flexibility
For Acceptance:	Depends on his or her playfulness
Measures Personal Worth By:	Acknowledgement, recognition, applause

Behavioural Characteristics:

Spontaneous actions and decisions

Likes involvement

Dislikes being alone

Exaggerates and generalises

Tends to dream and get others caught up in his or her dreams

Jumps from one activity to another

Works quickly and excitingly with others

Seeks esteem and belonging

Good persuasive skills

Environmental Clues:

Desk may look disorganised and cluttered

Walls may contain awards, motivational or personal slogans, or stimulating posters

Decorated in open, airy, friendly manner

Seating arrangement indicates warmth, openness, and contact

Theme: Notice me

ANNEX

RELATIONSHIP STRATEGIES FOR THE EXPRESSIVE

Strengths

The strength of an Expressive lies in his or her enthusiasm and exciting, playful nature- They quickly win people over and get others caught up in their drive to accomplish a task. They are fun to be with and can adapt easily to a changing situation. Another strength is that they always have something to say regardless of what the topic may be, and they usually **say** it in an interesting way.

Weaknesses

The weaknesses of an Expressive result from a extension of their strengths. They sometimes come on too strong and are seen as being artificial or "put on". Sometimes their playfulness and spontaneity is regarded as a lack of seriousness and unpredictability. They are not good detail people in that they are easily bored by anything that tends to be monotonous or has to be done alone.

General Strategies

Support opinions, ideas, and dreams.
Don't hurry the discussion.
Try not to argue.
Agree on the specifics of any agreement.
Summarise in writing what you both agreed upon.
Be entertaining and fast moving.
Use testimonials to positively affect decisions.

When Selling To Them:
PLAN to be stimulating and interested in them. Allow them time to talk.
MEET them boldly, don't be shy. Introduce yourself first. Bring up new topics openly

STUDY their dreams and goals as well as their other needs.

PROPOSE your solution with stories or illustrations that relate to them and their goals.

CLOSE with the details in writing. Be clear and direct.

ASSURE that they fully understand what they bought and can demonstrate their ability to use it properly.

When Managing Them:

TO MOTIVATE - offer them incentives and testimonials. They love to get "special deals".

TO COMPLIMENT - pay direct compliments to them as individuals.

TO COUNSEL - allow them plenty of opportunity to talk about things that are bothering them. Listen for the facts and for the feelings. Probe and direct with questions. Many times Expressives merely need to "get something off their chest" and talking itself can solve the problem.

TO CORRECT - specify exactly what the problem happens to be and what appropriate behaviour is required to eliminate the problem. Be sure you confirm in writing the agreed-upon behaviour changes.

TO DELEGATE - make sure you get clear agreement and establish check points so that there is not a long period of time between progress reports.

Above all be: interested in them.

ANNEX

THE RELATER

Demeanour:	Open and Indirect
Pace:	Slow and easy
Priority:	Relationships
Focus:	Building trust and getting acquainted
Irritation:	Pushy, aggressive behaviour
For Decisions:	Give them guarantees and reassurance
Question:	Why
Speciality:	Support
For Security:	Relies on close relationships
For Acceptance:	Depends on his or her conformity and loyalty
Measures Personal Worth By:	Attention from others

Behavioural Characteristics:

Slow at taking action and making decisions

Likes close, personal relationships

Dislikes interpersonal conflict

Supports and "actively" listens to others

Weak at goal setting and self-direction

Has excellent ability to gain support from others

Works slowly and cohesively with others

Seeks security and belonging

Good counselling skills

Environmental Clues:

Desk may contain family pictures and personal items

Walls may contain personal slogans, family or group pictures, or serene pictures

Decorated in open, airy, friendly, bright manner

Seating arrangement is open, informal, and conducive to building personal relationships

Theme: Notice how well-liked I am

ANNEX

RELATIONSHIP STRATEGIES FOR THE RELATER

Strengths

The strengths of the Relater are warmth and ability to build meaningful relationships with others. They're loyal and compliant. They're excellent team workers, willing to conform.

Weaknesses

Their weaknesses grow out of an extension of their strengths in that some people see them as too concerned about relationships to do an adequate job of completing the task. Directors perceive them to be slow and ineffective. They are often so sensitive to the feelings and needs of others that they are unduly influenced by them.

General Strategies

Support their feelings
Show personal interest.
Accurately spell out objectives.
When you disagree discuss personal opinions and feelings.
Move along in an informal, slow manner.
Show that you are "actively" listening.
Provide guarantees that any actions will involve a minimum of risk.
Offer personal assurances that you will stand behind any decisions.

When Selling To Them:

PLAN to get to know them personally. Be likeable and non-threatening, professional but friendly.

MEET them by developing trust, friendship and credibility. Go at a slow pace

STUDY their feelings and emotional needs as well as their technical and business needs Take time to get them to spell out what is really important to them.

PROPOSE by getting them involved Show the human side of your proposal. Show how it affects them and their relationships with others. CLOSE without pushing or rushing them.

Provide personal assurances and guarantees wherever you can

ASSURE by being consistent and regular in your communication. Give them the nurturing and reassurance that you would give someone who was highly concerned about the purchase they had just made

When Managing Them:

TO MOTIVATE - show them how it will benefit their relationships and strengthen their position with others.

TO COMPLIMENT - compliment the way they are regarded by other people, their relationship skills, their ability to "get along" with others.

TO COUNSEL - Allow plenty of time to explore their feelings and to understand the emotional side of the situation as well as the factual side. They tend to keep many of their feelings to themselves by stating tentatively what they mean. They are trying to express their feelings, but in an indirect way. Therefore, you'll need to draw them out through specific questioning and reflective listening techniques, i.e., "This is what I heard you say ... Is that what you meant?" Be sure to create a non-threatening environment for them. Don't push or make them feel that they're getting the 3rd degree

TO CORRECT - reassure them that what you are seeking to correct is the behaviour only. Don't blame or judge the person, but rather keep things focused on the behaviour and it's appropriateness. Relaters tend to take everything personally, therefore, you'll need to be extra cautious in the way you make your comments

TO DELEGATE - appeal to them personally and also appeal to their loyalty Give them the task, state the deadlines that need to be met and explain why it's Important to do it in that specific way

Above all **be:** Non-threatening and sincere.

THE THINKER

Demeanour:	Self-contained and indirect
Pace:	Slow and steady
Priority:	The task
Focus:	The details, the process
Irritation:	Surprises, unpredictability
For Decisions:	Give facts, details and documentation
Question:	How
Speciality:	Processes, systems
For Security:	Relies on preparation
For Acceptance:	Depends on being correct
Measures Personal Worth By:	Precision, accuracy and activity

Behavioural Characteristics:

Cautious actions and decisions

Likes organisation and structure

Dislikes involvement

Asks many questions about specific details

Prefers objective, task-oriented, intellectual work environment

Wants to be right and, therefore, over-relies on data collection

Works slowly and precisely by himself/herself

Seeks security and self-actualisation

Good problem-solving skills

Environmental Clues:

Desk may appear structured and organised

Walls may contain charts, graphs, exhibits, or pictures relating to job

Decorated functionally for working

Seating arrangement suggests formality and non-contact

Theme: Notice my efficiency

RELATIONSHIP STRATEGIES

FOR THE THINKER

Strengths

Thinkers tend to be precise, efficient and well organised. They are task oriented and will persevere on what might otherwise be considered a boring task.

Weaknesses

Their weaknesses come from an extension of their strengths in that they are often seen as too task oriented and too cool and impersonal. They are suspected of not being concerned about feelings because they place so much emphasis on facts. They may be perceived to be nit-pickers who are too much of a perfectionist to be effective.

General Strategies

Support their organised, thoughtful approach
Demonstrate through actions rather than word
Be systematic ,exact, organised: Prepared
List pros & cons of any plan you propose.
Give time to verify your words and actions.
Provide solid, tangible, factual evidence that what you say is true and accurate
Don't rush decision-making process.
Provide guarantees that actions can't backfire
Avoid gimmicks.

When Selling To Them:

PLAN to be well prepared and equipped to answer all their questions.

MEET them cordially but get quickly to the task.

STUDY their situation in a practical, logical manner. Ask lots of questions and make sure your questions show a clear direction. The better your questions fit into the overall scheme of things, the more likely they are to give you the appropriate answers.

PROPOSE logical solutions to their problems. Document the how and the why and show how your proposition is the logical thing to do.

CLOSE as a matter of course. Don't push, give them time to think. Offer documentation.

ASSURE them through adequate service and follow-through. Be complete.

When Managing Them:

TO MOTIVATE - appeal to their need to be accurate and to their logical approach to things.

TO COMPLIMENT - compliment their efficiency and their efficient thinking processes, i.e., "I like the way you think."

TO COUNSEL - describe the process that you'll follow and outline how that process will produce the results they seek. Ask questions to help them give you the right information

TO CORRECT - specify the exact behaviour that is indicated and outline how you would like to see it changed. Establish checkpoints and times.

TO DELEGATE - take time to answer all their questions about structure and guidance. The more they understand the details, the more likely they'll be to complete the task properly. Be sure to establish target times and deadlines.

Above all be: Thorough and well prepared.

ANNEX

BEHAVIOURAL STYLE SUMMARY

	RELATER	THINKER	DIRECTOR	EXPRESSIVE
BEHAVIOUR PATTERN	Indirect Emotive	Indirect Non-Emotive	Direct Non-Emotive	Direct Emotive
APPEARANCE:	● Casual ● Conforming	● Formal ● Conservative	● Businesslike ● Functional	● Fashionable ● Stylish
WORKSPACE:	●Personal ●Relaxed ●Friendly ●Informal	●Structured ●Organised ●Functional ●Formal	●Busy ●Formal ●Efficient ●Structured	●Stimulating ●Personal ●Cluttered ●Friendly
PACE:	Slow/ Easy	Slow/ Systematic	Fast/ Decisive	Fast/ Spontaneous
PRIORITY:	Maintaining relationships	The Task: the process	The Task: the results	Relationships interacting
FEARS:	Confrontation	Embarrassment	Loss of control	Loss of prestige
UNDER TENSION WILL:	Submit/ Acquiesce	Withdraw/ Avoid	Dictate/ Assert	Attack/ Be sarcastic
SEEKS:	Attention	Accuracy	Productivity	Recognition
NEEDS TO KNOW (BENEFITS):	●How it will affect their personal circumstances	●How they justify the purchase logically ● How it works	●What it does ●By when ●What it costs	● How it enhances their status ●Who else uses it
GAINS SECURITY BY:	Close relationships	Preparation	Control	Flexibility
WANTS TO MAINTAIN:	Relationships	Credibility	Success	Status
SUPPORT THEIR:	Feelings	Thoughts	Goals	Ideas
ACHIEVES ACCEPTANCE BY:	●Conformity ●Loyalty	●Correctness ●Thoroughness	●Leadership ●Competition	●Playfulness ●Stimulating environment
LIKES YOU TO BE:	Pleasant	Precise	To the point	Stimulating
WANTS TO BE:	Liked	Correct	In charge	Admired
IRRITATED BY:	●Insensitivity ●Impatience	●Surprises ●Unpredict-ability	●Inefficiency ●Indecision	●Boredom ●Routine
MEASURES PERSONAL WORTH BY:	●Compatibility with others ●Depth of relationships	●Precision ●Accuracy ●Activity	●Results ●Track record ●Measurable progress	●Acknowledge- ment ●Recognition ●Applause ●Compliments
DECISIONS ARE:	Considered	Deliberate	Decisive	Spontaneous

THEIR STYLE	YOUR STYLE			
	RELATER	**THINKER**	**DIRECTOR**	**EXPRESSIVE**
RELATER	• No change in openness or directness • Limit time spent on personal talk • Be responsible for initiating action • Establish deadlines/schedules	• Directness no change • Openness increase	• Directness decrease • Openness increase	• Directness decrease • Openness no change
	General Strategies: support their feelings; show personal interest; accurately spell out objectives; when you disagree, discuss personal opinions and feelings; move along in an informal, slow manner; show them how it will strengthen their position with others. • **To motivate:** show them how it will strengthen their position with others.			
THINKER	• Directness no change • Openness decrease	• No change openness/directness • Take control of direction of process, let customer control decisions/destiny • Accept less than perfection	• Directness decrease • Openness no change	• Directness decrease • Openness decrease
	General Strategies: support their organised, thoughtful approach; demonstrate through actions rather than words; give time to verify your words and actions; follow up personal contacts with a letter; provide solid, tangible, factual evidence that what you say is accurate; be systematic, exact, organised and prepared; list advantages and disadvantages of proposed plan. • **To motivate:** appeal to their need to be accurate and logical; provide guarantees that actions can't backfire; avoid gimmicks.			
DIRECTOR	• Directness increase • Openness decrease	• Directness increase • Openness no change	• No change openness/directness • Remain receptive; don't impose your view • Let customer feel in control	• Directness no change • Openness decrease
	General Strategies: support their goals, objectives; keep your relationship businesslike; if you disagree, argue facts, not personal feelings, give recognition to ideas, not the person; be precise, efficient, well organised; to influence decisions, provide alternatives and probabilities of their success. • **To motivate:** provide options; clearly describe probabilities of success in achieving Director's goals.			
EXPRESSIVE	• Directness increase • Openness no change	• Directness increase • Openness increase	• Directness no change • Openness increase	• No change openness/directness • Exercise discipline - establish agenda • Structure relationship by: note-taking, verification, follow-up • Summarise agreements in writing
	General Strategies: support their ideas, dreams; don't argue; don't hurry the discussion; nail down details verbally or in writing; be entertaining and fast-moving; use testimonials to positively affect decisions. • **To motivate:** offer them incentives and testimonials.			

ISBN 142516933-3

9 781425 169336